DATE DUE			

THE TRUTH ABOUT CORPORATE ACCOUNTING

By the same author

Unaccountable Accounting
More Debits Than Credits

ABRAHAM J. BRILOFF

The Truth
About Corporate
Accounting

HARPER & ROW, PUBLISHERS, New York
Cambridge, Hagerstown, Philadelphia, San Francisco
London, Mexico City, São Paulo, Sydney

1817

Portions of this work originally appeared in *Forbes*.

Grateful acknowledgment is made for permission to reprint passages from the March 7, 1979 transcript of the *MacNeil/Lehrer Report*, copyright © 1979 by Educational Broadcasting Corporation and Gweta; a quote reprinted from the December 31, 1979 issue of *Business Week* by special permission, © 1979 by McGraw-Hill, Inc.; and a quote from Harriet Van Horne's column, © 1978, *Los Angeles Times* Syndicate.

657.45
B76t
123147
Nov.1982

THE TRUTH ABOUT CORPORATE ACCOUNTING. Copyright © 1981 by Abraham J. Briloff. All rights reserved. Printed in the United States of America. No part of this book may be used or reproduced in any manner whatsoever without written permission except in the case of brief quotations embodied in critical articles and reviews. For information address Harper & Row, Publishers, Inc., 10 East 53rd Street, New York, N.Y. 10022. Published simultaneously in Canada by Fitzhenry & Whiteside Limited, Toronto.

FIRST EDITION

Designer: Sidney Feinberg

Library of Congress Cataloging in Publication Data

Briloff, Abraham J
  The truth about corporate accounting.

  Includes index.
  1. Corporations—Accounting. 2. Corporations—
Auditing. I. Title.
HF5686.C7B7 1980   657'.45   80–7584
ISBN 0–06–010479–1

---

81 82 83 84 10 9 8 7 6 5 4 3 2 1

For: Edith, Leonore, and Alice

To: Distinguished Professor Emeritus Emanuel Saxe

Contents

Acknowledgments

To the extent this work evolved from my prior endeavors, I begin by acknowledging my appreciation to Michael Schiff, David Norr, Phil Copelin, Harvey Segal, and Tadashi Akaishi.

Then there is the *Barron's* triumvirate, Steven S. Anreder, Alan Abelson, and Robert Bleiberg; without their encouragement, friendship, and confidence there is little question but that my ruminations over the past dozen years would have found their outlet, if at all, in the journals of my colleagues in practice or academe. As is spelled out in Chapter 12, this friendship survived an extraordinary test during the years that elapsed since *More Debits Than Credits.* When a company aggrieved by my writings in *Barron's* vented its anger by hauling us into court, the triumvirate responded by pledging their resources to the defense of our First Amendment rights. We are grateful to the court for confirming our rights to write and publish critical commentaries on corporate entities and their managements as fully as journalists are permitted to write about governments and their leaders.

Insofar as this present writing is concerned, I am indebted to Harper & Row's Joseph Vergara, who encouraged me to undertake this venture.

Because so much of what has transpired in the profession of accountancy between the writing of *More Debits* and this work is the consequence of the discovery of the profession by the United States Congress, I am indebted to John Chesson and Ira Shapiro of the Senate committee staff and Caroline Emigh of the House committee for their valiant efforts in the Congressional probes.

This writing has been more challenging than anything I had previously undertaken. Because my ability to read has all but gone, I have had to rely on a succession (sometimes relays) of readers who would track down relevant materials identified by me, and frequently to record the material on tapes. For this burden I relied importantly on my graduate assistants Joseph Streisfeld and Warren Strauss, the three Briloff ladies, and then for the "word processing" of the manuscript I turned to Pete Ballstra, Natalie Rusiecki, and especially Lucy Silva.

It was Casey Villard and Toni Mulett on whom I relied to weave together the various segments of the typed copy, controlling the segments to be superseded, revised, corrected, and updated. Their task was herculean indeed; my appreciation is correspondingly great.

It is again my most agreeable privilege to express my appreciation and devotion to Emanuel Saxe, Dean and Distinguished University Professor Emeritus, for his indispensable role in the writing of *Truth About Corporate Accounting*. For more than two score years I have looked to this great dean as my role model—relying on his guiding hand and keen eye to advance the scope of my knowledge, and to help me avoid some pitfalls.

Having thus extended credits to those who came to mind as I compose this, I want to make clear that all debits that may remain are to be charged to me in their entirety.

There is, however, one further acknowledgment—most sincere and sensitive—to persons yet unknown to me. I want here and now to express my appreciation to those who, in academe or practice, may, from my writings, recognize the exhilaration and intellectual stimulation that may be derived from investigative writing in the realm of accountancy, or economics generally, and who thereupon undertake its pursuit.

THE TRUTH ABOUT CORPORATE ACCOUNTING

1

We Often Paint Fakes

In his *The Act of Creation*, Arthur Koestler relates an incident of some relevance for corporate leaders and accountants:

> An art dealer bought a canvas signed "Picasso" and traveled all the way to Cannes to discover whether it was genuine. Picasso was working in his studio. He cast a single look at the canvas and said, "It's a fake."
>
> A few months later the dealer bought another canvas signed "Picasso." Again he traveled to Cannes and again Picasso, after a single glance, grunted: "It's a fake."
>
> "But *cher maître*," expostulated the dealer, "it so happens that I saw you with my own eyes working on this very picture several years ago."
>
> Picasso shrugged: "I often paint fakes."

In this context I am not alluding to the "accounting fakes" which we have witnessed over the years—Equity Funding, National Student Marketing, Four Seasons, for example, where the books were overtly cooked—and where the scoundrels were found out and punished. I am alluding to the pervasive "fakes" produced in the corporate accountability environment—where the unsophisticated public has been led to believe that an effective system of checks and balances assures the accountability by the professional managers, the stewards of the wondrous pools of resources concentrated in our major publicly owned corporations. Those knowledgeable of the corporate accountability process know that there is a gap between the myth and the reality of the independent audit function. Let's explore this myth-reality gap.

The Auditor's "Nihil Obstat"

To begin with, the independent auditor's *nihil obstat* which graces the client's financial statements may be exemplified by the approval United States Steel received from its audit accountants, Price Waterhouse & Co., at the conclusion of their 1979 audit (to the extent relevant here):

> We have examined the Consolidated Balance Sheet of United States Steel Corporation and Subsidiary Companies as of December 31, 1979 and December 31, 1978 and the related Statements of Income and Income Reinvested in Business and Statement of Changes in Financial Position for the years then ended. Our examinations of these statements were made in accordance with generally accepted auditing standards and accordingly included such tests of the accounting records and such other auditing procedures as we considered necessary in the circumstances.
>
> In our opinion, the accompanying financial statements present fairly the financial position of United States Steel Corporation and Subsidiary Companies at December 31, 1979 and December 31, 1978 and the results of operations and changes in financial position for the years then ended in conformity with generally accepted accounting principles consistently applied during the period. . . .

This might be read as a straightforward declaration by the certifying CPA that he has diligently probed the corporation's accounts and accountings, has assured himself that the statements describe accurately what is going on, and that the internal control procedures in force are appropriate to assure effective control of corporate resources (e.g., no off-balance-sheet cash accounts), that liabilities (e.g., the true amount owed to employees and others) have been fully and fairly set forth, and that he has assured himself that the corporation's transactions have been described in accordance with the fairest of the accounting alternatives subsumed in the phrase "generally accepted accounting principles" (GAAP).

In short, the public assumes that the auditor's certificate reflects his responsibility as clearly enunciated by one of the accounting profession's great eminences, Colonel Robert H. Montgomery, a half century ago:

> It is [the auditor's] duty, after fighting the figures and finding the facts, to assemble the figures and to tell the truth about them, with clarity, conciseness and intelligence so that he who runs may read. . . .

Things have become somewhat more complex since Colonel Montgomery expressed his credo. Perhaps today the reader should be expected to sit and read. Nonetheless, the public might still expect that the auditor has fulfilled his duty as Montgomery saw it.

Old Myths and New Realities

In fact, it might even be asserted that the auditor's certificate reproduced above induces this expectation in the public when it states that the statements "present fairly the financial position . . . [and] results of operations. . . ." The truth appears to be quite different.

A few years ago in *More Debits Than Credits* I argued that the public's assumption should become the standard for the auditor's performance; that the auditor should be responsible for the development of the statements which he deemed to be fair, i.e., not merely "fair in accordance with GAAP"—whatever that phrase might mean. In this connection I argued that decisions of the courts in a number of critical contexts called for "fair" to mean what people expect it to mean, without reference to accounting practices.

This argument met with disfavor from a distinguished accounting academician in a review for *Business Week:*

> The basic theme of the book can be briefly summarized: The financial statements should be fair. Briloff maintains that financial statements may be in accordance with generally accepted accounting principles and yet not be fair presentations of a corporation's financial position and the results of operations. Unfortunately, Briloff, like many other people (and at least one major public accounting firm) who have argued that fairness should be the basis of financial reporting, never defines what he means by fair. Fairness is an empty box, and the sooner we bury the term, the better off we will be. What Briloff apparently means by fair is something that agrees with his biases. The biases of other people are dismissed with contempt.

When a blue-ribbon committee (so high-level that it was dubbed a "commission") of the American Institute of Certified Public Accountants rendered its report, it cited the *Business Week* review with abject approbation. The AICPA Commission on Auditors' Responsibilities (referred to as the Cohen Commission in recognition of its chairman, the late Manuel F. Cohen) suggested in its 1978 report omission of the phrase "present fairly"; presumably to retain it would introduce the auditors' biases. Instead, the report would perpetuate reliance on the biases of corporate managements, the subjects of the audits.

This is not the place to plead again for fairness as determined by the independent auditor rather than corporate management. My intention is to emphasize the disparity between the popular myth and the reality known to sophisticates.

The critical "fake" may well lie in the phrase of the certification reproduced above which reads "our examinations of these statements." If one were to believe the Montgomery credo, he (or she) would presume that the auditor *prepared* the financial statements. Now look again; note that the auditor is merely saying that he has *examined* the statements. The difference between the two emphasized terms takes on a disparity of 180 degrees, especially when the auditor is confronted in litigation with statements which are patently unfair and which the auditor is constrained to agree are inherently unfair. He is then heard to proclaim that they are not *his* statements; they are those of *management,* which he has merely examined to determine whether they were fair in conformity with GAAP—and so the argument goes round and round.

There are times when I wonder who has fallen victim to the myth, the auditor or the public. Should not the auditor acknowledge that when push comes to shove, he must demonstrate the inherent fairness of the statements—within the framework of GAAP if he can, but ultimately fair nevertheless?

The *Continental Vending* landmark case involved three CPAs of a major national accounting firm. In the course of his opinion, Judge Henry J. Friendly, speaking for the United States Court of Appeals for the Second Circuit, stated the vital issue as follows:

> Defendants [CPAs] asked [the trial judge to give] . . . instructions which, in substance would have told the jury that a defendant could be found guilty only if, according to generally accepted accounting principles, the financial statements as a whole did not fairly present the financial condition of Continental at September 30, 1962. . . . The [trial] judge declined to give these instructions. Dealing with the subject in the course of his charge, he said that the "critical test" was whether the financial statements as a whole "fairly" presented the financial position of Continental as of September 30, 1962, and whether it accurately reported the operations for fiscal 1962.
> We think the judge was right. . . .

This critical conflict between the popular and elitist views of what the opinion clause means was reflected in defendants' unsuccessful petition to the United States Supreme Court for certiorari.

Thus the *Continental Vending* case provided a sharp contrast between the standards of the "town" and those of the "establishment," with a resounding confirmation of the judgment of the former regarding the meaning of the word "fair." The significance of the case was put into clear focus by former SEC Commissioner A. A. Sommer, Jr.:

More disturbing to the accounting profession . . . was the language in which Judge Henry J. Friendly, surely one of the most knowledgeable of federal judges in financial and accounting matters, wrapped the affirmance. He said in effect that the first law for accountants was not compliance with generally accepted accounting principles, but rather full and fair disclosure, fair presentation, and if the principles did not produce this brand of disclosure, accountants could not hide behind the principles but had to go beyond them and make whatever additional disclosures were necessary for full disclosure. In a word, "present fairly" was a concept separate from "generally accepted accounting principles," and the latter did not necessarily result in the former.

This judgment was subsequently applied by a federal district judge in the matter of *Herzfeld v. Laventhol,* as follows:

Traditionally, the accounting profession and the courts have recognized that an auditor or public accountant owes a duty to the public to be independent of his client and to report fairly on the facts before him. Thus, the SEC has said: "The public accountant must report fairly on the facts as he finds them whether favorable or unfavorable to his client. His duty is to safeguard the public interest, not that of his client."

*   *   *

Compliance with generally accepted accounting principles is not necessarily sufficient for an accountant to discharge his public obligation. Fair presentation is the touchstone for determining the adequacy of disclosure and financial statements. While adherence to generally accepted accounting principles is a tool to help achieve that end, it is not necessarily a guarantee of fairness.

*   *   *

Too much attention to the question whether the financial statements formally complied with principles, practices and conventions accepted at the time should not be permitted to blind us to the basic question whether the financial statements performed the function of enlightenment, which is their only reason for existence.

*   *   *

The policy underlying the securities laws of providing investors with all the facts needed to make intelligent investment decisions can only be accomplished if financial statements fully and fairly portray the actual financial condition of the company. In those cases where application of generally accepted accounting principles fulfills the duty of full and fair disclosure, the accountant need go no further. But if application of accounting principles alone will not adequately inform investors, accountants, as well as insiders, must take pains to lay bare all the facts needed by investors to interpret the financial statements accurately.

In light of the alarming accounting fakes of the past few years and the compelling reasons for application of the fairness standard independently of GAAP, the question persists: Why doesn't the accounting profession move to put up or shut up? I submit that a major part of the answer is that our profession enjoys the present state of ambivalence and ambiguity. After all, would society be willing to pay several billion dollars for auditing if they realized that those who were carrying on this function were not really willing to stake their credentials on the fairness of the statements they audit?

Lest the reader rely on the judicial process to assure fairness in statements, I urge that he wait till he has read Chapter 3.

A Plea from a "Blue Ribbon" AICPA Panel

But it should not have taken the *Continental Vending* trauma or *Herzfeld* to sensitize the accounting establishment to the fact that it was indulging in a myth regarding its responsibility for the "fairness *qua* fairness" of audited financial statements. Fifteen years ago a select committee of the AICPA created to study the Opinions of the Accounting Principles Board zeroed in on this very issue. In its report to the Institute's Council it expressed itself on the issue in strident tones:

> At the earliest possible time the [Accounting Principles] Board should:
> . . . . (*b*) define such phrases in the auditor's report as present fairly and generally accepted accounting principles.

The committee report went on to assert:

> . . . in the standard report of the auditor, he generally says that financial statements "present fairly" in conformity with generally accepted accounting principles—and so on. What does the auditor mean by the quoted words? Is he saying: (1) that the statements are fair *and* in accordance with GAAP; or (2) that they are fair *because* they are in accordance with GAAP; or (3) that they are fair only *to the extent* that GAAP are fair; or (4) that whatever GAAP may be, the *presentation* of them is fair [emphasis in original]?

But a myth dies hard, especially when a society (e.g., the accounting profession) believes it has a vested pocketbook interest in the perpetuation of that myth. *Continental Vending* and *Herzfeld* notwithstanding, the AICPA is still trying to get its fairness act together.

As the profession approached the decade of the 1980s, its Auditing Standards Board held public hearings on the matter of the auditor's report; a summary of the proceedings prepared by a task force of the Board reported the following consensus:

> What topics should the auditor's report cover?
>
> Issues related to the opinion—should the phrase "present fairly" be deleted? The public generally favored retaining the phrase; some commentators would accept a substitute phrase such as "in all material respects" or "reasonable." The task force unanimously agrees that the phrase should be deleted. However, the task force does not feel strongly about the issue, some believing that resolution is partly dependent on whether GAAP is described.

The fruits (or at least the flowering) of these ASB hearings are considered in Chapter 14; in the meantime the myth is alive and well—at least in the minds of the accounting profession's hierarchy.

The Gaps in GAAP

The other half of the "fairness in accordance with generally accepted accounting principles" myth pertains to the "gap in GAAP." There are still significant numbers of statement users and even some statement preparers who presume that accounting principles are really principles in the true sense of the word. To the contrary, GAAP is not of divine origin; it is, instead, something of a chimera derived from economics, law, mathematics, the behavioral sciences, ethics, communications. Over the past forty years the accounting profession has endeavored to codify this body of knowledge.

From 1940 to 1959 the responsibility was vested in the Committee on Accounting Procedure of the AICPA. Then, as a consequence of the agonizing reappraisal undertaken by all sectors of society post-Sputnik, the responsibility shifted to a more awesome AICPA body, i.e., its Accounting Principles Board.

That group undertook its mission on a high trajectory—but was soon shot down by the Securities and Exchange Commission, which refused to follow the APB lead on the investment-tax-credit accounting rules.

And when, in the late 1960s, that board became impotent in the face of the business combinations and oil and gas accounting issues, it was superseded (in 1973) by the current manifestation of the great noble experiment—the Financial Accounting Standards Board.

It will become clear in the following chapters that committees and boards have not yet been able to develop the ultimate wisdom to guide the accounting profession as it pursues its practice. The body of knowledge which the profession has evolved can lead to a fair presentation—most financial statements prepared in accordance with GAAP do provide a reasonable and responsible basis for decision making. But these very same precepts may be perverted and distorted in practice, so that we often paint fakes, as will become evident as we proceed.

2

The Godfather

A cynical aphorism says that "street crime will get you into jail; white-collar crime will get you into the Social Register." This is largely true, with a qualification: Only powerful, affluent white-collar criminals will have their marriages and other happenings recorded; only they will find themselves invited to the White House to consult with the President on matters of state; only they will find publishers to disseminate their self-exculpatory memoirs. Weak and poor white-collar criminals will find themselves banished to oblivion or, if they are fortunate, tucked away in the back offices of their firms or clients.

In this and in the succeeding chapter I consider the trinity of forces responsible for ferreting out substandard and/or illegal conduct by persons associated with corporate America. This chapter will consider the "godfather," the disciplinary apparatus of the American Institute of Certified Public Accountants (AICPA). The succeeding chapter will consider the role and effectiveness of the "enforcers," i.e., the Securities and Exchange Commission and the judiciary.

The AICPA has an elaborate apparatus committed to the implementation of its Code of Professional Ethics (COPE). This code, like similar professional codes, is intended as a consciousness-raising book of rules. It is presumed to require of those in the calling a standard of conduct higher than that expected of the masses. The profession then undertakes to administer this code to assure a level of performance higher than that which might be compelled by a court of law. I have made it one of my responsibilities to monitor the AICPA's disciplinary practices. The Institute does have a highly structured ethics apparatus, including a Professional Ethics Executive Committee and its subcommittees, the Professional Ethics Division, with its staff, Trial Boards, and sub-boards.

Box Score for the Decadent Seventies

What has this elaborate apparatus wrought? Since January, 1970, I have kept score of the published disciplinary actions against my colleagues in the American Institute of Certified Public Accountants. The following tabulation covers the entire decade of the 1970s:

For conviction of bribery	27
Because of revocation or suspension of member's certificate by state licensing body (where specific reasons are not indicated)	27
For failure to file (or for false filing) of personal tax returns	26
For conviction of grand larceny, embezzlement, misuse of funds, extortion, theft, perjury, and corresponding high crimes	22
For failure to pursue mandatory continuing education program	17
For substandard auditing and reporting	12
For conviction of mail fraud	9
For lack of independence	7
For failing to disclose (or for false disclosure) to the SEC or IRS	6
For conviction of involvement in the Equity Funding fraud	5
For moral turpitude and other undisclosed crimes	4
For solicitation and advertising	4
For violations of securities laws	3
For fraud on CPA exams or application thereto	2
For refusal to cooperate in grand jury or state investigations	2
For failure to return a form W-2 to client and to take an AICPA professional improvement course	1
For failure to respond to ethics probe	1
Involvement in fraudulent land deals	1
For failure to pay for securities	1
For obstructing justice	1
For failure to acquire sufficient information to support the audit report	1
For threatening to inform on client	1
Conviction of "false pretense"	1
For filing false reports with HUD	1
Retention of client's books	1
For inadequate disclosure in footnotes	1
A total of	184

These are all grievous offenses, and our colleagues have been made to pay for their transgressions. Yet, when I review these actions of the impressive disciplinary apparatus, I conclude that the disciplinarians are very much like the blind guides of Scripture—those who strain at the gnat while swallowing camels. Except for the convicted felon in the National Student Marketing fiasco and those involved in Equity Funding, the 178 cases have not addressed the horror stories which have induced the prevailing credibility gap—the cases which I call the Roll of Dishonor, running the alphabetical gamut from Ampex to Yale Express and involving all of the Big Eight accounting firms.

When I earlier criticized the profession's efforts, the then AICPA chairman, Ivan Bull, took umbrage, pointing to increased activity on the part of the Institute's disciplinary apparatus. True, there were no fewer than twenty disciplinary actions in the first nine months of 1976. Let us study those twenty reported cases to see how diligently the panoply of ethics division, committees, and boards pursued its responsibility to exorcise evil from our profession.

The initial 1976 issue of the *CPA Letter* reported five of the twenty cases. Three Equity Funding defendants pleaded guilty and their two colleagues were convicted after trial. The three were expelled, the other two suspended pending appeals. *Sic transit gloria mundi.* Two weeks later, the *CPA Letter* told of a member who was suspended for a period of time because he had been involved in the bribing of revenue agents. He had been granted immunity from prosecution and thereby avoided trial and possible conviction. That same issue told of another Institute member who had committed the cardinal sin of "soliciting engagements by letter and had conducted a practice under a fictitious name." He was sentenced to "take a course in professional ethics." (Ironically, that course conceivably may have been written, and possibly even taught, by a partner in one of the firms which produced the prevailing credibility gap and corporate accountability crisis.)

We heard nothing from the Institute's ethics apparatus for the next five months of 1976. Then we were advised that three members were expelled—two because of conviction for filing false returns, the third because his state had revoked his license. In August, the wheels of the gods ground out six judgments following convictions in court proceedings: one for embezzlement, three for filing false returns, and two for mail fraud. Finally, the ninth month of this test period produced two more expulsions and two suspensions. The expulsions were for grand larceny and perjury convictions; the suspensions followed revocation of CPA licenses by the members' state boards.

That adds up to twenty. As I reflect on these awesome judgments, I conclude that except for the poor unnamed member who did not know how to solicit professionally (the way our prestigious colleagues do), there was really no compelling need for committees or boards, to say nothing of a whole division. True, without this awesome apparatus the poor soliciting scoundrel would not have been apprehended and punished. By my standards, I am prepared to accept that lost opportunity in order to avoid the pretense that we are, in fact, administering a code of ethics worthy of its name.

Even a cursory review of critical commentaries on auditors in various contexts would demonstrate that the Ethics Division, *et al.*, has failed to fulfill its responsibilities. It may well be that the Division is under-funded and overworked (possibly kept deliberately lean so that it cannot fulfill its presumptive responsibilities), because it appears to be capable of little more than opening its mail to read how a particular state licensing board revoked a member's license or a final judgment from a court convicting a member of a crime deemed to require the automatic expulsion of a member.

A CPA's Obligations to His Colleagues

I maintain that the Ethics Division's and the AICPA's hierarchies are maintaining an attitude of benign neglect of these matters and they themselves are guilty of violations of our ethical precepts. Thus, COPE includes among its precepts the following [as AICPA Professional Standards, Ethics (55.03)]:

> A CPA has the obligation to assist his fellows in complying with the Code of Professional Ethics and should also assist appropriate disciplinary authorities in enforcing the Code. *To condone serious fault can be as bad as to commit it. It may be even worse, in fact,* since some errors may result from ignorance rather than intent and, if let pass without action, will probably be repeated. In situations of this kind, the welfare of the public should be the guide to a member's action [emphasis mine].

Among the rules of COPE clearly violated (as I see it—and generally, also, as the courts and/or the SEC have seen it) are the following, *inter alia:*

> Rule 201—Competence. A member shall not undertake any engagement which he or his firm cannot reasonably expect to complete with professional competence.

> Rule 202—Auditing standards. A member shall not permit his name to be associated with financial statements in such a manner as to imply that he is acting as an independent public accountant unless he has complied with the applicable generally accepted auditing standards promulgated by the Institute. . . .

Elsewhere in this book I question whether Haskins & Sells has filed a complaint against Peat, Marwick, Mitchell & Co. based on what H&S discovered regarding PMM's serious shortcomings in its audit of Sharon

Steel. I shall await their response. Meantime, to avoid the trap of benign neglect, I shall file a copy of this book with the Professional Ethics Division of the AICPA as a formal complaint against the firms which have been found out in the matters described here.

Blowing the whistle was the subject of a direct question I put to Russell Palmer, the head of Touche Ross & Co., at the conclusion of his Emanuel Saxe Distinguished Lecture at Baruch College on December 12, 1977. The question:

> Now, to a very important matter. It's one I raise with my students. I believe that our Institute has failed dismally in the administration of ethical standards. I'm referring to an important essay on the concepts of ethical standards. The essay says that when any of us becomes aware of a major aberration in terms of our colleagues' practice, we have a responsibility of moving towards the effective discipline of our colleagues. So, I turn to your firm. I know of the very effective job that you did on behalf of the trustees in Equity Funding. You discerned some serious aberrations on the part of Haskins & Sells as well as on the part of Seidman and Seidman. I know the important job that Arthur Andersen did on Lockheed. I know what Leidesdorf did with respect to Gulf Oil. I know what Price Waterhouse did with respect to Mattel Incorporated and Arthur Andersen. I also know the extent to which Haskins & Sells developed some insights on U.S. Financial. Now, the question. Why haven't the firms that made those discoveries—including yours—proceeded to the American Institute of CPA's, saying: "We are filing an ethics complaint; this is our responsibility pursuant to the rules of professional conduct?"

Mr. Palmer's response to this query was:

> There is no need for Touche Ross or Peat, Marwick or Haskins & Sells to go running to the Institute or the states. We don't have to go in and ring a bell or shoot off a flare. Everybody in the world knows about USF and Equity Funding. The question is, what's the Institute, what's the profession going to do about all of this? I don't believe, however, that we need to go in and file anything, because all of this is common knowledge.

This is as far as the edited version of the interchange goes. My memory tells me that Mr. Palmer went further to note that his firm might be subjecting itself to legal liability if its allegations turned out to be wrong. It appears that a CYA (Cover Your "Anatomy") approach is to retain a discreet detachment.

So there is no need, as Mr. Palmer sees it, for anyone to lodge a formal complaint against a colleague since it might well be presumed that the AICPA Ethics Division reads the same stuff I do—and is presumed to take the initiative where it deems it necessary and appropriate—

and if the Division is oblivious of the implications of the matter, well then, it's just too damned bad. (I refer to this at times as "the Kitty Genovese Syndrome.") Has Mr. Palmer considered the possibility that a particular matter never got itself adequately exposed in the public media? Or, has he considered that, conceivably, the real evidence was deep-sixed through some settlement before trial? I cannot and will not exculpate Mr. Palmer (and others who follow his lead) in their determination to play it safe, avoid getting involved, don't press too hard or you might find others who might reciprocate your criticism. At the least let these CYA's be made aware of the fact that our professional precepts would hold them *in pari delicto.*

A Christmas Gift from Maurice Stans

The Ethics Division does not proceed on its own initiative, which may be discerned from the following dramatic tale:

Christmas, 1978, found my stocking filled to overflowing—there was a copy of Maurice H. Stans' just-published work, *The Terrors of Justice.* To add to that season of felicity, the author was interviewed on television and reconstructed history to demonstrate that he was the victim of plots by sinister characters inside and outside the government.

There were, of course, those who disapproved the Stans version of history. For example, the *New York Post* for December 28 carried the following review of his *magnum opus:*

> During Nixon's last campaign in 1972, Maurice Stans raised an obscenely rich campaign chest. All kinds of strings, veiled threats and promises were involved in the pledges. Said one industrialist, after writing a handsome check to Stans' committee, "I have just been visited by the angel of death."
>
> As Stans tells it, the Watergate affair maligned and damaged a lot of splendid, high-minded Americans, himself among them. Though he was indicted on several counts of conspiracy, obstructing justice, lying to a grand jury, violating election laws and soliciting illegal contributions, the former accountant says all the charges were hokum.
>
> This despite the fact that he entered a guilty plea to some (the fine was $5000) and was acquitted of others in a trial blessed by a jury kindly disposed to all Nixonian devices and strategies.
>
> As you might expect from an author elected to The Accountants' Hall of Fame, Stans has written a neat, bloodless book. He denies everything. His heart bleeds for all the lovely people who made Watergate possible. He's particularly sad to see John Connally's political career in the deep freeze. An incredible book.

But my special interest was piqued by what appeared at pages 383–84 of his book, where Stans wrote:

The final and most heart-searing blow was from the accounting profession in which and for which I had worked thousands of hours over more than twenty-five years. At the instigation of a renegade CPA named Briloff, a bombastic professor at New York University [sic] who made unounded [sic] public assertions against me from 1973 to 1975 while knowing little of the circumstances, the Committee on Professional Ethics of the American Institute of Certified Public Accountants concluded it had to file charges against me for conduct discreditable to the profession. The specific counts before the Institute panel were that the five offenses in my plea of guilty in the Federal Court in Washington constituted discreditable actions.

I had served the Institute through the years as a member of several of its major committees, had been its vice president and then president by 1954, had received its annual award for outstanding service, had received the annual award of the American Accounting Association, an organization of teachers of accounting, and had been elected to the Accounting Hall of Fame. My private life had been exemplary and my business and government service had been beyond reproach. Yet I was forced to go through the indignity of a trial before the Institute's Trial Board.

The hearing lasted a full day and ended when the Board, after only fifteen minutes of deliberation, acquitted me by unanimous vote on all counts. It was, in a manner of speaking, a trial by my peers, and to have their evaluation of the evidence so strongly in my favor was gratifying. It fortified my recurring feeling that had I been willing to take the strain of a court trial by jury in the first instance I would have won (although I realize that a jury may have been less qualified to understand the details and reasoning which justified my actions and more likely to be influenced by adverse publicity).

Maurice Stans' Vindication by His Peers

The Stans affair manifests so much that is perverse in the administration of the system of ethics in my profession and others. Be that as it may, Stans is right: He was absolved by his peers in the accounting establishment. Those glad tidings were conveyed to all the world by the initial 1976 *CPA Letter:*

AICPA member Maurice H. Stans, former Secretary of Commerce, has been found by a sub-board of the Trial Board of the AICPA to be not guilty of charges brought by the AICPA's division of professional ethics.

The ethics division's charges arose from Mr. Stans' plea of guilty in Federal Court in Washington in March of last year to five misdemeanors relating to his conduct as Chairman of the Finance Committee to Re-elect the President. It was alleged that the subsequent conviction tended to bring discredit to the profession. Mr. Stans contended that the offenses were minor and technical, that they had been found by the court to be unwillful and that the transactions upon which the convictions were based had been handled by him in good faith.

Following a full-day hearing, the sub-board, on October 28, 1975, found that the charges of the ethics division had not been proved. Mr. Stans requested publication of this finding and the sub-board has authorized this notice.

I will leave it for you to determine whether the regulation of conduct within a profession should be left to a group comprised of Stans' peers.

The circumstances under which Stans' peers at the Institute were constrained to bring a proceeding against him are interesting. They demonstrate that Russell Palmer's assumption that the Ethics Division reads the same stuff he and I might read, and read it in the same way, may be unfounded. An April 1, 1973, article in *The Washington Post* by Morton Mintz, "CPA Asks Probe of Stans Donation," included the following:

> The accounting profession got a shove yesterday toward a possible investigation of the "Sordid Stories" of how one of its former leaders, Maurice H. Stans, chairman of the Finance Committee to Re-elect the President, handled a $200,000 campaign contribution from financier Robert L. Vesco.
>
> Abraham J. Briloff, a certified public accountant and accountancy professor at City University of New York, criticized Stans' "major money manipulations" in a speech at Tulane University in New Orleans.
>
> Stans is a former president of the American Institute of Certified Public Accountants and is still a member.
>
> Briloff, in a telephone interview from New Orleans, said he will send a copy of the speech to the Institute's executive director, Wallace E. Olson, with a plea that its Ethics Division—"on its own initiative"—make an investigation of Stans' handling of the Vesco contribution.
>
> In New York City, Olson told a reporter that the division will investigate any formal complaint and "possibly" would act on the basis of a plea such as Briloff promised to make.

So despite extended critical press coverage of Stans, the AICPA required a shove from Briloff before they would even consider initiating a probe. In light of all the conceded violations of the law (and those which somehow got themselves submerged in the plea bargaining), one can only wonder who were Stans' peers and just what they looked for in the record to determine discreditable action by one of its members.

Mr. Stans in the course of a television interview asserted that he was never found guilty in the crimes of Watergate; it should be pointed out that neither was Richard M. Nixon ever found guilty of Watergate crimes.

If it is my judgment of Mr. Stans which causes him to describe me as a "renegade" to *his* peers, I wear that badge with some distinction.

Let us revert to Stans' discourse on his "trial by [his] peers" and the resulting acquittal—a judgment which Stans said "fortified [his] recurring feeling that had [he] been willing to take the strain of a court trial by jury . . . [he] would have won. . . ." Stans did add parenthetically that this felicitous projection is rooted in the assumption that a lay jury would be as qualified as the AICPA "jury of his peers" to "understand the details and reasoning which justified [his] actions. . . ."

Who Were Stans' Peers?

Because I wanted to know what "details and reasoning" were so convincing to the AICPA "jury," I wrote to the Ethics Division requesting access to the proceedings of that "professional trial." I was rebuffed! A January 12, 1979, letter from the Director of the Ethics Division read in part as follows:

> In reply to your recent letter, I must inform you that there has been no change in the status of confidentiality with respect to disciplinary matters which come before the Regional Trial Boards. Therefore I am unable to meet your request regarding the Trial of Mr. Stans.

Whereupon I wrote asking that at the least I be informed regarding the identity of that "jury" so that I might gain some perspective on the persons who were chosen to sit in judgment on Mr. Stans' conduct, insofar as it may have reflected on our profession. I believed (and believe) this disclosure to be especially significant in this case, first, because of the national importance of the matter being adjudicated and, second, because Mr. Stans was a principal partner of the same accounting firm as the AICPA's chief executive officer. The persons selected for this proceeding should have been patently and overtly free from bias—both in fact as well as in appearance.

Even this most limited request was rejected by a letter from the Director of the Ethics Division which read in part:

I am responding to your letter of January 18, 1979. You inquired about the names of trial board members and I must tell you that this information continues to be confidential. As recently as the AICPA Council meeting of October 1978, a proposal was made to open the trial board hearings to the public and it was voted down. Thus Council continues to support the policy on confidentiality of the trial board's processes while making it clear that the names of respondents found guilty by a trial board hearing panel must be published.

As this essay was being brought to a conclusion, I again queried the AICPA Ethics Division in the hope that during the intervening period there may have been a change of heart on the part of the Institute, as an incident to its commitment to the "sunshine standard." Alas, the response was, if anything, even more categoric. It took the form of a letter (dated April 21, 1980) from Donald J. Schneeman, Esq., the AICPA's secretary, which read in part as follows:

> The rules of practice and procedure provide that matters coming before the board are confidential. In fact, in the *Stans* case, of which you inquire, the following instruction was given at the beginning of the hearing:
>
> > Again, I would like to repeat the same thing that I said yesterday concerning the confidential nature of all matters coming before this Sub-Board. The only information on trials which is to be released is the official decision, to be published in *The CPA*. Even the names of all persons involved—Board members, respondents, attorneys, staff, and the Ethics Committee representatives—are confidential.
>
> Accordingly, we are unable to give you the information you requested.

3

The Enforcers

The staff study, *The Accounting Establishment,* compiled for the late Senator Lee Metcalf's Subcommittee on Reports, Accounting and Management (of the Senate's Governmental Affairs Committee), had this to say about the SEC's disciplinary practices as they pertained to the accounting profession:

> After receiving complaints that individual CPAs and small accounting firms are treated unfairly by the SEC, the subcommittee staff reviewed the SEC's procedures designed to ensure that independent auditors perform their responsibilities properly. The staff's review of SEC disciplinary proceedings against independent auditors since 1969 showed that individual CPAs and small accounting firms apparently were treated more harshly than large national accounting firms by the SEC. . . .

> *   *   *

> In its response to this subcommittee, the SEC defended its uneven application of disciplinary sanctions by saying that it would be unfair to punish innocent members of large accounting firms by imposing harsh sanctions.

The Matter of Peat, Marwick

A dramatic illustration of what the Metcalf staff study was protesting is the SEC's Accounting Series Release No. 173, issued July 2, 1975, captioned "Opinion and Order in a Proceeding Pursuant to Rule 2(e) of the Commission's Rules of Practice in the Matter of Peat, Marwick, Mitchell & Co."

19

This was a monumental promulgation if for no reason other than its bulk. The Commerce Clearing House format covers no fewer than 52 tightly printed pages of text. It needed all of those pages and columns of text to spell out the firm's dismal performance in case after case. Thus, the Accounting Series Release chronicles Peat, Marwick, Mitchell's (PMM) most serious aberrations in:

National Student Marketing
Republic National Life Insurance Co.
Penn Central
Stirling Homex
Talley Industries

The release also accused PMM of dissembling regarding Stirling Homex in conferences with the SEC staff.

This prestigious accounting firm also gave us Bar Chris, Liberty Equities, and a piece of Equity Funding. What penance was set for Peat, Marwick's sins? According to that release:

1. A review of PMM's audit practices will be conducted by a committee composed of persons agreed upon by PMM and the SEC. Follow-up reviews are to be carried on in the two succeeding years.
2. For the six-month period of May through October, 1975, PMM is prohibited from accepting new engagements (with some exceptions) calling for SEC filings.
3. PMM consents to the entry of orders of injunction in the four civil actions previously instituted by the Commission (i.e., NSM, Penn Central, Talley, and Republic National). Thus, PMM may not repeat its naughty deeds.
4. PMM will review and improve its operating practices.

I cannot avoid the rhetorical question, almost as a *cri de coeur*: "If it had been John Jones who had perpetrated but a scintilla of what that firm had done, would he even be permitted to affix his signature to another set of financial statements for filing with the SEC? Would he even be permitted to retain his right to call himself a certified public accountant—much less presuming to be prestigious? Could he (or anyone associated with his firm) aspire, much less succeed, to the chairmanship of the entire American Institute of CPA's and the chairmanship of the giant-firm section (SEC-Practice Section) of the AICPA?" John Jones could not conceivably indulge in such absurd hallucinatory visions; PMM can and, in fact, partners of that firm have succeeded in just such attainments. Be that as it may, this lament is little more (possibly even less) than its iteration in my *More Debits Than Credits*: so what's new?

To begin with, a few months after Accounting Series Release (ASR) 173, Peat, Marwick disseminated a press blitz worthy of a Madison Avenue introduction of a new perfume. This was occasioned by PMM's release of the peer review report which it had received from Arthur Young & Co. (AY—an eminent, prestigious co-worker in the vineyards of the accounting establishment) for a cost of upwards of a half million dollars.

That report, to the extent released for public consumption, concluded with the following paragraph:

> In our opinion, the prescribed audit practice quality control procedures of Peat, Marwick, Mitchell & Co. (United States) for the period April 1, 1974, through March 31, 1975, were appropriately comprehensive and suitably designed for a multioffice firm to conform with the requirements of generally accepted auditing standards. Substantial efforts have been expended on quality control procedures relating to the Firm's audit practice and comprehensive audit practice guidance material has been made available to audit personnel throughout the Firm. Further, in our opinion, the prescribed quality control procedures were generally being applied during the period at the Firm's Executive Office and in the other segments of the practice we reviewed. We were favorably impressed with the extent of the Firm's commitment to the conduct of its practice in accordance with professional standards.

There may have been more than was permitted to meet the public eye: PMM refused (and still refuses) to release the complete text of the AY report.

Surely either firm would condemn any of its clients if it were to release nothing but the covering letter of a detailed accounting report while that report and its footnotes (possibly revealing warts, scars, and blemishes) were cloaked in confidentiality. In short, I have branded the AY peer review report as insidious press agentry.

Let us turn to the presumptively more independent review, that mandated by ASR 173. A Review Committee was created by Peat, Marwick with the consent of the SEC, and comprised:

Donald J. Bevis, CPA, retired partner of Touche Ross & Co.—a Big Eight accounting firm
J. Michael Cook, a partner of Haskins & Sells, ditto
Paul Lambert, Jr., CPA, a partner of Lambert & Jones, of Washington, D.C.
Ralph F. Lewis, editor of *The Harvard Business Review*

Marvin L. Stone, a partner of Stone, Gray & Co., a regional accounting firm, and a former chairman of the AICPA

Arnold Bauman, of Shearman & Sterling (a very large Wall Street law firm), and a former federal judge, the committee's attorney

The committee rendered its report on December 22, 1976, and it became a matter of public knowledge some months later. This report was somewhat less glowing than the one PMM obtained from AY.

There are at least two curious aspects about this report:

1. Despite the fact that the Special Review Committee relied heavily on the prior AY report, and despite the fact that this committee must logically be seen as a quasi-public body, the SEC was not provided with a copy of that earlier study.

2. Inasmuch as the Sharon Steel imbroglio (see pp. 76–80) was festering while the special review panel was making its rounds, it is incomprehensible to me that the matter was not subjected to a pathological review. Is it conceivable that PMM told the SEC group to "buzz off" and so it did?

What did the Special Review Committee determine? The "Overall Conclusions" segment of the 31-page report imparts the flavor:

Policies and Procedures

While we have made recommendations for modifications, on balance, we believe that PMM's prescribed policies, procedures and practices are comprehensive, are effectively communicated and are appropriate for the conduct of its SEC audit practice. We also believe they are appropriate to provide reasonable assurance of conformity with the objectives of generally accepted auditing standards.

Compliance

*   *   *

Although in certain areas, the level of compliance was not, in our opinion, adequate, we believe that compliance with prescribed policies, procedures and practices was generally satisfactory.

So enthralled was the Securities and Exchange Commission with this report that it issued Accounting Series Release 173A on May 9, 1977, shortening PMM's period of penance.

Regardless of what AY and the Special Review Committee might have discovered and reported, the SEC must have known that PMM had again fouled the accountants' nest in its Sharon Steel audit. And this occurred months after it had entered into the long-winded consents documented in ASR 173. In my view, the SEC should have sought contempt citations rather than produced a superseding ASR.

Enter Saul P. Steinberg

But the accountants are not the only beneficiaries of the SEC's propensity for saying one thing and doing another. In July, 1976, Saul Steinberg (no stranger in my writings) negotiated a consent decree arising from a complaint filed by the SEC in the Federal District Court (Southern District of New York, 78 CIV. 4044). That complaint alleged that Steinberg had given hot tips to his secretary and good friends to buy shares in Pulte Home Corporation, of which he had been a director and, "as of January 1, 1976, . . . beneficial owner of 187,666 shares. . . ."

According to the complaint, Steinberg was touting the stock on the basis of alleged negotiations between Pulte and International Basic Economics Corporation (IBEC), a Rockefeller vehicle. On the strength of this *wunderkind*'s representation, his friends and associates purchased 80,200 shares. They initiated the purchases in July, 1976, when Pulte shares were selling at $4.50, and continued to do so through September 22, by which time the price was bid up to $6.75.

Steinberg, on the other hand, started selling on September 8 (at $5.25 per share) and continued to do so until September 22, by which time he had unloaded 37,600 shares.

It is of interest to note that on September 10 one of Steinberg's friends (sic!) bought 12,000 shares while on the same date Steinberg himself sold the identical number of such shares. Why he didn't just sell his shares directly to his friend on that date and avoid the brokerage fees at both ends is not entirely clear. Maybe Steinberg felt that there are certain things one doesn't tell even to his secretary or good friends.

The clincher is paragraph 25 of the complaint: "By reason of the activities set forth in paragraphs 11 through 24 above, Steinberg . . . directly and indirectly violated Section 10(b) of the Exchange Act, and Rule 10b-5 thereunder."

What was the punishment meted out to fit the alleged crime? As indicated, this litigation was terminated by a consent decree, whereby Steinberg is "permanently enjoined" from:

1. employing any device, scheme or artifice to defraud;
2. making any untrue statement of material fact, or omitting to state a material fact necessary in order to make the statement made, in light of the circumstances under which they were made, not misleading;
3. engaging in any act, practice or course of business which operates or would operate as a fraud or deceit upon a person.

The allegations paint a chintzy performance on the part of Steinberg, who had earned the plaudits of certain segments of the financial press as boy genius, captain of industry, and the like. It is difficult to comprehend touting a stock to his secretary and friends to unload a measly quarter of a million dollars' worth—difficult unless one recalls that in September, 1976, Steinberg was in hock to his favorite bankers, that he was indebted to his own public corporation to pay the interest on those loans, that he was reneging on pledges to Woodmere Academy, even though that school had agreed to name a library to memorialize the Steinbergs. Consequently, Saul Steinberg must have been desperate—in any event, he appears to have moved with desperation. Should such a person be permitted to sit on top of an empire of billions of dollars of other people's money?

One cannot avoid thinking of the irony. Few if any of us have entered into a corresponding consent decree enjoining us from doing that which Steinberg is enjoined from doing. Nevertheless, the law restrains us from such felonious activity; the judgment against Steinberg restrains him.

The settlement document was subscribed also by Robert Hodes, partner of Willkie Farr & Gallagher, the prestigious Wall Street law firm. It is the same Robert Hodes we regularly encounter when we come up against Saul Steinberg. Hodes is a member of the boards and had been a member of the audit committees of Steinberg's nexus of corporations flying under the Reliance flag; he also turns up as Steinberg's co-defendant (in *Feit v. Leasco,* for example); and when the circumstances call for it, Hodes is Steinberg's spokesman to the press—e.g., from the *Wall Street Journal* of August 30, 1978: The settlement "concerned personal investment transactions conducted in good faith with no intention of impropriety." Mr. Hodes said Mr. Steinberg "agreed to the settlement on our advice solely to avoid the distraction and expense of protracted and pointless litigation."

These disclosures by the SEC provoke some personal resentment. Steinberg's disposal of his Pulte shares under circumstances ostensibly violative of the Securities Acts pivots around September 14, 1976. That is precisely the date that Hodes's firm was filing a complaint at the behest of his client against *Barron's* and myself because Steinberg and his colleagues were unhappy about my article, "Whose Deep Pocket?" in the July 19, 1976, issue.

That complaint alleged, among other things, that *Barron's* and I had violated Rule 10b-5 of the SEC regulations. The story of this litigation is set forth in Chapter 13 of this work.

What I find galling in this context is the timing—at the moment

Steinberg was allegedly violating the securities laws, he was hiring Hodes's law firm to make the allegations in the complaint—expecting to chill the critical reporting by Briloff and *Barron's*.

The SEC in its consent decree proclivities is doing little more than notching up numbers of cases adjudicated and settled—but to what end?

The ITT Embroglio

In the matter of International Telephone and Telegraph Corporation (ITT) and Lazard Freres & Company (Release No. 14049, October 13, 1977), the Securities and Exchange Commission evidenced its abject respect for the epitome of the hierarchy of corporate America.

This saga revolves around ITT's hot pursuit in 1969 of the Hartford Fire Insurance Company (HFI). ITT required a favorable ruling from the Internal Revenue Service whereby the Hartford shareholders would be permitted to swap their shares for new ITT preferred stock without paying a tax at the time of the swap.

There was a serious stumbling block. ITT had purchased 1,741,348 Hartford shares at an average cost of about $51 a share. To get the required IRS ruling, ITT had to absolutely dispose of all of those shares prior to proceeding with the merger.

Because such a disposition on the open market would have had a serious adverse impact on the market price, ITT endeavored to find an "institutional investor" to relieve it of the Hartford block. According to the SEC:

> After concluding that a domestic entity was not available to enter into an agreement that would accomplish the foregoing objectives, Felix Rohatyn, a partner of Lazard and a director of ITT active in ITT's HFI acquisition effort, requested Andre Meyer, Senior Partner of Lazard, to suggest a foreign institution which could enter into an agreement that would accomplish ITT's objectives. Thereafter, Meyer asked Dr. Enrico Cuccia of Mediobanca di Credito Finanziario S.P.A. whether Mediobanca would be interested in an agreement that would accomplish such objectives. Discussions ensued regarding a possible agreement between ITT and Mediobanca.

A deal was then negotiated in which Mediobanca agreed to acquire the Hartford block for a price predicated on certain subsequent happenings.

With this deal in hand, ITT got the favorable ruling from the IRS and completed the transaction with Mediobanca. The essential aspect of the deal was that Mediobanca remained riskless. What is more, there was no exchange of money and the shares were transferred from ITT to Lazard Freres in Switzerland as "custodian." Mediobanca established a restricted account in the name of ITT, to which $88.8 million, the nominal purchase price, was credited. Mediobanca's risklessness was implicit in the cleverly rigged pricing arrangement.

On the merger the 1,741,348 Hartford shares of Mediobanca were swapped for a like number of ITT Series N Preferred shares. Portions were thereafter sold, but only after obtaining the advice and consent of Lazard Freres. The proceeds from these sales were effectively credited to ITT.

The SEC allegations concentrate on two such dispositions, demonstrating that they were, in fact, used to effectuate certain ITT acquisitions rather than representing true dispositions for the account and risk of Mediobanca as the presumptive owner of the shares.

One of these deals involved 400,000 of the Series N shares which, according to the SEC, was the catalyst for acquiring an Italian auto parts manufacturer, Way Assauto; the other involved Eurofund International, Inc. (a regulated closed-end investment company), where the sale of 100,000 shares to a Mr. Charles Engelhard at a bargain price represented something of a "sweetener."

The text of the SEC Release, comprising thirteen pages of an issue of the Commission's Docket (complete with 31 footnotes), describing the involvements of ITT executives, Lazard Freres partners, and various foreign interests, is a Byzantine scenario. And, *malheureusement* for our understanding of some of the most critical happenings, prestigious members of our nation's corporate and financial establishments suddenly develop amnesia. Events somehow happened parthenogenetically—or at least coincidentally. These leaders have testified that they had no "contemporaneous knowledge" of critical events.

So the Internal Revenue Service and the SEC were seriously and overtly misled back in 1969 and 1970—overtly lied to in most serious and deliberate circumstances—offenses which could and should put ordinary mortals into the dock.

How did Lazard Freres and ITT manifest a *mea culpa* for this alleged plotting, scheming, and intrigue? Briefly:

1. ITT agreed to amend its reports for 1969 through 1976 by filing a copy of the SEC's promulgation.
2. Lazard Freres agreed to adopt procedures to "record all fees received by it and the basis for such fees."
3. Lazard Freres also agreed to inform corporations to which it has a consultative or fiduciary relationship whenever there is a potential conflict of interest.

4. ITT was to establish a committee of independent directors to review the corporation's procedures to avoid a recurrence of aberrations like those here in issue.

This ends the tale as told by the SEC Release. The Internal Revenue Service and the SEC were not the only governmental agencies cuckolded by the Geneen Machine; the State and Justice Departments, the Central Intelligence Agency, and the U.S. Senate were also among those victimized.

But I do have some questions to put to Internal Revenue and ITT's independent auditors insofar as the foregoing saga is concerned:

Should it not have been evident to the IRS that Mediobanca was nothing but a "warehouseman" in this elaborate deal?

Should not the pricing arrangement have alerted the IRS that ITT was not effectively disposing of the Hartford shares, a condition precedent to the favorable tax ruling?

And what about Arthur Andersen, ITT's independent auditors? Recognizing the critical connection between the tax ruling and the Mediobanca transaction, should they not have probed just a little bit further to ascertain precisely why the $88.8 million proceeds from the transaction were not remitted to its client but, instead, put into a restricted account?

Is it at all conceivable that both the IRS and Arthur Andersen preferred not to have all the facts lest they might thwart that which our entire government seems to have been committed to seeing accomplished—Hartford's being absorbed into the Geneen Machine?

As if to expiate ITT of its sins of omission and commission *vis à vis* the Securities and Exchange Commission and the Internal Revenue Service, counsel for the corporation sent me a copy of the February 6, 1979, opinion by the Tax Court of the United States in the matter of *C. Reeves v. Commissioner of Internal Revenue.*

This case involved a Hartford shareholder who had swapped his shares for ITT stock; the shareholder succeeded in convincing the Court (with four judges abstaining and five dissenting) that ITT's earlier cash acquisition of Hartford shares should not contaminate the subsequent exchange so as to make it a taxable, rather than a taxfree, reorganization.

While counsel might rationalize the deceptions detailed in the SEC Release by asserting that the end justifies the means, by my standards, the fact that ITT might not have required the anticipatory benediction from the Internal Revenue Service does not condone the fact that ITT did seek such a ruling and was allegedly mendacious in the process.

As it turns out, as of this writing in early summer, 1980, at least two Federal Circuit Courts of Appeal (the First and Seventh) have determined that ITT was wrong on its view of the tax law. In so doing these courts reversed decisions of the Tax Court and a District Court which were favorable to the company.

In the course of its opinion the First Circuit observed:

> In March 1974, the Internal Revenue Service retroactively revoked its ruling approving the sale of Hartford stock to Mediobanca, on the ground that the request on which the ruling was based had misrepresented the nature of the proposed sale. Concluding that the entire transaction no longer constituted a nontaxable reorganization, the Service assessed tax deficiencies against a number of former Hartford shareholders who had accepted the exchange offer. Appellees, along with other taxpayers, contested this action in the Tax Court, where the case was decided on appellees' motion for summary judgment. For purposes of this motion, the taxpayers conceded that questions of the merits of the revocation of the IRS rulings were not to be considered; the facts were to be viewed as though ITT had not sold the shares previously acquired for cash to Mediobanca. The taxpayers also conceded, solely for purposes of their motion for summary judgment, that the initial cash purchases of Hartford stock had been made for the purpose of furthering ITT's efforts to acquire Hartford.

In short, even if ITT were to have prevailed on the technical tax issues involved in the reorganization, ITT and its corporate executives stand accused of having contrived an elaborate scheme to deceive vital agencies of our government.

The Matter of Ernst & Ernst re Westec

On May 31, 1978, the Securities and Exchange Commission issued another of its blockbuster Accounting Series Releases. This one, numbered 248, was the "Matter of Ernst & Ernst, Clarence T. Isensee and John F. Maurer." This promulgation marked the end of a decade's so-called "Section 2(e) proceedings"—brought by the Commission as an administrative matter to determine the appropriateness of the respondents' conduct in a particular case or cases—and to determine their right to continue to practice before the SEC.

Here I will let the release speak for itself in laying out the allegations and the SEC's consideration.

At the outset we have the Securities and Exchange Commission's synopsis of the case:

> Where firm of certified public accountants certified two years' financial statements which were materially false and misleading in that, among other

things, earnings of companies acquired or purportedly acquired by issuer after balance sheet dates were included in earnings under pooling-of-interests accounting even though pooling requirements were not met, and one year's earnings statements also reflected huge profit on property sale which was not arm's-length transaction; and the firm, its partner in charge of the audits and the audit manager failed to comply with generally accepted auditing standards as to those and other transactions and failed to fulfill responsibilities as independent accountants by reliance on management's unsupported and questionable representations, held, the firm and the individual respondents engaged in improper professional conduct. . . .

As an overture to the dramatic presentation, Accounting Series Release No. 248 informed that Ernst & Ernst (E&E), a large national accounting firm, and two of its partners, Clarence T. Isensee and John F. Maurer, were charged with professional misconduct. Following lengthy hearings, the administrative law judge filed a decision sustaining most of the charges against them. Some of the background facts are: E&E became auditors for Western Equities, Inc. (Westec) in September, 1964. Isensee had been an E&E partner since 1959; Maurer was, at the time, the "audit manager"—he became a partner in 1970.

The charges were based on their audits and E&E's certification of financial statements of Westec for the fiscal years ended December 31, 1964, and 1965.

Westec was a Houston-based conglomerate which combined the talents of the two arch villains of the scenario, James W. Williams and Ernest M. Hall. For their misdeeds they were convicted and incarcerated. Westec stock was traded on the American Stock Exchange; under the Hall-Williams aegis the price rose from 3 to 67. In August, 1966, when the shares were at 45, trading was halted because Hall was unable to pay for $8 million worth of the company's stock he had bought through nominees.

It was indispensable to the Williams-Hall scheme to create the impression that Westec was a dynamic conglomerate with soaring earnings. The 1964 and 1965 financial statements and the shareholder messages based on them clearly conveyed that impression. In Westec's 1964 annual report, Williams and Hall reported that the year had been the most successful in the company's history. Earnings were reported at a record level of 43 cents a share, compared to only 12 cents the year before. Williams and Hall advised shareholders that their objective—which they expected to achieve—was to increase earnings by at least 75 percent in 1965. According to the 1965 report, the results far surpassed expectations. Earnings were reported as $1.10 per share. Williams and Hall forecast another 75 percent increase in 1966. Soon thereafter the bubble burst.

Some specific allegations contained in the SEC promulgation, concerning the 1964 financial statements:

The principal focus of the Chief Accountant's allegations of misconduct in connection with Westec's 1964 financial statements is on three transactions reflected in the reported net earnings for that year of $1,331,966, or $.43 per share:

1. The sale by Westec's Instrument Corporation of Florida (ICF) division of a plant and real estate in Florida to one Donald McGregor, a friend and business associate of Hall and Williams, for a reported gain of $89,984.
2. Westec's acquisition in March 1965 of two companies, Doliver Corporation and Beco, Inc., and the accounting treatment given those acquisitions as "pooling of interests." That treatment resulted in the inclusion of those companies' 1964 earnings in Westec's consolidated earnings for that year, with Doliver contributing $115,364, or $0.03½ per share, and Beco $79,360, or $.02½ per share.

As for the following year's aberrations:

E&E's audit report for Westec's 1965 financial statements was dated April 28, 1966, and was authorized for printing in final form on that date. The annual report to Westec's shareholders was mailed a few days later. According to the statement of earnings, Westec had consolidated net earnings of $4,868,913, or $1.10 per share. The earnings were attributable in their entirety to the following ... . transactions effected at or after the end of the fiscal year.

1. The acquisitions by Westec in April 1966 of two companies, Seacat-Zapata Offshore Company, S.A. (Seacat) and Engineers and Fabricators, Inc. (Efco), which were accounted for as poolings of interests and contributed $684,805 and $896,178, respectively, to Westec's 1965 earnings.
2. The sale, in late December 1965, of so-called "carved-out production payments" by Camerina Petroleum Corporation, a Westec subsidiary. The reporting of this transaction under the "current income method" resulted in the inclusion of almost $1.3 million in Westec's 1965 net earnings.
3. The sale, also in late December 1965, of oil and gas properties by Weco Petroleum Co., another Westec subsidiary, for a reported gain of over $2 million.

The Commission, sitting in an essentially judicial capacity to review the findings and recommendations of the administrative law judge, rendered its independent judgment on each of the foregoing transactions.

As to the charade regarding the ICF sales:

> This conclusion [that the auditors should have obtained independent verification of the critical elements of the ICF transaction] is buttressed by the context in which the ICF transaction was presented to respondents. Among other things, it was a last-minute transaction and was followed after year's end by several other transactions . . . which had the effect of further increasing 1964 income. Moreover, as the administrative law judge found, Isensee and Maurer were aware of an earlier transaction involving McGregor that was of a questionable nature. . . .

As to the dirty pooling proclivities of Westec, *et al.*, the Commission provides us with the following footnote to history:

> It is not surprising that the ability of pooling accounting to create instant sales and earnings endeared it to the managements of the conglomerate companies which were proliferating in the 1950's and 1960's, and contributed to the pressure to liberalize the conditions under which its use was acceptable to the accounting profession. And, for such managements, purchase accounting had significant disadvantages. . . .

It may be of some significance to note that Ernst & Ernst, and Isensee particularly, were in the vanguard of making pooling-of-interests accounting applicable beyond anything that might have been contemplated by the original concept.

As to Doliver Pool:

> In our judgement, the inclusion of the Doliver earnings in Westec's 1964 income through pooling accounting was clearly improper and respondents' audit of the transaction was inadequate. . . .
>
> The frontiers of that concept may have been hazy. But there were some clear limitations. . . .
>
> Not only was the audit of the transaction itself inadequate, but the surrounding circumstances cried out for a thorough scrutiny. Among other things, the transaction was on its face a last-minute effort to augment Westec's 1964 earnings. There was no written contract covering it. The board of directors' minutes did not reflect board approval. And Isensee had already been subjected to management efforts to puff up 1964 earnings through inclusion of a 1965 transaction. . . .

As to the other 1964 *nunc pro tunc* contrived pooling injection (from the Beco acquisition):

We find it difficult, if not impossible, to believe that Isensee and particularly Maurer, who acknowledged dipping into the audited Beco statements, did not actually read note 1 to those statements before the 10-K was filed with us. Maurer would have been incredibly myopic in either not noting or not following up the reference to Beco as a Metric subsidiary on the very page he concededly looked at. But even on the unlikely assumption that respondents did not read note 1, they clearly should have. Dr. Glen A. Welsch, one of the respondents' own experts, testified that in this kind of situation, "you would normally expect" that the audit manager or someone under him would read the audited financial statements.

An Especially Exotic Pooling of Interests

Turning now to the perfidious conduct impacted into Westec's 1965 certified financial statements: First we are told of a Seacat-Zapata deal which was initiated three months after Westec's 1965 books were ostensibly closed but which nevertheless got itself pooled into 1965—and that year's financial statements were cooked to the tune of almost $700,000. The deal was exotic, involving a swap of Westec shares for some of Seacat's, a contract for the buyout of some other of the latter's shares owned by Zapata, and a management contract with Zapata.

As something of a student of the exotics and esoterics of pooling-of-interests accounting, I have yet to see one as convoluted as what E&E and Isensee determined to be an appropriate pool. This isn't just dirty pooling, it's the *reductio ad absurdum*. According to the SEC:

> The administrative law judge concluded that pooling accounting was not proper for the Seacat acquisition, principally because of the management contract. We agree that aside from any other factors, that contract precluded pooling treatment for the transaction. . . .

The 1965 books were left open for yet another month—all the way to the last days of April—permitting yet another dirty pool to be infiltrated *nunc pro tunc*. This concoction injected about $900,000 into Westec's 1965 reported bottom line.

Now here there was a catch which for Westec and its auditors was a mere detail. Efco's principal shareholders wanted a cash deal, not Westec's stock. Accordingly that would preclude pooling-fooling accounting. Whereupon Tupper, a company ostensibly independent, came on the scene as Westec's fairy godmother—it bought the shares from the Efco holders and proceeded to swap them for a bundle of $6.4 million in Westec stock. And so:

The administrative law judge concluded that the transaction was not properly accounted for as a pooling because (1) Tupper was only used by Westec as a mere conduit and the transaction between the two companies was not arm's-length, and (2) there was a 100% change in ownership immediately preceding Westec's acquisition. We fully agree with his conclusion to the extent that it rests on the first ground. Clearly, Tupper was merely a tool of Westec and was interposed to create the appearance of an acquisition for Westec stock notwithstanding the refusal of Efco shareholders to take such stock. In substance, the transaction amounted to a purchase by Westec for cash. We further find that respondents should have known or discovered the sham nature of the arrangements with Tupper.

Did Westec's auditors know that this deal was a fake? The release doesn't use this precise language but it does go on to assert that only persons determined to be blind and deaf and especially dumb could fail to recognize that they were on a dung heap. And so E&E permitted this pile created in late April, 1966, to be dumped into Westec's 1965 income accounts.

Next we were told of how Westec generated more than a million dollars (about 25 percent of its reported 1965 numbers) from a sale of so-called "carved-out production payments." The contract price went into 1965 income even though the income was properly to be attenuated over the period of ultimate, actual production.

Westec's practice was discredited by 1965 but, apparently no one had yet said "Absolutely not!"—so E&E and Isensee decided to go along.

Here the Commission rejected the determination of the administrative law judge and accepted the respondents' response. This leads us to the Weco Oil Property Sales matter.

According to the release, this was the "largest single profit item reported by Westec for 1965." The income injected by the transaction amounted to more than $2 million. The SEC then asserted that:

> . . . The sale was in fact a sham transaction engineered by Hall and Williams to inflate Westec's income. Irving [the purchaser] was a corporation created by Hall's brother at Hall's instance for the purpose of effecting the transaction. Respondents did not know that the transaction was not bona fide. But the administrative law judge found, as charged by the Chief Accountant, that their lack of knowledge resulted from a failure to comply with generally accepted auditing standards in their examination of the transaction. We agree.

In my *Unaccountable Accounting* I impeached E&E for lack of independence in the Westec audit, principally on the basis of what I asserted was its direct and overt involvement in the pooling transactions. The administrative law judge also used the poolings as the focus of his attack on E&E's lack of independence. The SEC, on review, concurred in a finding that there was a failure of independence—but rooted its indictment in other grounds:

> . . . But we are in accord with the law judge's finding of lack of independence insofar as it rests on respondents' repeated dependence on management representations concerning significant information. As noted above, it was particularly in connection with the last-minute pooling transactions, which contributed significantly to the appearance that Westec's earnings were soaring, that respondents uncritically accepted such representations when the circumstances called for independent inquiry or investigation. Perhaps the most flagrant example is the Efco transaction. The respondents simply accepted management's representation concerning Tupper, the "new non-related stockholder," when, as noted, the circumstances surrounding the transaction—and respondents' experience with management representations in the Beco situation—cried out for a thorough independent investigation.

The Punishment to Fit the Crime

Having thus spelled out the tales of the sordid involvement by E&E, *et al.*, in this monstrous hoax, the Securities and Exchange Commission, that prestigious regulatory agency, proceeded to its ultimate judgment, to decree the punishment to the professional persons and their firm responsible for this perfidious conduct. Here is the judgment from the mount:

> Notwithstanding the seriousness of respondents' misconduct, however, we have concluded that the sanctions imposed by the administrative law judge are unduly severe. Among the factors which lead us to that conclusion are the fact that we have set aside certain of the law judge's findings, and that, in the years since 1965, the respondents have been subjected to an extensive series of investigations and proceedings which, combined with the sanctions that we impose and the publication of this decision, cannot fail to have a powerful deterrent effect.
>
> With respect to E&E as a firm, the record does not reflect an involvement sufficient to warrant a sanction greater than censure.
>
> Under all the circumstances, we shall issue an order suspending Isensee from appearance or practice before us for one year and Maurer for three months, and censuring E&E.

"Deterrent effect?" Humbug!! The august Securities and Exchange Commission may have overlooked the irony of their determination. At

the moment they were writing about the deterring effect which this obloquy might have on E&E, the SEC was concluding its report to the Congress of the United States entitled *The Accounting Profession and the Commission's Oversight Role.* That report stakes the SEC's faith in the future of
the profession on the newly structured peer review procedures of the
AICPA's SEC-Practice Division. And who is it that's at the head of that
peer review group? None other than an E&E partner. If the SEC were
to reread the ways in which E&E sought to justify their actions in the
Westec case, could they not recognize the standards by which peers
will judge peers?

There is, of course, ample precedent for this hypocrisy. Remember
that the other blockbusting landmark disciplinary action enshrined in
an Accounting Series Release was Number 173 against Peat, Marwick,
Mitchell.

And so it came to pass that when the SEC-Practice Division was
carved out by the accounting establishment, where did it turn to find
the chairman of its Executive Committee? You guessed it—to the managing partner of PMM. And he sat in that awesome spot to regulate the
conduct of his peers while another partner in that firm was ensconced
as Chairman (chief elected officer) of the whole establishment as represented by the AICPA. "Deterrent effect?" Humbug!!

The Westec fiasco, and especially E&E's overt and direct involvement,
have been much on my mind for over a decade (witness my *Unaccountable
Accounting*). It is my considered view that the Westec imbroglio was, if
anything, even more horrendous than Continental Vending or National
Student Marketing.

The Matter of Touche Ross

Let's turn now to the May, 1979, decision of the United States Court
of Appeals for the Second Circuit, in *Touche Ross & Co. v. Securities and
Exchange Commission*, which begins on the following lament:

> On September 1, 1976—more than two and one-half years ago—the
> SEC, pursuant to Rule 2(e) of its Rules of Practice . . . entered an order
> which provided for a public administrative proceeding against the accounting
> firm of Touche Ross & Co. and three of its former partners, Edwin Heft,
> James M. Lynch and Armin J. Frankel. The firm and the three partners,
> all appellants, will be referred to collectively as "Touche Ross" or "appel-
> lants."
>
> The proceeding was instituted to determine whether appellants had en-
> gaged in unethical, unprofessional or fraudulent conduct in their audits of
> the financial statements of Giant Stores Corporation and Ampex Corporation.

The SEC's September, 1976, grievous allegations against Touche Ross (TR) included, first, that in its audit of Giant Stores' 1972 financial statements TR failed to follow GAAS and misapplied GAAP in (among other things):

a. Accepted theories and accounting entries which were contrary to generally accepted accounting principles, such as, the improper recording of certain credits by Giant. . . .

b. Accepted the recording of certain items, without performing adequate auditing procedures with respect thereto and without a reasonable basis for such acceptance.

c. Accepted inconsistent representations and contradictory explanations by Giant management as to the basis and reasons for certain items. . . .

d. Overruled the conclusions of certain members of Touche's audit staff without a reasonable basis and continually placed excessive reliance on the representations of Giant management despite, among other things, the warnings of certain members of the Touche audit staff as to the suspect credibility of Giant management. . . .

e. Failed to obtain proper and sufficient confirmations or to follow sufficient alternative procedures to support the recording by Giant of certain items, and disregarded contrary information in its possession. . . .

f. Disregarded evidence obtained by Touche's audit staff. . . .

g. Disregarded or failed to adequately respond to numerous facts and circumstances which raised questions as to the credibility of Giant's management and the propriety of the recording by Giant of certain items. . . .

h. Negotiated with Giant management the dollar amount of certain items to be recorded, including the allowance for bad debts and an accounts payable accrual. The amounts agreed upon were arbitrarily determined, were without any reasonable basis or support, and were materially at variance with evidence developed by the Touche audit staff.

Second, regarding the TR audit of Ampex's 1971 financial statements:

a. The allowance for doubtful accounts receivable as it appeared on the Consolidated Balance Sheet of Ampex as of May 1, 1971 was substantially understated. Touche knew that a significant adjustment was needed to increase the allowance for doubtful accounts. . . .

b. Touche ascertained that as of May 1, 1971, current royalty payment commitments arising out of minimum guarantee provisions of licensing agreements, not recoverable from tape sale revenues, approximated $10 to $15 million. This would have represented an additional fiscal 1971 cost of Ampex. Touche and Ampex, through negotiation of a "trade off," arrived at a 1971 addition of only $5 million to the then existing provision of $1 million. . . .

c. In addition to the inadequate provision for losses arising out of minimum guarantee provisions of licensing agreements . . . the Music Division of Ampex had on May 1, 1971 firm obligations to pay approximately $80 million in royalties to various music companies in years subsequent to fiscal 1971. . . .

The Circuit Court proceeded unanimously to reject Touche Ross's endeavors to forestall the SEC's administrative probe. Having been repulsed by the circuit court, Touche Ross might have gotten its Washington superlawyers (Arnold & Porter) to petition the Supreme Court to get the SEC off its back and not make it go through the ignominy of an administrative Rule 2(e) proceeding.

Instead, through an *entente cordiale* proceedings were terminated with a June 27, 1979, edict from the Securities and Exchange Commission which amended an earlier 1974 Accounting Series Release (No. 153, which faulted Touche Ross for its performance in the U.S. Financial audits). Putting everything else aside, TR's negotiators attained a *tour de force* since all of their client's sins are combined into a unitary presentation—one which is pushed back five and a half years in the SEC annals—where only some cantankerous scholar would go hunting. But the negotiators achieved even more, as will be pointed up presently.

What does this June, 1979, supplement (labeled ASR 153A) tell us?

First, it turns out that the 1974 release had ordered a review of TR's practices and procedures. Because the Giant Stores–Ampex matters had surfaced by that time, the review then ordered was put into deep-freeze. (In the meantime, it should be noted, a retired Touche Ross partner was designated with the SEC's concurrence to serve as a member of the Peat, Marwick review panel required by ASR 173, promulgated against that firm in 1975. And the managing partner of TR turns up in 1977 as the chairman of a select Financial Accounting Foundation panel to study the structure and operation of the Financial Accounting Standards Board. And then, too, during the hiatus TR managed to merge into itself one of the old-line, second-tier accounting firms. All this, mind you, when the firm should have been devoting all of its talents to purging itself of the sins of the past.)

The 1979 promulgation proceeded to a further recapitulation of Touche Ross's failings in the Giant Stores–Ampex audits, essentially along the lines set forth in the September 1, 1976, order directing the litigated and now aborted 2(e) hearings. In addition this later promulgation devoted an extensive section to "The Conduct of Touche Ross's

Supervisory Personnel." This section included the following critical comments:

> Faced with . . . difficulties (in the audit) Frankel (the TR partner in charge of the audit) in early April, 1972, requested assistance. A Touche Ross partner, who was a retail expert, was assigned to handle the inventory and accounts payable area. Another partner was assigned to assist Frankel in formulating an audit program for the difficult items. This partner's assignment ultimately resulted in conflict with Frankel and confusion among the audit staff. When the inability to accept certain items continued into mid-April, the head of Touche Ross's Boston office referred Frankel and the other partners working on the Giant audit to Heft, one of six regional accounting directors.
>
> The Boston partners working on the audit met with Heft in New York on April 13 but did not inform him of the doubts of the Touche Ross staff concerning the integrity of client management, the auditing conflicts which had developed, or the rancorous nature of the client relationships. In fact, Frankel, in response to an inquiry by Heft, stated that he had found no evidence that the client was dishonest.
>
> At the April 13, 1972, meeting in New York, the facts concerning the problem items were not sufficiently developed to fully inform Heft. . . .
>
> On April 18, 1972, Touche Ross's representatives met with Giant at Giant's request. . . .

> *   *   *

> The Commission finds that Heft functioned at the April 18 meeting more as an arbitrator than an auditor. . . .
>
> During this meeting, Giant personnel continuously calculated earnings per share on a pocket calculator. When the calculations reached Giant's reduced target earnings figure of $.83 per share (before extraordinary items) Giant ceased to be contentious. . . .
>
> On April 18, when the final decisions were to be made, certain Touche Ross personnel failed to effectively communicate their own doubts or took such a vacillating stand that several of their proposed adjustments were reduced or not accepted. . . .
>
> A similar matter arose in a Commission investigation of Ampex. In the financial statements for fiscal year ended May, 1971, which statements were audited by Touche Ross, the Commission found that Touche Ross agreed to reduce the proposed allowance for uncollectible accounts by $8 million because of counterbalancing "hidden reserves." The Commission finds this to be improper because the allowance for uncollectible accounts should have

been correctly portrayed to reflect a trend of significant increase and sufficient competent evidence was not obtained to support the allowance.

All these allegations of grievous errors of omission and commission led the SEC to conclude that Touche Ross's audit of Giant "failed to meet those requirements which the accounting profession has established for itself."

Further, according to the Commission, "the audit was permeated with undue reliance placed on the representations of Giant management." The SEC summed up its conclusion with the following obloquy:

> . . . Touche Ross was presented with a large number of suspicious and inadequately documented last-minute adjustments, replete with incongruities and audit problems. The troublesome elements were rationalized with contradictory explanations by a client pressuring for an unqualified opinion on a favorable earnings statement and for a quick conclusion of the audit.

Again, the Punishment That Fits

All this is but prologue to the punishment deemed to fit TR's aberrations; that punishment is enshrined as Section V of the June, 1979, release:

> Respondents Touche Ross and Frankel have submitted offers of settlement in which, without admitting or denying the allegations of the September 1, 1976, Order for Proceedings under Rule 2(e), they consent to the issuance of this Opinion and Order, waive their rights to further Court and Commission hearings in these matters, and waive their right to filing of proposed findings of fact and conclusions of law. Touche Ross, in its offer of settlement, agrees that the Commission in the Opinion and Order may impose a censure upon the firm for its conduct of the 1972 audit of Giant discussed herein.
>
> The Touche Ross offer of settlement contemplates that the peer review required by ASR 153 will be conducted during 1979. . . .

In addition Frankel agreed not to engage in practice before the SEC for five months and Heft, having retired five years ago, asked that no sanctions be imposed against him.

And lest we forget, the respondents agreed that they would not pursue their right to appeal the May, 1979, decision of the United States Circuit Court. Whereupon: "After careful consideration the Commission has determined to accept the Offers of Settlement submitted by respondents Touche Ross, Frankel, and Heft."

Strangely, even though ASR 153A recapitulates the SEC's allegation of the firm's failures on the Ampex audit, there appears to be no censure meted out to anyone for the serious transgression. Somehow Ampex appears to have fallen through the cracks. Inquiry of the SEC brought forth the response that the Commission was of the view that the general censure meted out to Touche Ross adequately covered both situations; further, there did not appear to be particular persons prominently identifiable with the Ampex aberrations.

What are my misgivings regarding this SEC expedition?

To begin with, the "consent decree" mechanism, with its nonadmission and nondenial of the allegations, is an abomination. Either the allegations are true and determined or they are to be rejected. If the parties to a dispute cannot agree on the facts, then the judicial process requires that we turn to a judge or jury to make the determination. In this process testimony is presented under oath and with penalties for perjury.

As a consequence of this hammering on the anvil of justice, other proceedings might ensue—including disciplinary proceedings within the profession. Failing court action, the respondents (e.g., Touche, et al.) might insist that the profession (i.e., the AICPA, if it should get around to it) proceed de novo.

Further, I find the punishment meted out in this instance (and generally where respondents are giants in the accounting and possibly the legal professions) lack symmetry with that accorded ordinary mortals.

The objection might be voiced that you cannot condemn the whole international operation of a giant accounting firm because of transgressions, however serious, in one, two, three offices. My response is that these giants command positions of importance and honor not necessarily because of the competence of particular individuals, but because of the very giantism of the firms. Consequently, I maintain, the firm as a whole should bear the onus of sins in its various offices. Only by clipping their wings will these giants be made effectively responsive to the standards which govern everyone else.

Finally, the bargained outcome of the Touche Ross affair moved the probe of the firm's practices (partners apparently dissembling) from public scrutiny to the confidentiality of a review committee designated by Touche Ross from a roster suggested by the Commission.

By so doing, according to the SEC promulgation, "the contents of the examination, the working papers, files and other documentation (except the Committee's Report) and the deliberations of the Committee will be kept confidential, except from Touche Ross and the Commission, to the extent permitted by law."

And as a result, documents which might have been scrutinized by those responsible for administering a code of professional ethics or by scholars generally are to be hidden from view.

Finally, despite my misgivings about the final judgment reached by the SEC in Accounting Series Release 248, regarding Ernst & Ernst, it should be noted that in that proceeding we may see the findings of fact and law of an independent administrative law judge. In addition we see reported the specific recommendations from the staff of the SEC, and the defenses advanced by the respondents. In short, the open judicial process and its adversary nature are the most effective means for informing the public regarding the circumstances of a controversy—assuming, of course, that this process does not end in plea bargaining.

And any member of the American Institute of CPA's who may be in the office of the chief accountant of the Securities and Exchange Commission and has access to the files involving, say, the Touche Ross aberrations has a positive obligation to file a formal complaint with the Ethics Division of the AICPA. This is a burden vested in members under the Institute's Code of Professional Ethics. If these persons fail to file such an advice with the Ethics Division, then I maintain that these officers of the Securities and Exchange Commission have themselves violated our Code of Professional Ethics.

Again we must give guidance to good conduct from the leaders in our society, including those who have been elevated to important positions in our government.

The Courts on Trial

The courts deserve a share of the responsibility for the prevailing malaise in corporate accountability.

The consent decree, as I've asserted in the preceding section, is a poor way to encourage righteousness. In such a disposition, the court typically incorporates the euphemism, "without admitting or denying. . . ," and then instructs defendant to behave himself henceforth as a law-abiding citizen is supposed to. Judges who put their seals on such decisions can't claim to be upholding the dignity of their courts; they are merely clearing the dockets and producing neat statistics for themselves and the Securities and Exchange Commission.

The courts may also be faulted for low numbers of cases heard. Note the front-page headline of *The New York Times* (July 15, 1979): "U.S. Attack on Corporate Crime Yields Handful of Cases in 2 Years." Of course the courts are not alone to blame for this condition. The

Justice Department, which must initiate and prepare cases, is ensnarled by lawyers, often politically powerful, representing corporate defendants, and by the occupants of the executive suites.

However, a general criticism of the courts is not my present objective. But we must recognize that the strict-constructionist philosophy of the majority of the incumbents of the Supreme Court of the United States has endangered the effective administration of the federal securities laws.

The courts had been an effective ally of those of us who hoped for higher standards of performance by the accounting profession in its fulfillment of the attest function, especially when it involved the audit of publicly held corporations. In this service the profession performs its responsibility as the historian in the economic microcosm. For this service the accountant is entitled to the status and stature of a professional. Legal actions, brought generally on a class-action basis under Section 10(b) of the Securities Exchange Act of 1934 and Rule 10b-5 of the SEC's regulations thereunder, have forced the profession to a higher standard of responsibility than it was willing to undertake on its own initiative.

The Hochfelder Setback

In May, 1976, when I was asked to testify before Congressman John E. Moss's Committee on Oversight and Investigations, I said that the hope for upward mobility had been seriously set back by the decision of the Supreme Court of the United States in *Ernst & Ernst v. Hochfelder* (425 U.S. 185, March 30, 1976). The majority opinion of the Court stated the issue at the outset (it should be noted that Ernst & Ernst, the auditors, were the defendant-petitioners; Hochfelder the euchred plaintiff-respondent):

> The issue in this case is whether an action for civil damages may be under Sec. 10(b) of the Securities Exchange Act of 1934 . . . and Securities and Exchange Commission Rule 10b-5 . . . *in the absence of an allegation of intent to deceive, manipulate or defraud* on the part of the defendant [emphasis mine].

After an exhaustive analysis of the semantics of the 1934 congressional enactment, the Court decreed that ". . . the language of Section 10(b) . . . clearly connotes *intentional misconduct* . . ." (emphasis supplied). Since there were no allegations made that Ernst & Ernst were accomplices of the perpetrator of the fraud against Hochfelder, *et al.*, they were exculpated. The language of the decision would appear to require a direct or conspiratorial involvement on the part of the auditors to support an action under Rule 10b-5. The majority's decision was put into clear perspective by the opening paragraph of a sharply worded dissent by Justice Blackmun:

> Once again . . . the Court interprets Sec. 10(b) . . . restrictively and narrowly and thereby stultifies recovery for the victim. This time the Court does so by confining the statute and the Rule to situations where the defendant has "scienter," that is, the "intent to deceive, manipulate, or defraud." Sheer negligence, the Court says, is not within the reach of the statute and the Rule, and was not contemplated when the great reforms of 1933, 1934, and 1942 were effectuated by Congress and the Commission.

Blackmun's dissent includes an impassioned plea for holding the auditors responsible for their apparently conceded negligence, pointing up the critical role played by the auditor accountants in the securities arena.

Nevertheless, the Court has decreed that negligence by a professional person is not sufficient to hold him liable to those victimized by his negligence, even though the person claims competence, expertise, and responsibility. For me this pretentious claim is a fraud if negligence is a hidden factor in the profession's tool box. To make matters even more confusing, there are those legal experts who are asserting that even reckless negligence would not support an action against an auditor under 10(b).

By *Hochfelder* the Court has set back the process of the accountant's responsibility in securities matters by forty years. In a *Yale Law Journal* article, December, 1933, William O. Douglas (then a professor at Yale) and George E. Bates commented on the impact of the developing securities legislation on accountants. They took careful note of Justice Cardozo's 1931 decision in the *Ultramares v. Touche* case, where he asserted that negligence per se would not support an action by third parties; instead, he decreed a standard of *gross* negligence (hence, constructive fraud). The Douglas-Bates article asserted:

> To say the least the Act goes as far in protection of purchasers of securities as plaintiff in *Ultramares Corp. v. Touche* unsuccessfully urged the New York Court of Appeals to go in the protection of a creditor. The change which that court thought so "revolutionary" as to be "wrought by legislation" has been made. And the duty placed on experts such as accountants has not been measured by the expert's relation to his employer but by his service to the investor.

The authors went on to observe that this burden may be so onerous as to discourage "reputable and substantial persons" from serving as experts. "Nevertheless," they continued, "it may be predicted that the fees of these experts will measurably increase. . . ." Assuredly accountants' fees have increased measurably since then. But the Court has now put the investors back to square one, insofar as their relying on the auditors' professed expertise under the 1934 Act.

As a consequence of the Supreme Court's introduction of the "*scienter* standard,*" it becomes necessary for a plaintiff in a Section 10(b) action to prove without a doubt that the auditor was a willing accomplice.

The Supreme Court did, however, leave an open door with footnote 12 to the *Hochfelder* decision:

> [T]he term scienter refers to a mental state embracing intent to deceive, manipulate, or defraud. In certain areas of the law recklessness is considered to be a form of intentional misconduct for purposes of imposing liability for some act. *We need not address here the question whether in some circumstances reckless behavior is sufficient for civil liability under Section 10(b) and Rule 10b-5* [emphasis mine].

That footnote has produced exhausting analysis by courts, lawyers, and law review editors.

The Supreme Court's judgment in *Hochfelder* has not been unanimously accepted by congressional committees responsible for the oversight of the accounting profession. For example, from the October, 1976, report of the Moss Committee: "Legislation amending 10(b) of the Securities and Exchange Act of 1934 is needed to protect the public against negligence by accountants and others, regardless of intent to deceive or defraud."

And from the November, 1977, Report of the Subcommittee on Reports, Accounting and Management—the one headed by the late Senator Lee Metcalf:

> The goals set forth in this report are designed to strengthen the practice of independent auditing in the private sector so that government involvement, especially at the Federal level, will be minimized. Accordingly, the subcommittee strongly supports enforcement mechanisms to make the system work in the private sector without extensive Federal participation. Testimony during the subcommittee's accounting hearings clearly demonstrated that potential legal liability for negligence is the most effective mechanism for assuring that independent auditors perform their public responsibilities competently and diligently.
>
> The subcommittee believes that independent auditors of publicly owned corporations should be liable for their negligence to private parties who suffer damages as a result. The "private attorney-general" concept—which

permits private parties to recover damages through the judicial system—serves the public best because it provides incentive for independent auditors to perform responsibly while compensating private parties who have actually suffered damages through the proven negligence of errant auditors. To be effective, the system must allow access to the judicial process for parties claiming damages, and auditors found negligent should not receive special treatment by having their liability artificially limited by law.

And when, in late 1978, Congressman Moss introduced his bill to regulate the accounting profession, he addressed the *Hochfelder* issue as follows ("Liability of Accounting Firms"):

Sec. 10. *(a)* Any independent public accounting firm shall be liable for any damages sustained by any private party as a result of such party's reliance on an audit report by such firm with respect to a financial statement, report, or other document filed with the Commission under any Federal securities law, if such accounting firm was negligent in the preparation of such audit report.

(b) Any person suffering damages described in subsection (a) of this section may bring an action in the appropriate district court of the United States against the allegedly negligent independent public accounting firm.

The Redington Decision of the Supreme Court

But then, in June, 1979, the Supreme Court dropped another shoe—its decision in *Touche Ross & Co. v. Edward S. Redington, 442* U.S. *560.*

Justice Rehnquist's opener (in the opinion written in behalf of himself and six of his colleagues) was as follows:

Once again, we are called upon to decide whether a private remedy is implicit in a statute not expressly providing one. . . . Here we decide whether customers of securities brokerage firms that are required to file certain financial reports with regulatory authorities by Section 17(a) of the Securities Exchange Act of 1934 have an implied cause of action for damages under Section 17(a) against accountants who audit such reports based on misstatements contained in the reports.

The case arose from the fact that Weis Securities, Inc., a registered broker-dealer, went "belly up" in 1973. Edward Redington was designated as the trustee in liquidation, whereupon he instituted suit against Touche Ross for the benefit of the Securities Investors Protection Corporation (SIPC), which had provided the funds to discharge Weis's liability to its customers as required by the act which created SIPC.

Touche Ross, as Weis's auditors, had prepared for filing with the

SEC the annual reports on Weis's financial condition, as required by Section 17(a) of the Securities Exchange Act of 1934. The theory of the plaintiffs' case was essentially that proper audits by Touche would have revealed Weis's difficulties at an earlier stage—permitting "remedial action to forestall liquidation or to lessen the adverse financial consequences of such a liquidation to the Weis customers," and that Section 17(a) gave rise to an implied right of action against Touche to recoup customer losses which could have been prevented.

The Court rejected Redington's theory that 17(a) gave rise to a private cause of action against the auditors; instead, according to the majority:

> . . . Section 17(a) simply requires broker-dealers and others to keep such records and file such reports as the [Securities and Exchange] Commission may prescribe. It does not, by its terms, purport to create a private cause of action in favor of anyone. . . .
>
> The intent of Section 17(a) is evident from its face. Section 17(a) is like provisions in countless other statutes that simply require certain regulated businesses to keep records and file periodic reports to enable the relevant governmental authorities to perform their regulatory functions.
>
> . . . The information contained in the Section 17(a) reports is intended to provide the Commission, the Exchange and other authorities with a sufficiently early warning to enable them to take appropriate action to protect investors before the financial collapse of the particular broker-dealer involved. But Section 17(a) does not by any stretch of its language purport to confer private damage rights or, indeed, any remedy in the event the regulatory authorities are unsuccessful in achieving their objectives and the broker becomes insolvent before corrective steps can be taken.

Justice Marshall, as the lone dissenter, lamented the majority's view, asserting ". . . because the SEC lacks the resources to audit all the documents that brokers file, it must rely on certification by accountants. . . . Implying a private right of action would both facilitate the SEC's enforcement efforts and provide an incentive for accountants to perform the certification functions properly."

The Geotek–Arthur Young Matter

In a decision involving neither *Hochfelder* nor *Redington,* the Circuit Court of Appeals for the Ninth Circuit rejected an SEC endeavor to reprimand Arthur Young & Co for its alleged failings in the *Geotek* case:

To accept the SEC's position would go far toward making the accountant both an insurer of his client's honesty and an enforcement arm of the SEC. . . . The difficulty with this is that Congress has not enacted the conscription bill that the SEC seeks to have us fashion and fix as an interpretive gloss on existing securities laws.

The early history of the administration of the securities acts indicates that the independent auditors argued successfully for the privilege of becoming paid mercenaries in enforcing those laws. This view is supported by the frequently quoted assertion by the SEC that:

The Commission and its staff do not and cannot investigate representations made to it, but must be able to rely on their completeness if this process is to work. The objectives of the securities laws can only be achieved when those professionals who practice before the Commission, both lawyers and accountants, act in a manner consistent with their responsibilities. Professionals involved in the disclosure process are in very real sense representatives of the investing public served by the Commission, and, as a result, their dealings with the Commission and its staff must be permeated with candor and full disclosure. It cannot resemble an adversary relationship more appropriate to litigants in court, because the Commission is not an adverse party in this context. All who are familiar with the Commission's policies know that too much importance is attached to the word of the professional, to permit his or her word to become the subject of question. A professional's word is often the functional equivalent of his or her reputation.

While *Hochfelder* and *Redington* are, in my view, inimical to the public interest and, as a consequence, to the profession, I am constrained to accept them as representing judicial interpretations of the law *qua* law— however much I might despair at the narrow interpretation accorded the law.

It is the Geotek case I find particularly disturbing; this is because in that case the court deliberated on the auditing firm's course of conduct and then determined that in the court's view the firm had proceeded in accordance with generally accepted auditing standards. Based on my review of the facts, and by my standards for GAAS, the court's determination was an unfortunate denigration of the profession.

Briefly, in Geotek the auditors were engaged to make an independent examination of the accounts of a nexus of oil-drilling ventures managed by one Jack Burke. It may well be that the venturers to whom the auditor's pursuit was intended were more desirous of depleting the resources of the United States Treasury than of Mother Earth. Nonetheless, the auditors were presumed to be pursuing their tasks in accordance with generally accepted auditing standards. And how did they pursue this noble aim?

They found, *inter alia*, that checks were being *predated* by a substantial period of months (to permit tax deductibility one year earlier for the "investors"); the funds of the venturers were commingled by Jack Burke in an unaudited (and apparently unauditable) entity owned by him called Fundamental; properties were being transferred among and between the venturers and Jack Burke and/or Fundamental as though they were markers in some parlor game. All this the auditors saw (or should have seen had they not, as the SEC put it, conducted their audit "with blinders on"). The auditors' reports on the cash basis went forth without any whistle being blown—all this, the court said, in accordance with GAAS. And, as noted, the court observed that if society expected anything more, it would presume that the auditing profession was "conscripted."

While I congratulate the accounting firm on having been thus exculpated, I nevertheless lament the court's low esteem for our profession's standards. To the extent that our colleagues hail these decisions as victories for our profession because they relieve us of responsibilities to the public as our constituents, let them be reminded that the decision thereby seems to make the external audit responsibility vestigial.

The High Court's Third Strike

Ironically, had AY been able to stall the litigation into mid-1980, the firm could have avoided the agonies of the trial and subsequent appeal. Thus, both the District and Circuit Courts assumed, for the purposes of their determinations, that the *Hochfelder scienter* standard did not apply in actions by the Securities and Exchange Commission seeking prophylactic relief, by an injunction, against a defendant who, it is alleged, violated the antifraud provisions of the Securities Acts. The issue, the respective courts had indicated, was still unresolved at the time of the Geotek determinations.

But then, on June 2, 1980, the Supreme Court of the United States decided the so-called *Aaron* case against the SEC insofar as the 10(b)–10(b)-5 issue was concerned. The case involved a broker-dealer in securities; after a strict linguistic analysis of the statutory provision worthy of the medieval scholastics, the Court decreed that the Commission had to meet the *Hochfelder* standard, just like an ordinary private citizen.

There was a dissent on this issue by Mr. Justice Blackmun (joined by Justices Brennan and Marshall); nevertheless, by the 6 to 3 majority the Court further rendered impotent the Securities and Exchange Commission in its endeavors to exorcise deceptive practices from the securities marketplace. It is now up to the Commission, if it so chooses, to endeavor to regain its effectiveness in the enforcement of the Securities Acts.

Thus, the SEC might proceed under its Administrative Rule 2(e) to discipline the persons and/or firms who had perpetrated the deceptions. It might, since it has to demonstrate wilfulness anyway, urge the Justice Department to institute criminal proceedings. Or the Commission might importune the Congress to reaffirm that which for more than twoscore years had been presumed to be the mandate handed to the Commission by the Securities Exchange Act of 1934.

As of this writing, the question arises as to whether the Commission is, in fact, desirous of undertaking any of these courses of action, thereby courting the displeasure of the "Corporate Establishment."

I can see that the accounting profession will rue the day when the determinations in the *Hochfelder, Redington,* and *Arthur Young* cases became the law of the land. This will occur when the public becomes aware that rings of protection surround the auditors. The public will soon be asking whether the independent audit function is really cost efficient. The question has already been asked, inimically to the profession, by Profs. Richard Briston and Robert Perks in their article, "The External Auditor—His Role and Cost to Society" (*Accountancy,* November, 1977).

I ask my colleagues how they would feel as passengers of commercial airlines if the Supreme Court were to decree (following *Hochfelder*) that the airlines can be held responsible for performance failure only if the plaintiffs could prove that the airlines were bent on ignoring safety precautions. Or (following *Redington*) the plaintiffs were told that the Civil Aeronautics Board rules and regulations are privy only to the CAB— and that their violation by the airlines will not give rise to a private action in behalf of an injured passenger or his estate.

4

Fiddlers on the Roof

There are two numbers which the members of the Financial Accounting Standards Board (FASB) undoubtedly wish they never heard of: 8 and 19. Number 8 was assigned sequentially to its October, 1975, promulgation, "Accounting for Translation of Foreign Currency Transactions and Foreign Currency Financial Statements." Number 19 was assigned to the December, 1977, Statement of Financial Accounting Standards, "Financial Accounting and Reporting by Oil and Gas Producing Companies."

These two major promulgations have characteristics in common. In both cases the FASB wrestled with accounting problems for which, over the years, divergent practices had evolved, and for each the Board decreed a rule, as contrasted with the formulation of a standard.

It was clearly recognized in both circumstances that the rules decreed might or might not reflect economic reality. Nonetheless, presumably to make the accountant's tallying easier, a single yardstick was to be imposed.

While decreeing rules was not unique to foreign currency translation or oil and gas accounting, in these instances the Board found itself aligned against powerful adversaries. In the number 8 situation it found itself up against the giant multinational corporations; in the number 19 situation the Board found that the smaller, independent oil and gas producers had some powerful allies in the Congress. Using that clout (combined with these companies' ability to obtain the best professional counsel that money could buy), the producers were capable of getting the Securities and Exchange Commission to finesse the FASB's Statement 19.

The presumptively imperial standard-setting board had to back away in both of these situations. At the outset I want to point out that I believe the fate of the Board in these instances (and others) was well earned; in both, it made itself vulnerable by insisting on the establishment of a rule which could be shown, in various contexts, to distort economic reality. And while the Board may have endeavored to make an invidious distinction between such reality and the accountant's numbers, those opposed to the particular rule could undercut the FASB by demonstrating the economic absurdity which would be portrayed.

The Foreign Currency: Translation Brouhaha

Let us consider these two FASB Waterloos. First, Statement 8 was undoubtedly well motivated; the Board sought to address itself to the variety of alternative accounting practices which had evolved for the translation of amounts represented in foreign currencies into the United States dollar amounts which were then to be introduced into the presumptively definitive statements to be submitted to shareholders.

This variety of experience might be categorized as follows:

A. *Conversion Rates to Be Applied:*

1. Current vs. noncurrent items: Here all current assets and current liabilities would be translated into dollars at the rates prevailing as of the close of the accounting period; the remaining items would be translated at the rates in effect when the transaction was initiated. Cash, current receivables, inventories, prepayments, and amounts currently payable would be converted at the exchange rates prevailing as of the current balance sheet date. On the other hand, plant and equipment, land, franchises, bonds payable, and deferred income taxes would be converted at the rates which prevailed as of the date when the asset was acquired (or the liability incurred).

2. Monetary vs. nonmonetary: Pursuant to this alternative, items which represent "mere" rights to money or obligations "merely" to pay money would be converted at rates prevailing as of the balance sheet date. All other items (including inventories) were to be converted at the rates prevailing when the asset was acquired or the liabilities were established.

3. Hybrid method: Pursuant to this procedure the monetary vs. nonmonetary approach would be implemented excepting that inventories would also be translated into dollars at the current exchange rates.

B. *As to Time of Recognition of the Resultant Gain or Loss:*

After the differentials resulting from the translation were determined (again, gains if the exchange rates moved favorably after the initial translation, losses if the fluctuation was adverse), the question arose as to whether the resultant gain or loss should be recognized in the current income statement, or attenuated over a period of time (during which the year-to-year pluses might vitiate the minuses from other years, and vice versa). Or, in some instances, the differences might have been footnoted but otherwise ignored in the accounts until they were realized by ultimate conversion into dollars.

The FASB first moved into this quagmire in 1973 when it promulgated its Statement 1, which merely decreed that whatever method was followed was to be fully disclosed. But then it dug itself into the mire with its ill-fated number 8. The Board opted for the monetary vs. nonmonetary alternative (albeit with a semantic quibble—it called it the "temporal method"); the Board further decreed immediate recognition on financial statements, including interim statements, of the gain or loss from the exchange fluctuations—and the feathers flew.

The effect of FASB 8 may be discerned from U.S. Steel's 1975 report (the one in which the company made the new standard operational); that report included the following as footnote 11:

> Foreign Currency Translation—U.S. Steel adopted in 1975 Financial Accounting Standards No. 8 related to foreign currency translation. The effect in 1975 was to increase income by $5.4 million or $.10 per share. As required, prior years have been restated. The net effect was to reduce income by $4.6 million or $.08 per share in 1974 and to reduce income Reinvested in Business at the beginning of 1974 by $12.8 million.
>
> The aggregate exchange gain (loss) included in income was $3.9 million in 1975 and $(9.5) million in 1974.

For 1978 U.S. Steel reported the consequences of foreign exchange fluctuations in footnote 21, as follows (in millions):

Loss on the fluctuations in the dollar value of its debt payable in foreign currencies	$ 9.1
Other foreign exchange losses (i.e., on net monetary items)	7.0
Aggregate foreign exchange loss	$16.1

For 1979 the fluctuations went the other way, to wit (in millions):

Gain re debt	$1.3
Other gains	4.2
Total gain	$5.5

The intensity of the controversy led the FASB to commission two research studies: one by Prof. Donald F. Dukes of Cornell University, "An Empirical Investigation of the Effects of (FAS 8) on Securities Return Behavior"; the other by Profs. Thomas G. Evans, William R. Folks, Jr., and Michael Jilling of the University of South Carolina, "The Impact of (FAS 8) on the Practices of American Multinationals: An Economic Impact Study."

Professor Dukes maintained that FASB Statement 8 did not significantly affect the behavior of investors. But then there are those dubbed the "efficient market aficionados" who maintain that nothing the accountants do can affect the securities pricing apparatus. This philosophy, hardly flattering to the accountant's craft, holds that all facts are known to the marketplace and are impacted into securities prices—all that accountants do is to put into some kind of a formal matrix the data already known by the investment community. And Professor Dukes presents all kinds of tables to support his conclusions.

On the other hand, the trinity from South Carolina demonstrated that the corporate decision makers are frightened out of their wits by the implications of FAS 8 and engage in all kinds of maneuvers—all legal, many inimical to the corporation's economic well being and possibly having adverse impacts on the value of the dollar in the foreign exchange markets.

It may be true that the investor doesn't give a hoot what the accountant might say—but corporate managers may perceive things differently and might, therefore, initiate prophylactic procedures—negating the presumptive neutrality of the accounting precepts.

(Ironically, to the extent the FASB is convinced by the Dukes study, they should then recognize the sterility of the Board's pursuit—and thereupon proceed to take a sabbatical or disband.)

The Conference Board Studies the Controversy

Another study, the June, 1978, Conference Board Information Bulletin 40, "Corporate Experience with FASB Statement 8" by Vincent G. Massaro, is of special interest. This study was undertaken by the Conference Board "in order to assess the impact . . . on important corporate decisions."

It did this by conducting "a survey of current practices in transnational money management . . . in which financial executives of 117 companies participated, examined corporate experience with FASB Statement 8. . . ." The 117 respondents were identified principally as chief financial officers, representatives of many of the largest companies in the nation. The sales of the respondent companies place them in the top 250 manufacturing firms.

The result of this study: "After roughly two years of corporate experience with FAS 8 the majority of respondents—60 executives—favor its repeal. Twenty-four favor modifying or substantially amending FAS 8. Only 17 financial executives favor retaining FAS 8. . . ."

According to the Conference Board study, the bases for the anti-8 feeling were as follows: On the one hand, FAS 8 did not call it like it is; on the other hand, FAS 8 changes the way it is. Thus from the Conference Board:

> . . . The broad reason given most frequently for opposing FAS 8 is that, because of FAS 8, the reported fluctuations in earnings distort real earnings and mislead shareholders and investors. The chief financial officer of a large company notes that the importance of short-term swings "is blown out of proportion." Several executives cite the increased volatility of reported earnings and increased difficulty in comparing period-to-period operating results on a consolidated basis, especially for the small investor.

A particular irritant noted by the Conference Board stemmed from the FASB requirement that inventories be translated at historical rates; the reason for this irritation is readily apparent from the following simplistic (but not unrealistic) illustration. Assume that during the quarter ended June 30, 1979, a dealer in chocolate bars buys 100,000 bars at one Swiss franc each—when a franc was worth 50 cents. The transaction was booked: Inventory, $50,000; Accounts Payable, $50,000. Assuming that the chocolate is still in inventory at the end of June (and the account remains unpaid), the Inventory would remain at $50,000 (100,000 francs converted at the 50-cent historic rate), whereas the Accounts Payable of 100,000 francs would be converted at the June 30 rate of (say) 60 cents—hence $60,000. As a consequence there would be an immediate recognition of a $10,000 loss on the monetary item Accounts Payable without any reflection of the profit implicit in the inventory (since it will, presumably, be sold by reference to the June 30 or subsequent value of the Swiss franc).

According to the Conference Board:

> . . . A large number of respondents think inventories should be valued at current rates. In fact, this is the reason for opposing FAS 8 given most

frequently by the 80 largest respondents in this survey. The chief financial officer of one of these large companies states: "The pegging of inventory creates a short position (since liabilities exceed assets), which gives rise to an unrealized foreign exchange loss when foreign currency is appreciating *vis à vis* the dollar. However, when the inventory is sold in the next reporting period, this loss is recovered through the translation of higher foreign operating earnings into U.S. dollars." Many of the executives who criticize the valuing of inventories at historical exchange rates point out that their inventories turn over roughly two to four times a year and are, therefore, really monetary, rather than nonmonetary, assets.

For some further insights into the confusion, here are some additional excerpts from the Conference Board study:

. . . A number of executives from both large and medium-sized companies indicate an increase in the use of foreign exchange forward contracts to hedge translation exposures, since translation losses are recognized quarterly. One executive from a very large company, however, points out that FAS 8 has precluded the use of hedging as a management technique since "It is not possible to hedge both the accounting and economic exposures simultaneously." The same executive sees the translation of inventories at historic rates to have the effect of reporting gains or losses "that are precisely the opposite of the ultimate economic effect." Another executive from a large company sees the treatment of inventories as "not only wrong but . . . just not understandable."

A large number of respondents also oppose the immediate recognition of foreign exchange gains or losses, particularly as regards long-term foreign debt. The chief financial officer of a large food company, for instance, points out FAS 8 does not allow a correct measure of conservatism since it requires immediate recognition of unrealized exchange gains. Another from a chemical company criticizes FAS 8 for failing to distinguish between realized losses on transactions, and unrealized losses on translation, since the latter may never occur.

An executive from a medium-size company notes that last year his company took large exchange gains on long-term debts in British pounds and Australian dollars and this year it is taking losses on the same debts—the swing representing over one-third of the company's 1976 net income. Another executive from a large company points out that the assets associated with long-term debt are translated at historical rates while the debt is translated at current rates.

The concluding segment of the Conference Board study might well serve as the ultimate judgment on FASB's "foreign exchange expedition":

Finally, despite the increased attention management devotes to international activities because of FAS 8, the majority of respondents do not think that FAS 8 has led to a better appreciation within their companies of the real effects of foreign exchange borrowing and investment decisions.

In mid-October, 1979, the FASB was reconsidering the entire Statement 8. It was anticipated that a new promulgation would come forth at year end. The Board came forth with nothing by year end. However, the flowers that bloomed in spring, 1980, included an announcement that the FASB had, by a narrow four to three majority, determined upon its tentative conclusions to resolve the foreign currency translation dilemma. These conclusions were:

1. A current rate method best achieves the following objectives of foreign currency translation:

    a. The process for translating foreign currency transactions and financial statements should retain as the primary unit of measure each functional currency in which elements of financial statements are measured, so that translated results and relationships express, in a single reporting currency, the essence of foreign currency transactions and financial statements.
    b. Adjustments resulting from translating foreign currency transactions and financial statements should be generally compatible, in terms of direction of change and financial statement classification, with the expected effects of a rate change on an enterprise's exposure to foreign exchange risk.

2. There is a presumption that a foreign entity's assets and liabilities are best measured in the currency of the country in which the entity is located, but in certain instances some other foreign currency or the U.S. dollar might be a more appropriate unit of measure.
3. Nonmonetary assets and related expenses of foreign entities operating in hyperinflationary economies should be restated prior to translation to approximate changes in general purchasing power but not in excess of recoverable amounts, and the resultant adjustment should be reported as a separate component of stockholders' equity.
4. Adjustments from settlement or translation of unsettled foreign currency transactions constitute exchange gains or losses and should be currently recognized in income unless (a) the foreign currency transaction is intended to be an economic hedge of a net investment in a foreign entity or (b) the adjustment is attributable to translation of foreign currency balances or transactions between a parent and

its subsidiary, in which cases, the adjustments would be reported as a separate component of stockholders' equity.

5. Adjustments resulting from translation of foreign currency financial statements should be reported as a separate component of stockholders' equity pending substantial or complete liquidation and provided that the investment does not become permanently impaired, in which cases accumulated net adjustments to the extent of the liquidation or impairment would be currently recognized in income.

Assuming that these conclusions are ultimately enshrined in a FASB statement, I submit it will have issued a catalog of catch-22s. This, in turn, will keep the Board and its staff occupied during the 1980s promulgating amendments and interpretations paralleling those of the preceding years for accounting for leases.

I offer the following proposal to the FASB: Return to your relatively virginal state and reinstate Statement No. 1 (December, 1973), wherein you permitted any of the existing translation options to prevail provided that there was full and fair disclosure of the procedure being followed. But then I would add one further directive to the FASB: Direct a "statement of position" to the American Institute's Auditing Standards Board whereby the latter board would enjoin the independent attesting accountant to assert, on the basis of his responsibility and credentials, that the particular option applied was the one which, in his opinion, most fairly reflects "economic reality."

FASB's Oil and Gas Petard

The second of the petards on which the Financial Accounting Standards Board determined to hoist itself was its December, 1977, Statement 19 on "Financial Accounting and Reporting by Oil and Gas Producing Companies."

The accounting dilemma is hardly new. There are those who have asserted that the Accounting Principles Board's demise stemmed from its failure to resolve the burning issue—should oil and gas producers be constrained to apply "full-cost" or "successful-efforts" accounting or should they be permitted to perpetuate the permissiveness of free choice.

The FASB tackled this hot issue in the manner in which porcupines are reputed to make love, very gingerly. The Board did not put the matter on its agenda until late 1975. And it might not have done that had it not been put on notice by the Congress that it had better act before December 22, 1977, or else the SEC would be made to answer for this failure on the part of the awesome private-sector accounting-standard-setting Financial Accounting Standards Board.

This two-year ultimatum flowed from the so-called Title V of the Energy Policy and Conservation Act of 1975, added by an amendment proposed by Congressman John E. Moss. (Congressman Moss's shock on learning the confused state of the accountant's craft in the hearings on this Act may have prompted him to use his position as Chairman of the Oversight and Investigations Subcommittee to explore the accounting environment in its entirety.)

Because of its importance, not only to this particular accounting controversy but for accounting in general, it may be well to recite the provisions of this title:

(a) For purposes of developing a reliable energy data base related to the production of crude oil and natural gas, the Securities and Exchange Commission shall take such steps as may be necessary to assure the development and observance of accounting practices to be followed in the preparation of accounts by persons engaged, in whole or in part, in the production of crude oil or natural gas in the United States. Such practices shall be developed not later than 24 months after the date of enactment of this Act and shall take effect with respect to the fiscal year of each such person which begins 3 months after the date on which such practices are prescribed or made effective under authority of subsection (b)(2).

(b) In carrying out its responsibilities under subsection (a), the Securities and Exchange Commission shall:

(1) consult with the Federal Energy Administration, the General Accounting Office, and the Federal Power Commission with respect to accounting practices to be developed under subsection (a), and

(2) have authority to prescribe rules applicable to persons engaged in the production of crude oil or natural gas, or make effective by recognition, or by other appropriate means indicating a determination to rely on accounting practices developed by the Financial Accounting Standards Board, if the Securities and Exchange Commission is assured that such practice will be observed by persons engaged in the production of crude oil or natural gas to the same extent as would result if the Securities and Exchange Commission had prescribed such practices by rule.

Full Cost vs. Successful Efforts Accounting

Why the fuss? Briefly, the full-costing option permits a greater amount of costs to be capitalized presently. This reduces the current charges to income account, and gives a plus to the bottom line. By way of an oversimplified example:

Assume that a petroleum producer in a given year spends $1 million in exploratory costs on each of five tracts. Two of these turn out to be productive, the others produce only salt water. The two productive sites are expected to produce 10 million units of oil, and 1 million such units are produced in the current year (and sold for $15 each).

The comparative arithmetic would be as follows:

	"Full Cost"	"Successful Efforts"
Gross revenues		
(1 million @ $15)	$15,000,000	$15,000,000
Costs:		
Write-off of dry-hole costs		
for 3 unproductive tracts	0	3,000,000
Depletion	500,000*	200,000†
Total costs	$ 500,000	$ 3,200,000
Income	$14,500,000	$11,800,000

* Total capitalized costs ($5 million) divided by 10 million anticipated units equals a depletion charge of $.50 per unit. Hence, 1 million produced units at $.50 equals $500,000.

† Total capitalized costs ($2 million) divided by 10 million anticipated units equals a depletion charge of $.20 per unit. Hence, 1 million produced units at $.20 equals $200,000.

OXY's 1978 Flip-Flop

To demonstrate the implications of this accounting duality in practice, let us consider the flip-flop by the Occidental Petroleum Corporation in mid-1978.

According to its Form 10-K for 1978, this switchover triggered the following consequences (from footnote 2 to the financial statements):

Change in accounting for oil and gas exploration and production operations and oil shale operations

In December, 1977, the FASB issued Statement 19, "Financial Accounting and Reporting by Oil and Gas Producing Companies," for companies adopting "successful efforts" accounting which would require that capitalized acquisition costs of proved oil and gas properties, wells, and related equipment and facilities be amortized to become part of the cost of oil and gas produced, and that capitalized acquisition costs of unproved properties and related exploratory wells be charged to expense when the likelihood of finding proved reserves has been impaired.

Occidental elected at the end of the second quarter of 1978 to apply the Statement, which requires retroactive implementation through restatement of the financial statements of prior periods.

This accounting switch for crude (as well as a corresponding switchover for the accounting for oil shale) impacted on Occidental's income history as follows:

	Income as Originally Reported	Reduction (Increase) in Pre-Tax Income	Reduction (Increase) in Income Tax Provision	Reduction (Increase) in Net Income
	(Amounts in Thousands)			
1977	$217,912	$ 68,419	$ 4,257	$ 64,162
1976	183,721	68,615	13,806	54,809
1975	171,956	2,607	6,993	(4,386)
1974	307,082	34,699	8,382	26,317
Subtotals	—	$174,340	$33,438	$140,902
Prior to 1974	—	$245,757	$34,896	$210,861
Totals	$836,564 [a]	$420,097	$68,334	$351,763

[a] Represents balance in Retained Earnings as of December 31, 1977, as originally stated.

Occidental stripped $352 million out of its previously reported income and reduced its accumulated deferred tax liability by some $68 million. As a consequence of these adjustments, the company was able to reduce the net carrying value for its oil and related properties by $420 million—thereby allowing it to reduce future depletion charges by that amount.

This kind of retroactive adjustment permits something of a double dipping since the $352 million, having been counted as income once in the years through 1977, will find its way into income once again in subsequent years.

But what is especially noteworthy about this process of restatement is that the company was able to go through its past history using full costing and is now able to go back and rewrite it year by year under the alternative accounting calculus. This restatement process is remarkable since oil and gas producers had been regularly resisting the plea to show the numbers both ways—and to let the marketplace make its own judgment with all the salient facts at hand. Their resistance was predicated on "excessive burden." It would appear, however, that where the company is determined to make the change, it can, in fact, accomplish the feat going back to Genesis. This leads to the conclusion that all of their protestations about can'ts are nothing but a lot of won'ts.

Tenneco's Full-Cost Accountings

That there is fuller costing, as well as full costing (just as there is more—or less—successful-efforts accounting) is evidenced by Tenneco's footnotes to its 1979 financial statements regarding a change in its accounting practices. After stating Tenneco's full-cost accounting premise and summarizing the SEC's promulgations regarding accounting by oil and gas producing entities, the footnote continues (page 34):

In 1979, Tenneco adopted the SEC full-cost method of accounting for oil and gas properties. Certain elements of the SEC's form of the full-cost method differed from that previously followed by Tenneco. The financial statements of prior periods have been restated to reflect the application of the SEC full-cost method. This accounting change resulted in a reduction of 1978 retained earnings of $305 million and a decrease in net income of $6 million and $14 million for 1979 and 1978, respectively. Corresponding earnings per share were decreased 6 cents and 14 cents, respectively. The reduction of prior years' retained earnings was due primarily to (1) the adoption of comprehensive interperiod allocation of income taxes for periods prior to 1974 and (2) the inclusion in the amortization calculation of estimated future dismantlement costs and the impaired portion of the cost of properties not being amortized.

So it is that Tenneco washed out $305 million from its accumulated earnings as of December 31, 1978 (an amount equal to 9.6 percent of the common stock equity as of that date). The debit/credit balancing act that led to this restatement went as follows (in millions):

	Debits	Credits
Accumulated earnings (a decrease)	$305	
Deferred federal income taxes (an increase)		$142
Deferred credits and other liabilities (an increase)		40
Long term debt (an increase)		31
Long term receivables and other investments (a decrease)		16
Plant, property, and equipment—net of depreciation (net decrease)		107
Deferred income from production payments (a decrease)	31	
Totals (nearest million)	$336	$336

The Politics of Oil and Gas Accounting

Financial analysts asserted they were up a tree trying to develop comparability among oil companies following divergent accounting methods. Each company had a vested interest in its particular method. And as we should know, when a major oil company has a vested interest in anything, it will soon find allies (including even accountants) who will make certain these interests are not disturbed.

In December, 1977, the FASB just barely met the Title V deadline by promulgating its Statement 19, "Financial Accounting and Reporting by Oil and Gas Producing Companies." In brief, the FASB edict banned the full-costing alternative and decreed the universal application of successful-efforts accounting. In addition the statement directed that the entities involved in this activity disclose substantial data regarding their available resources. The FASB and the accounting profession might have expected that the Securities and Exchange Commission would countersign the Board's decree—making it the law of the land, thereby responding to the requirements of Title V. After all, the SEC in its Accounting Series Release No. 150 had indicated (December, 1973) that the FASB's wisdom would be given full faith and credit.

Alas, agreement did not greet this particular standard. Instead, the Board's promulgation became the target of heated controversy first within the Department of Energy and then the Justice Department and the Federal Trade Commission—with the Securities and Exchange Commission under fire.

The matter was being presented at the highest levels of our government as a replay of David and Goliath. The ostensibly small, independent producers were asserting that Statement 19 rewarded the proclivities of the giants since they were all almost uniformly on a successful-efforts basis already. Further, for a mature company the distinction between the two alternatives might produce a negligible difference—since the greater current write-offs resulting from expensing the dry-hole cost would be offset (at least in part) by the lesser current-depletion charge (because of the reduced capitalization of costs incurred in yesteryear). And, significantly, the Goliaths were already enjoying profits beyond their dreams (thanks to OPEC), while the parvenus were still endeavoring to accumulate additional capital resources (and the red ink resulting from the increased write-offs in the earlier years required by successful-efforts would have a deleterious impact on them).

The Davids got some support from academe, the financial community, the Congress, and, as noted, several high-level governmental agencies who were concerned that the inimical impact on the independents might adversely affect the supply of energy resources and produce even further concentrations of these resources in the few Goliaths.

And what may be of particular significance, the FASB made itself vulnerable once again by presuming that it was setting a standard when it was doing nothing more than decreeing a somewhat arbitrary rule. In my view the FASB pronouncement ignored the fact that full costing is more consistent with the traditional accounting model than successful-efforts, predicated on the following reasoning:

1. In a process-cost accounting situation where 1,000 units are required to be started to obtain 700 salable units, the cost of the thousand is burdened against the 700.
2. In valuing inventories under the lower-of-cost-or-market standard, accountants have traditionally been permitted to compare the cost with the market by reference to the *total* pool of inventories so that any unrealized minuses could be offset to the extent that there have been unrealized pluses.
3. In constructing a building requiring the burying of three nonproductive stories to produce a structure with seven productive stories above ground, the entire ten-story cost is capitalized and then depreciated against the revenues derivative from the seven.
4. Etc., etc.

The SEC's Solomonic Wisdom

The Securities and Exchange Commission was faced with a hard choice in the spring and early summer of 1978. If the Commission supported the FASB (consistent with its ASR 150 covenant), it would be rejecting the executive branch of the government as represented by the Departments of Energy and Justice and the FTC. If, on the other hand, the Commission placated Energy, Justice, and the FTC, the FASB's death knell would have been sounded. The SEC's response to this awesome dilemma entitles it to the highest award for diplomacy. It finessed the situation beautifully; it said that neither full-costing nor successful-efforts accounting was suitable for the accountings by oil- and gas-producing companies. Instead, the FASB should go back to the drawing board to develop the procedures for implementing the Reserve Recognition Accounting (RRA) concept (referred to by its detractors as Ra Ra Accounting).

Then—*après moi le déluge*—the SEC decreed implementation within three years, i.e., after the administration will have passed out of office (or survived the 1980 election).

The SEC Introduces "RaRA Accounting"

Through a series of promulgations from mid-1978 through 1979, the Commission expanded its ideas regarding Reserve Recognition Accounting. In its Accounting Series Release 269 (September 24, 1979) it provided an illustration of the kind of disclosure major oil and gas producers might be expected to provide with their 1979 financial accountings. In part, the illustration provided by the SEC was as follows:

SUMMARY OF OIL AND GAS PRODUCING ACTIVITIES ON
THE BASIS OF RESERVE RECOGNITION ACCOUNTING

Year ended December 31, 1979
(Thousands)

	Net Present Value of Proved Reserves	Results of Oil and Gas Producing Activities
Additions to estimated proved reserves, gross	$1,110	$1,110
Revisions to estimates of reserves proved in prior years:		
Changes in prices	683	683
Other	(239)	(239)
Interest factor	749	749
Subtotal	$2,303	$2,303
Evaluated acquisition, exploration, development, and production costs:		
Costs incurred, including impairments		(577)
Present value of estimated future development and production costs	(873)	(873)
Expenditures that reduced estimated future development costs	337	
Sales of oil and gas and value of transfers, net of production costs of $231	(967)	
Sales of reserves in place	(238)	
Purchase of reserves in place	483	
Subtotal	$1,045	$ 853
Provision for income taxes		(356)
Net change of amount	$1,045	$ 497
Balance—beginning of year	7,490	
Balance—end of year	$8,535	

As should be evident from this presentation, RRA would factor in as an income item the net discounted value of the revenues which might be contemplated from the net additions to the proved reserves. The Results of Oil and Gas Producing Activities starts with the addition to the year's income for the gross additions to the estimated reserves and then makes some adjustments for changes in prior years' projections (e.g., changes in price). And then because each passing year brings the future that much closer to the present, there is added the "imputed interest" factor; since the standard discount rate used was 10 percent per annum, there was deemed "earned out" 10 percent of the beginning-of-the-year's balance of reserves, i.e., $7,490—imputed interest of $749 was picked up as this year's increment.

There are some pluses and minuses shown for costs incurred during the year for expenditures, acquisitions, and transfers—some affect this year's results from producing activities, others merely affect the carrying value of the proved reserves in place.

The net avails from the year's operation are determined and a potential tax is calculated—to produce the bottom line under the RRA alternative for income determination by oil and gas producers.

How did the FASB—this prestigious private-sector body—respond to the SEC rebuff? Rather than respond with indignation that its prerogatives had been usurped, the FASB backed away. It suspended the most critical provision of Statement 19—the requirement that the full-costers switch to the successful-efforts alternative.

It remains to be seen whether the blow struck by the SEC will be fatal; at the least it must have been unnerving to the Stamford Seven.*

RaRA in the "Real World"

To discern the ways in which the RRA experiment works in the real world I turned to the SEC form 10-K disclosures by three of the oil giants, Exxon, Mobil, and Texaco. The following data were abstracted from those statements:

---

* A euphemism I sometimes apply to the seven members of the Financial Accounting Standards Board.

SUMMARY OF OIL AND GAS PRODUCING ACTIVITIES ON THE BASIS
OF RESERVE RECOGNITION ACCOUNTING FOR THREE SELECTED COMPANIES

Year Ended December 31, 1979
(Billions)

	Exxon	Mobil	Texaco
Additions to estimated proved reserves	$ 3.2	$ 1.5	$ 1.0
Revisions to estimates of reserves proved in prior years:			
Changes in prices	27.9	14.6	9.4
Other*	(9.1)	(1.5)	(3.8)
Interest factor (accretion of discount)	2.7	1.8	1.7
Subtotal	$24.7	$16.4	$ 8.3
Evaluated acquisition, exploration, development and production costs:			
Cost incurred, including impairments	(1.2)	(.8)	(.7)
Present value of estimated future development and production costs	Deducted Above	(.5)	Deducted Above
From equity in investees' reserves and foreign contracts	1.0	1.8	—
Pre-tax results RRA Basis from Oil and Gas Operations	$24.5	$16.9	$ 7.6
Provision for income taxes	14.7	11.5	3.6
Net results from Oil and Gas Operations	$ 9.8	$ 5.4	$ 4.0

* Represents generally (e.g., as stated in the Texaco presentation): "Other revisions, including changes in costs, revisions of previous volume, estimates and timing of production."

I find this SEC-induced experimentation intellectually stimulating and conceptually intriguing. It seeks to tackle from the revenue side the economic impact of inflation on those who are in possession of resources acquired at various times at lower prices that are presently capable of generating substantially greater amounts of revenues. As a consequence, the "economic reality" for those entities is that they have been enriched not only by the amounts they determined to realize currently by the conversion of the resources to cash or other assets, but in addition their enrichment should be measured by the increased amount of potential yields.

By this Reserve Recognition Accounting process, in my view, the results are far more congruous than those induced by the FASB-directed experiment decreed by its Statement 33. (This is the subject of extensive discourse in "Write-offs or Rip-offs," Chapter 8.)

That the major companies (at least the three sampled by me) do not agree with my judgment can be discerned from caveats in the respective 1979 forms 10-K, to wit:

Exxon Corporation

. . . information depart significantly from prior reporting of historical information and attempt to portray 1978, 1979 and future activities of EXXON in oil and gas producing in a highly arbitrary fashion. Therefore, EXXON believes it should warn that the remaining data set forth in this section, . . . are not to be interpreted as necessarily representing current profitability or amounts which EXXON will receive, or costs which will be incurred, or the manner in which oil and gas will be produced from the respective reserves. The arbitrary ten percent discount rate used in the determination of the present value of estimated future net revenues represents neither a cost of capital nor a borrowing rate, and, additionally, does not necessarily reflect political risks. Actual future selling prices and related costs, development costs, production schedules, reserves and their classifications, and other matters may differ significantly from the data portrayed or assumed.

Mobil Corporation

The information regarding oil and gas producing activities contained herein is filed in accordance with SEC and FASB reporting requirements. *Mobil cautions investors and analysts against simplistic use of these data.*

Mobil has urged the SEC to suspend implementation of the rule that requires publication of the new SEC-required information. Mobil believes that further study of Reserve Recognition Accounting (and also of the related disclosures contained herein) is needed. Mobil believes that after the necessary study is done, the likely conclusion will be that the SEC's Reserve Recognition Accounting (RRA) does not provide useful information.

*   *   *

Texaco Inc. and Subsidiary Companies

The reader is cautioned that the foregoing . . . should not be considered indicative of Texaco's earnings or cash flow from exploration, development, and producing activities during 1979. Rather, this amount is merely a notional computation derived under an experimental account concept.

Note these relationships (in $ billions):

	Pre-Tax Income RRA Basis (1)	Amount Thereof Representing Mere Adjustment Price of Previously Reported Re- sources (2)	Percent Column (2) Divided by Column (1)
EXXON	24.5	27.9	113.9
MOBIL	16.9	14.6	86.4
TEXACO	7.6	9.4	123.7

Note how the cases of Exxon and Texaco 1979 RRA results were the consequence of the enormous increase in the number assigned to *old* resources—hence, not the result of net resources added to our energy pool. The companies might be seen to be living off the fat of yesteryear ballooned by the actions of the Organization of Petroleum Exporting Countries. Of course, this fat, as it is rendered into revenues, drips down into the bottom line, producing the appearance of managerial efficiency—with concomitant bonuses and other perquisites. But where is the "muscle" for which we are looking to these companies? These companies rationalize their enormous profits by asserting they are required to expand our energy pool; instead, in good measure, they go to buying up other companies—sometimes to acquire existing blobs of accumulated fat, other times to acquire manufacturing and retailing enterprises.

Only of tangential interest to this RRA inquiry, in the course of my study of the Texaco 1979 statements the following footnote intrigued me:

Note 20, Belridge Oil Company

On December 10, 1979, a majority of the shareholders of Belridge Oil Company (Belridge), in which Texaco owned a capital stock interest of 17.04%, approved a merger offer of Shell Oil Company to acquire the outstanding shares of Belridge for $3,665 per share. . . . Texaco voted its 17.04% capital stock interest in Belridge against the merger offer.

As of December 31, 1979, and until January 11, 1980, at which time Texaco delivered its shares in Belridge, Texaco remained a shareholder in Belridge entitled to the rights and privileges of a shareholder. On January 17, 1980, Texaco received $3,665 per share for its interest in Belridge, or a total of $622,600,000. This transaction was reflected in the Company's accounts in January, 1980 and resulted in net earnings of approximately $400,000,000 after provision for applicable income taxes.

I maintain that this is nothing but a contrived deferral of $400 million of after-tax income from 1979 to 1980. I have seen this in other instances where a particular year's results are rich beyond dreams of avarice, inducing management to contrive some fiction for putting the income into the ensuing years (thereby providing a cushion for that later year).

In short, "income management" frequently calls for the contrived acceleration of income; sometimes it calls for a reverse tactic.

Of course, the independent auditors are supposed to cut through these fictions, both ways; after all, this is what we're supposed to do under the substance over form rubric. But, alas, what are we to do when the client confronts us with the legal documents? Is he going to "bite the hand that feeds him"?

SOP's to the FASB

When appearing before the public and even Congress and the Securities and Exchange Commission, the Financial Accounting Standards Board likes to appear independent, omnipotent, and, especially, omniscient. When, however, FASB representatives confront the American Institute of CPA's, FASB's creator, they are obsequious. From the minutes of a meeting of the prestigious Accounting Standards Executive Committee (AcSEC) of the AICPA, we learn that there was a serious confrontation between AcSEC and emissaries from the FASB.

According to the minutes of the April 18–19, 1979, meeting, the two FASB representatives "led a discussion of the status of the FASB projects." During the course of the colloquy, "AcSEC members expressed the view that the Board is not responding quickly enough to the projects on which AcSEC task forces and committees have worked so hard."

The FASB representatives appear to have become most contrite, attributing the Board's failures to:

1. Recent turnover of Board membership
2. Screening committee's ineffectiveness
3. AcSEC's sending to the FASB projects that are not emerging issues
4. Existence of a priority system at the FASB.

One AcSEC member expressed the view that "if the FASB does not stop 'trash-canning' its projects, AcSEC might have to ask the Institute to change Rule 203 to allow the AICPA to issue accounting standards."

If the FASB persists in "trash-canning" the Statements of Position (SOP) which emanate from AcSEC, there may yet be some hope for the Board. Recent AcSEC promulgations are uniformly matters of significance for a particular industry and pertain to a particular transaction. They are, accordingly, rules in application rather than a "standard." In some instances the SOP appears to have been designed to give absolution for a past transgression. By pretending that a situation had no known correct response, thereby requiring the adoption of a new standard, AcSEC permits those who may have perpetrated evil to find their sins washed clean.

When testifying before Senator Eagleton's committee in August, 1979, I commented on SOP 78-8 ("Accounting for Product Financing Agreements"), asserting that the profession would be better served if AcSEC forwarded the dossiers on those following the practices described in the SOP to the Institute's Ethics Division for punishment rather than to the FASB for absolution. (The basis for this acerbic comment is set forth on pages 208–209.)

Confronted with this challenge from its "patron saint" the FASB responded with a remarkable *tour de force.* By its Statement No. 32 (September, 1979), entitled "Specialized Accounting and Reporting Principles and Practices in AICPA Statements of Position and Guides on Accounting and Auditing Matters," the Board bestowed its priestly benediction on the AICPA promulgations.

Statement 32 says that the principles and practices in the AICPA documents are "preferable accounting principles" for justifying an accounting change. This does not mean that a business enterprise must adopt the AICPA recommendations, but it may not change away from such a recommended precept.

As to whether such a pragmatic statement deserves the dignity of being designated a "statement of accounting standards" I leave to the reader to judge.

FASB's Conceptual Framework Project

Let us now direct our attention to the herculean conceptual framework project undertaken by the FASB shortly after its organization. In December, 1976, the Board released a Discussion Memorandum on its "Conceptual Framework for Financial Accounting and Reporting Elements of Financial Statements and Their Measurement." In a prefatory essay the Board sought to respond to the question, "Why is a Conceptual Framework necessary?"

> Perhaps because accounting in general and financial statements in particular exude an aura of precision and exactitude, many persons are astonished

to learn that a conceptual framework for financial accounting and reporting has not been articulated authoritatively. . . .

A conceptual framework is a *constitution*, a coherent system of interrelated objectives and fundamentals that can lead to consistent standards and that prescribes the nature, function, and limits of financial accounting . . . [emphasis supplied].

So the Board set out to write a constitution. If there were among its members the Randolphs, Jeffersons, Hamiltons, Madisons, and Adamses whose inspired vision provided us with our Constitution, I might applaud this undertaking even though it might be little more than the rediscovery of the wheel (but restated in a prose style to inspire the profession). Analysis of the composition of the Board over the past half dozen years gives, regrettably, little basis for exhilaration in this regard. It might further have been hoped that the Board would have taken the lead from our Founding Fathers and drafted a Declaration of Independence for accountants, calling upon them to manifest the independence, integrity, initiative, intrepidity, and intellectual qualities which society expects. Instead, the Discussion Memorandum concentrated on definitions of assets, liabilities, cost, revenues, and stockholders' equity, and then proceeded to an exegetic analysis of those elements.

True, the Memorandum did question whether an entity's results are better measured by the traditional Revenue minus Cost equation or whether an Asset minus Liability calculus would be more informative. This latter alternative, it should be noted, is rooted in the controversy regarding historical cost versus some current cost alternative. This theme is of major import, but it does not call for an awesome Conceptual Framework Project, implying that the accounting profession has been bereft of a doctrine by which to steer a course toward fair accountability.

I have referred to this project as a red herring to distract the attention of the public (including the Congress and the various regulatory agencies) from the real problems of the profession, i.e., the psyches of the accountants involved in aberrant conduct.

Let us examine the fruits of this FASB project. In November, 1978, we were presented with a "Statement of Financial Accounting Concepts No. 1," entitled "Objectives of Financial Reporting by Business Enterprises."

Before proceeding to the Statement per se, the Board points out that there is nothing really binding about its pronouncement—the Statement does not call for compliance. The first constitutional promulgation will have nothing new for those exposed to the literature of our discipline; if there is a difference, the prose style in the FASB promulgation lacks the inspiration observable elsewhere.

It appears that the members of the FASB do not necessarily read the stuff they're turning out (or do not necessarily take it to heart). Two promulgations issued almost concurrently point to that conclusion. Here is paragraph 37 from the aforementioned Objectives statement:

> Financial reporting should provide information to help present and potential investors and creditors and other users in assessing the amounts, timing, and uncertainty of prospective cash receipts from dividends or interest and the proceeds from the sale, redemption, or maturity of securities or loans. The prospects for those cash receipts are affected by an enterprise's ability to generate enough cash to meet its obligations when due and its other cash operating needs, to reinvest in operations, and to pay cash dividends and may also be affected by perceptions of investors and creditors generally about that ability, which affect market prices of the enterprise's securities. Thus, financial reporting should provide information to help investors, creditors, and others assess the amounts, timing, and uncertainty of prospective net cash inflows to the related enterprise. . . .

In the month following the publication of the Objectives statement, the FASB promulgated an "Exposure Draft" on "Capitalization of Interest Costs" (December, 1978); this called for "standards of financial accounting and reporting for capitalizing interest cost as a part of the historical cost of acquiring an asset that requires a significant period of time to bring it to the condition and location necessary for its intended use."

As the Securities and Exchange Commission observed in a 1974 Accounting Series Release (No. 163), such capitalization is at odds with the "conventional accounting model." That model, the SEC alleged, was applicable because:

> First, it is impossible to follow cash once it has been invested in a firm. . . .
>
> Second, the cost of capital is extremely difficult to measure. . . .
>
> Third, it has been felt that interest costs were generally costs of a continuing nature, usually fixed by contract, and that deferral of certain of these costs might leave an erroneous impression as to the level of interest expense (and the cash outlay for interest) that might be expected in the future. . . .

This third item is particularly relevant. As the SEC noted, the capitalization of a portion of interest cost could lead to an erroneous impression regarding the expected cash outlays for this cost. Consequently this FASB position (its Statement 34) is patently at odds with its paragraph

37 quoted above regarding the importance of informing the users of financial statements regarding the "amounts, timing, and uncertainty of prospective net cash inflows. . . ."

Surely a promulgation coming hot on the heels of the framing of a constitution should have been consistent with that awesome document. But, as I said, this would have meant that the Board really read and believed what it said was its constitution. In short, that initial statement of accounting concepts (and, I predict, those that will follow) will be little more than persiflage—the FASB will continue to ruminate and reach its determinations on the basis of pragmatism—just as the Accounting Principles Board steered its course.

At page 72 reference was made to "two promulgations issued almost concurrently" that followed in the wake of the initial FASB concepts statement. I then proceeded to discuss but one of these promulgations; the other, having to do with accounting during periods of inflation (FASB Statement 33) is considered presently in Chapter 8.

5

Big Steel—Little Steals

LIFO, we know, is the four-letter word standing for "last-in–first-out." That phrase is, in the real world, preposterous—except for passengers in a crowded elevator and, of course, for the way in which costs are assumed to flow, and be matched against revenues, in certain inventory situations.

Let us turn to the exhilarating fun and games permitted by LIFO dynamics. It might be noted in passing that a decision to go LIFO is like deciding to ride a tiger; you cannot dismount or you'll end up inside. (But as will soon be obvious, there are those who do want to end up that way—for reasons best discerned by them.)

To understand this point it is important to see how the decision to replace or not replace the inventory before year end affects the resultant bottom line.

U.S. Steel's LIFO Ploys

Let's look at the accounting by United States Steel in this context. The 1976 Inventories footnote carried the following legend: "For the effect on income of the penetration of LIFO inventory layers see page 4." That page stated: "A computation of the effect of LIFO quantity reductions made in conformance with the Internal Revenue Service procedure would indicate that income benefited approximately 6% in both years (1976 and 1975). . . ."

The subsequent year's footnote reference was to page 23 of that year's report; there we were told, "Included in cost of products and services sold and income before taxes were credits from inventory liqui-

Year	1 Entire Pre-Tax Net Income	2 Steel Manufacture Pre-Tax Income	3 Entire Net After-Tax Income	4 Per 1976 10-K LIFO Penetration, % of Net	5 (3 × 4) LIFO Penetration, Dollars	6 Per 1977/79 Reports LIFO Penetration, Pre-Tax $	7 (6 ÷ 2) LIFO Penetration, % of Steel Pre-Tax	8 (6 ÷ 1) LIFO Penetration, % of Entire Pre-Tax
	(a)	(b)	(c)	(d)	(e)	(f)	(g)	(h)
1973	483	299	313	13	40.7	87.5	29.3	18.1
1974	1033	572	630	6	37.8	85.1	14.9	8.2
1975	824	318	560	6	33.6	58.3	18.3	7.1
1976	518	170	410	6	24.6	55.9	32.9	10.8
1977	102	(45)[a]	138	N/A[c]	N/A	88.2	Inf.[d]	86.5
1978	250	33.4	242	N/A	N/A	124.5	373	49.8
1979	(676.4)	(102.5)	(383.4)[b]	N/A	N/A	118.7	Inf.	Inf.

[a] ( ) represents loss or deficit.
[b] Excludes the cumulative effect on prior years of change in accounting principles.
[c] N/A = not available.
[d] Inf. = Infinity.

dations of $88.2 million in 1977 and $55.9 million in 1976."

The 1979 and 1978 Inventories footnotes (there were no cross references) informed that: "Included in Cost of sales and Income before taxes on income are estimated credits of $118.7 million in 1979, $124.5 million in 1978 and $76.0 million in 1977 and LIFO inventory liquidations." (I saw no explanation of how the $88.2 million originally indicated from 1977 became $76.0 million shown in the 1978 report for 1977. For present purposes the gap is not especially significant.)

From these data we can develop a number of intriguing relationships as is evident from the table on page 75.

Note that the additional income in 1977 resulting from the LIFO penetration amounted to $88.2 million. When we see that even after this infusion the corporation sustained a $45 million loss from steel manufacturing, it follows that absent the penetration effect, the loss would have been over $133 million.

Even more dramatic, in view of the fact that the company's entire pre-tax income in 1977 was $102 million, the LIFO penetration contributed almost seven out of each eight dollars earned during 1977. Clearly this is an enormous portion of that year's income generated out of what is, in fact, an "inventory kitty" resulting from price rises extending over past decades. What is especially potentially insidious is that the suppressed kitty is, to an important degree, capable of being manipulated by management—possibly without the awareness of even the most astute observer.

Having discussed the income surfacing from inventory penetration on the part of Big Steel, let us study a manipulation by what might be alluded to as Little Steal.

Sharon Puts Old Wine into New Bottles

On April 20, 1977, Federal District Judge C. F. Poole of the Northern District of California handed down his opinion and order "granting preliminary injunctions and partial summary judgment" against Victor Posner, Sharon Steel, et al. In that opinion Judge Poole summarized Foremost's allegation that Sharon had implemented a campaign involving "fraud and thus violated the Securities Act and the Williams Act," in order to make its securities more attractive to the market. The court then went on:

> Foremost charges that the sinister scheme culminated in Sharon's filing the S-1 statement purporting to describe the exchange offer but containing numerous falsities and misrepresentations. Certain of these allegations are

based on material filed under seal as required by an existing protective order.

In connection with ancillary discovery proceedings in the District Court for the Eastern District of Ohio, that court ordered sealed certain information which had been obtained by discovery from the records of Sharon's outside accountants, Peat, Marwick, Mitchell & Co. For the purposes of this ruling, no present necessity requires more than a generalized reference to the specific documents. Revelation of this material has been limited. Some of its content necessarily has had to be discussed.

Mere "generalized reference" notwithstanding, Judge Poole made devastating points regarding Sharon's debits and credits.

In Sharon's consolidated financial statements portrayed in the S-1 statement for the year 1975 and for the three months ended March 31, 1976, attractive earnings are shown. The 1975 pre-tax earnings from operations are set at $25,620,000 and after a tax liability deduction of $11,054,000, net earnings of $14,566,000 are claimed. For the three-month period ending March 31, 1976, Sharon reported pre-tax earnings of $5,652,000, a tax liability of $2,349,000, and a net of $3,303,000. According to Judge Poole:

> The evidence (e)stablishes overstatement of Sharon's pre-tax earnings for 1975 by at least $7,891,000 and failure to disclose that $2,730,000 resulted from nonrecurring events. Foremost also contends that the figures for the first quarter 1976 earnings (listed at $5,652,000) in fact constituted an over-statement of between $11,000,000 and $14,000,000 because Sharon should have reported a pre-tax *loss* of between $5,278,000 and 8-plus million dollars. The conflict with respect to these 1976 earnings centers around opinions as to the propriety of manner in which Sharon applied its accounting method to its inventory.
>
> Most consistently Sharon adopted the LIFO method under which the most recently incurred costs are charged to costs of sales, and the first costs incurred, including the beginning inventory, are used to value inventory at the balance-sheet date. Sharon is in what is called "the dollar value, single pool, double extension (100%) LIFO inventory method" for its iron ore inventory.

The essence of Sharon's scheme was rooted in the company's creation of a blend of ores derived from their existing ores; this "new" item was designated "TPV." A new base cost was then calculated using the average 1975 cost of the three constituent ores, resulting in an increase in the ending inventory at base cost of approximately $3,000,000. This created a LIFO layer by which, according to Sharon's own evidence, the ending inventory at LIFO value was increased by approximately $4,100,000. The effect on earnings, of course, was profound.

According to Judge Poole:

> Before putting this new application into effect, Sharon considered the question whether TPV was indeed a "new" product, and if so, whether the change in valuation was proper. There is indication that some of Sharon's officials, including members of its outside accountant staff, were understandably concerned over the potential effect of this change in valuation.

>   *   *   *

> . . . Sharon computed the increase in its LIFO reserve for the period ending March 31, 1976, at $16,880,000 and made adjustments which totaled only $5,950,000. The remainder ($10,930,000) represented an amount which . . . should have been charged to costs of sale but was not so charged. Had Sharon done so, that is, had it reflected inventory in its financial statement in accordance with its historic LIFO policy, instead of reporting pretax earnings of 5.65 million dollars, there would have been a pre-tax *loss* for that period of approximately the same amount.

Further, the evidence showed some "management" by Sharon of its inventory in the crucial second half of 1975 through the medium of increasing the levels of certain items while reducing the levels of others. The result of change in the mix of the inventory components was to reduce the required LIFO reserve and correspondingly to increase pre-tax earnings by approximately $8,742,000. Especially dramatic is the following highly critical determination by the court:

> Specifically with reference to the TPV product, the Pioneer and Victor inventories had been carried on the books at low historical costs. Replacing these inventories with TPV valued at higher current costs had the effect of increasing the [carrying value] of Sharon's ending inventory by 4.7 million dollars which increased its 1975 pre-tax earnings by the same amount. It also increased substantially the company's tax burden. Given the obvious impact on earnings, it is impossible to subscribe to the alchemy by which the mixing of ores from three mines having essentially the same material characteristics could create a "new" product. It is also questionable that IRS would have *required* the use of current costs or to accept the contention of defense experts that Sharon could not feasibly have reconstructed discrete costs to comply with tax regulations using its normal cost accounting practice.

> The parties vigorously disputed whether TPV represented a new product in accordance with generally accepted accounting principles and the bona fides of Sharon's treatment here. But pursuit of these paths is diversionary

because the real issue is whether the end product was misleading in its message, and the court finds that it was. It told the world that Sharon had earned 4.7 million dollars in 1975 from operations when that figure was simply the consequence of using a method giving a higher valuation to ores essentially of similar components. This in connection with a bid to take over a target company whose own net income for that same year was $31 million could, unless fully disclosed, completely distort the reality of the tender offeror's capacity and financial strength.

The court concluded section VI of its opinion with a sardonic commentary on the accountant's art:

> To attempt to harmonize the warring expert opinions whether TPV technically could be called a new product; whether IRS permitted, or possibly might even require, application of current costs; Sharon's "title" to its written-off ores; its precise arrangements with SCOT [Steel Corporation of Texas]; and the labels which accountants might select—all would embark the traveler on endless excursions. The pertinent inquiry is whether the earnings picture which Sharon presented, and on which the investing public was expected to rely, sufficiently informs them in the particulars required for sound investment decision. However may be the outcome of the debate of experts in their jousts for the guerdons of accountancy, the investor—his money on the line—is entitled to candor about a company's earnings when he reads a registration statement or sees a report.
>
> It is this court's opinion that this standard was not reached here. What Sharon did, upon the urging of its corporate officers with some concurrence of respected outside accountants, was to give out information about its financial picture which, though highly attractive on the surface, was at best the cultivated product of questionable fluctuations and self-serving maneuvering of accounting procedures. . . .

Who Blew the Whistle on Sharon?

Who deserved the credit for blowing the whistle on Sharon's machinations? Was this proceeding initiated by Sharon's "respected outside accountants," who having certified these statements in early 1976 developed conscience pangs and sought to amend their past errors? That would be cause for hosannas. To the contrary, as is evident from the foregoing, Posner and Sharon had the temerity to move toward a takeover of Foremost-McKesson, Inc. Whereupon that company, seeking to ward off its suitor, engaged its accountants, Haskins & Sells, to probe Sharon—and this H&S did effectively, as Judge Poole's opinion makes clear.

Did H&S thereupon proceed to file an ethics complaint against Sharon's auditors, Peat, Marwick, Mitchell, for being incompetent or worse in the Sharon audit? If so, such an intrepid action has escaped my attention.

The SEC Enters the Picture

There is another chapter to the Sharon Steel saga. The scene shifts to Washington, where on September 20, 1977, the Securities and Exchange Commission filed a Complaint for Injunction and Ancillary Relief with the federal district court accusing the corporation and its principal executives of a host of securities laws violations.

The complaint catalogued Sharon's transgressions including (numbers represent relevant paragraph numbers of the complaint):

48:      1975 Misrecording of Iron Scrap Inventory
49–50: Recording 1976 Sales as 1975 Sales
51:      Transfers of Earnings from 1974 to 1975
52:      1974 Prepayment of 1975 Insurance Premium
53–60: Improper Transfer of Stainless Steel Between LIFO and FIFO
61:      Inconsistent Inventories of Reserve Ore
62:      Nondisclosure of Nonrecurring Ore Adjustment
63–65: Prior Years Errors

All these are, of course, serious deviations from full and fair accountings; but the really diabolic maneuvers were those especially relevant to this chapter on LIFO manipulations, and complement the obloquy expressed by Judge Poole in his *Foremost v. Sharon* opinion.

As you might know, this action terminated in a consent decree, so that Sharon and its principal executives will be constrained from commiting mayhem again in the same place, in the same way, and in the same time. (Change any of these factors and all bets are off.) But in addition, Sharon was made to establish an independent audit committee.

Sic transit gloria mundi!

The LTV–Jones & Laughlin Ploys

In the final days of October, 1978, LTV Corporation (Ling Temco Vought Corporation when it was the power base for Jimmy Ling) sent out its Notice of Annual Meeting of Stockholders, comprising about 250 pages. This volume served as the prelude for the December 5 nuptials of LTV (which already owned Jones & Laughlin Steel Corporation) with the Lykes Corporation (the owner of Youngstown Steel Corporation).

In the course of LTV's Management's Discussion and Analysis of the Summary of Consolidated Operations we were told, beginning at page 54, under Inventory Accounting Commentary, that:

> Since 1941, J&L Steel has accounted for its inventories, other than supplies, on the last-in, first-out (LIFO) method. J&L Steel has computed its LIFO inventory under a dollar value procedure. J&L Steel's application of this procedure requires costing inventory items at both base-year costs and current-year costs. The relationship between these costs (the "LIFO index") is used in calculating the LIFO cost of increments in the inventory. From 1961 through 1976, J&L Steel used 1960 base-year costs in computing this index. . . . In applying this procedure to items entering its inventory for the first time in a year subsequent to 1960 ("new items"), J&L Steel has treated the current-year costs of such items as their base-year costs and has not attempted to reconstruct or otherwise establish base-year costs. The effect of this procedure was to increase year-end inventory values which in turn had the effect of reducing cost of goods sold and accordingly of increasing pre-tax income.
>
> In the opinion of management and of Ernst & Ernst, this procedure is in conformity with applicable Treasury regulations and generally accepted accounting principles. There is substantial authoritative support for such procedure and no contrary position of the Commission has been expressed in rules, regulations, or other official releases of the Commission including the published opinions of its Chief Accountant.
>
> As a result of an extensive review of J&L Steel's inventory accounting, it has now been determined that in computing its LIFO inventories during the years 1974 through 1977, J&L Steel incorrectly treated as new items certain inventory items which have been identified as having previously been in J&L Steel's inventories. . . .

This statement might appear innocuous, especially when we were told by LTV's management and its auditors that J&L's procedures were "in conformity with applicable Treasury regulations and generally accepted accounting principles."

Before responding to that assertion by management, let us examine somewhat more closely J&L's LIFO method. On page F-12 of the meeting notice, LTV's auditors tell us that "LTV's steel subsidiary computes its LIFO inventories on a *dollar-value, single-pool base-year double-extension* basis and has done so in substantially the same manner since 1960 . . ." [emphasis mine].

What is the meaning of that cryptic phrase? First, "dollar-value" tells us that there is no presumption that the identical physical units are carried forward from year to year; instead, aggregate dollar values are calculated for the inventory and such aggregate is then subjected to a transmutative process by the application of an index number. The "single-pool" implies that all of the steel subsidiary's inventories (other than supplies) are taken on a unitary basis, rather than subdividing them into ores, coal, etc.

Some Exotic LIFO Practices

"Double-extension" is a somewhat more exotic concept. An illustration based on the Internal Revenue regulations follows:

A taxpayer using the dollar-value method has an opening inventory, or base-year cost, of $14,000 at January 1 of the first tax year the method is used. At December 31, his closing inventory at current-year prices is computed as follows:

Item	Quantity	Unit Cost	Amount
A	3,000	$6.00	$18,000
B	1,000	5.00	5,000
C	500	2.50	1,250
Total (at current-year cost)			$24,250

The cost of the items in the closing inventory at base-year unit prices was $5, $4, and $2 for A, B, C, respectively. The closing inventory would thus be restated at base-year cost as follows:

Item	Quantity	Unit Cost	Amount
A	3,000	$5.00	$15,000
B	1,000	4.00	4,000
C	500	2.00	1,000
Total (at base-year prices)			$20,000

Since the closing inventory at base-year cost, $20,000, exceeds the opening inventory at base-year cost, $14,000, there is an increment of $6,000. This increment would be multipled by 121.25% (the ratio of the closing inventory at current-year cost to its base-year cost, $24,250/$20,000, or taxpayer's price index for the year), and the increment at cost of acquisition would be $7,275. The LIFO value of the closing inventory would be $21,275 (base-year cost, $14,000, plus the adjusted increment, $7,275).

In short, the "double-extension" phrase relates to the mechanics for determining the transmutative index factor.

Now then, what did J&L do during recent years which brought the company (and its parent) into a confrontation with the SEC? Very simply, it used LIFO as something of a computer game—in order to manage (or more likely massage) its bottom line. Before detailing the ways in which J&L played out its game, let's examine the double extension illustration which showed that inventory costing $24,250 becomes $21,275. Notice that the increase in the unit value for item A was 20 percent ($6 in relation to $5), whereas that for B and C was 25 percent ($5 against $4 and $2.50 against $2, respectively). The resultant weighted index for A, B, and C showed an increase of 21.25 percent.

Suppose that the astute management is determined to increase the reported income (and, as we know, a convenient way is to increase the closing inventory—all other things being equal). Management could direct that any inventory items which would show a price increase *greater* than the overall average be sold before year end and not replaced; emphasis was to be placed on building up the stock of items with a less-than-average increase factor.

We will assume that all B and C units are liquidated and that the entire closing inventory, still assuming a $24,250 aggregate cost, is comprised of 4,042 units of A with a cost of $6 each.

Going through the calculus of the original example, at a base-period price of $5 each the inventory would cost $20,210 (4,042 units). At base-period prices there would be an increment of $6,210 ($20,210 minus $14,000). Converting this year's increment up to current-year prices gives $7,452 ($6,210 × 120 percent). Adding that sum to the base-period inventory of $14,000 gives a current closing inventory of $21,452—clearly better than the $21,275 toted up originally.

Now that you can see how the game can be played on a penny-ante basis, let's see how it's played in Texas (where LTV was born and bred). Here are some excerpts from the Securities and Exchange Commission complaint filed in mid-October, 1978 (which was followed by a judgment by Federal District Judge W. M. Taylor, Jr.). The SEC complaint makes the following conclusionary assertion regarding the LTV–J&L statement for 1975 and 1976:

> In J&L's 1975 Form 10-K Annual Report, the Consolidated Balance Sheet reported inventories of $280,156,000, and the Summary of Significant Accounting Policies included in the financial statements of J&L represented that "inventories, other than supplies, are stated principally at the lower of last-in–first-out cost or market." J&L's Consolidated Statement of Income

and Income Retained in the Business reported income before taxes on income of $10,302,000. LTV consolidated the above amounts with its operating results and reported in its Form 10-K Annual Report Statement of Consolidated Operations net income of $13,142,000.

J&L's ending inventory was overstated and, as a consequence, income and losses before tax provisions, net income, retained earnings, and other financial accounts and representations were misstated for J&L and for LTV consolidated. J&L's ending inventory and reported income were overstated primarily because of the incorrect designation of certain commodities as new products and the procedures employed in the valuation of such new products.

The J&L *modus operandi* for playing the game is described in the following colorful passages:

Realizing the opportunity to affect the results of operations by not using base-year cost for new products and in the absence of written guidelines defining new products, J&L misdesignated new products, did not establish adequate internal accounting controls to prevent the treatment as new products of items previously in J&L's inventory, and timed certain transactions to realize LIFO income benefits as a consequence of LIFO inventory valuation procedures.

J&L maintained a separate LIFO index for each commodity in inventory. This index, or the current-year unit cost divided by the base-year unit cost of each commodity, provided information concerning the LIFO impact of the acquisition and disposition of inventory items. Under the LIFO method employed by J&L, pre-tax income was benefited to the extent that commodities having an individual LIFO index less than the overall J&L LIFO index were inserted or increased in the ending inventory and commodities having an individual LIFO index greater than the overall J&L LIFO index were removed from the ending inventory.

To help fulfill its objectives J&L created an "inventory management team"; the SEC complaint then went on:

. . . J&L corporate accounting personnel prepared, from time to time, documents captioned "Opportunity List." These opportunity lists included calculations for "LIFO improvement options" which showed the effect on reported income of given transactions.

In September, 1975, senior management of J&L was aware of the urgency of reducing inventory levels to conserve cash. In the context of the inventory reduction program, senior management was further aware of the LIFO impact of the sale of inventory commodities having an individual cost index higher than the average cost index of all inventory and was aware that lower year-end inventories of high-index items would benefit the earnings of J&L. Specifically, J&L management, in considering whether to sell some of the nickel inventory, was given calculations purporting to show that there would be a substantial benefit to the value of the LIFO inventory and reported earnings if nickel ore was sold at market prices lower than original cost.

Another dimension of the J&L–LIFO game plan centered around the "new products ploy." If something is described as a new product it does not get itself subjected to the rollback for the inflation factor. The way J&L played it, these new products plopped into the closing inventories at the current-year costs. This, the SEC complaint alleged, was naughty. In that connection the SEC zeroed in on an especially intriguing sneak play:

> 32. In 1975, J&L found it temporarily uneconomic to operate the Pittsburgh plant. During the time in which it was uneconomic to manufacture certain steel slabs and other products in Pittsburgh, J&L shifted the manufacture of these products to its Cleveland plant. When these commodities were manufactured at the Cleveland plant, J&L used the different cost basis associated with their manufacture as a basis for designating them as new products. Thus, while the products themselves remained essentially the same, the switch in production facilities resulted, under J&L's LIFO inventory practices, in J&L's classifying these items as new products. This classification substantially increased pretax income. . . .

The SEC filing described a mind-boggling operation whereby J&L transmuted an actual loss on the sale of its nickel inventory into a bookkeeping profit. J&L had found Aladdin's lamp.

Where were Ernst & Ernst, LTV's and J&L's auditors? Can they assert, as they did when they prevailed in the landmark decision by the Supreme Court in *Hochfelder v. Ernst & Ernst,* that there was no *"scienter,"* i.e., that the firm was ignorant of the fakes in the financial statements? Hardly, it might appear from the SEC filing:

> 16. In connection with the 1975 audit, J&L's independent accountants informed J&L that they had noted various items which had a base-year cost much in excess of what they anticipated the base-year costs should be. The result thereof was, through the LIFO calculation, to substantially increase the LIFO cost of J&L's inventory.

> 17. In connection with the 1975 audit, J&L's independent accountants expressed the view that since J&L could not or did not wish to reconstruct the base-year cost of a new product, J&L should consider the link-chain method of LIFO. This method would mitigate the effect of entering new products without using base-year cost. J&L did not adopt the link-chain method.

The link-chain version of dollar-value LIFO is another approach to the development of the index. According to the Commerce Clearing House *Federal Tax Service:*

> Under the link-chain method, a cumulative price index showing the price level change from beginning of base year to current year is used to compute base-year cost and acquisition cost (of an increment). Each year's cumulative index is the product of annual indexes (ending inventory at current cost divided by its cost at beginning-of-the-year prices) for all LIFO years through that year.

J&L Steel had determined to exaggerate its reported income for the years 1975 and 1976. Now we must know that inflating the closing inventory has a corresponding impact on a company's taxable income and resultant tax liability. And, it would appear, J&L did reflect such augmented sums. But, alas, our government's fiscal deficit was not relieved. This was because the tax collectors had, for all intents and purposes, deputized LTV to act as their intermediary in the excising of the tax from J&L. And then, as the SEC pointed up:

> Expressing a concern of the independent accountants, voiced at a meeting in January, 1976, a J&L corporate accounting employee stated that "one of the subjects they were groping for is whether or not they wish to suggest any change in how we did LIFO. And in connection with that, they made the observation that the new-product policy that they had been following tended to generate more income, and accordingly would trigger the payment of more taxes than what another alternative policy might do." J&L rejected the suggestion to consider alternatives partially because of the availability of consolidated tax-loss carry-forwards. Increases in tax liability to J&L generally resulted in additional cash payments to LTV because of J&L's tax consolidation agreement and LTV's net operating loss carry-forward.

How to Succeed in Business

As a consequence of these clever maneuvers, LTV not only got an inflated bottom line, thereby contributing to its stature with the gnomes of Wall Street, but extra cash to boot. Who said that the wages of sin are death?

Perhaps in this context the opposite is true. The SEC complaint was lodged against LTV and J&L—but in addition named as a defendant James J. Paulos, described in paragraph 9:

Defendant Paulos is the senior vice president and chief financial officer of LTV and has held these positions since June, 1976. From December, 1975, to June, 1976, Paulos was vice president for planning at LTV. Prior thereto, Paulos was vice president and treasurer of J&L and had held these positions since 1972. Defendant Paulos is a certified public accountant and has been such at all times relevant herein.

That is a meteoric rise for someone who as recently as 1970 was an assistant controller at J&L. He certainly must have endeared himself to Jimmy Ling. Paulos's role in these LIFO machinations at J&L is not described in the complaint but in each of its eight counts he is alleged to have aided and abetted LTV and/or J&L in perpetrating the fakes.

Apparently these alleged transgressions did not make the Commission see him in an adverse light. The second signatory to the Form S-1 which registered the securities to be issued on the Lykes takeover was none other than "J. J. Paulos, Senior Vice President and Chief Financial Officer and Principal Accounting Officer."

According to the SEC there was a "subordinate corporate accounting employee" whose conscience was burdened by what he saw going on in the manipulation of the inventory figures; he was unhappy that LTV's financial statements did not disclose the effects of the steel company's inventory maneuvers. Of particular concern to this subordinate employee were the following:

> J&L, for the years prior to 1976, had established certain allowances or write-downs for excess and slow-moving items in inventories. J&L, near year end 1976, changed this practice and did not create allowances for such items, thereby increasing pre-tax income by approximately $4,000,000. J&L and LTV did not disclose in their 1976 financial statements that 1976 reported income was increased in this manner by such amount.
>
> J&L included in its 1976 LIFO inventory certain subnormal goods previously reported on a first-in–first-out basis and incorrectly designated them as new products, thereby overstating pre-tax income by approximately $8,000,000.

I congratulate that "subordinate J&L corporate accounting employee" for his perception, but I can assure him that he will never become LTV's Senior Vice President, etc. (assuming that he is still employed by that complex).

How did all of this inventory manipulation affect the financial statements of LTV and J&L? As to LTV, based on data included on page F-14 of the meeting notice, we can see the following:

	For the year 1975	For the year 1976
	(amounts in millions)	
Income as originally reported	$13.1	$30.7
Inventory reduction	$13.1	$19.7
Less reduction in tax related to the inventory adjustment (assumed @ 50 percent)	6.5	9.8
Net reduction	6.6	9.9
Percent of reported income	50.4%	32.2%

The distortion becomes even more egregious when the data are related to the reported net income of J&L (rather than for its parent company on a consolidated basis). The income as published by Moody's was:

	1975	1976
	(amounts in millions)	
Income as reported	$ 7.4	$26.7
Adjustment (as above)	6.6	9.9
Percentage of distortion	89.2%	37.1%

Let us return to the LTV management's allegation that in its opinion, as well as that of Ernst & Ernst, J&L's procedure was "in conformity with applicable. . . . generally accepted accounting principles . . ." and that "(t)here is substantial authoritative support for such practice and no contrary position of the (SEC) has been expressed in rules, regulations, or other official releases of the (SEC), including the published opinions of its Chief Accountant."

It is just this kind of pettifoggery which has brought the crisis in confidence to my colleagues and all too many of their clients. Surely, Ernst & Ernst should have learned some lessons from their involvement in the Westec quagmire. Surely someone in that firm should have read the decision in the so-called *Continental Vending* case where, as pointed up in Chapter 1, the court decreed that financial statements must be more than "GAAP-fair"—they must be "fair *qua* fair."

Even a modicum of awareness of the objectives of financial accounting should have informed Ernst & Ernst that the initial (November, 1975) SEC Staff Accounting Bulletin (Topic 10-H) should have directed disclosure. That item reads:

LIFO Liquidations

Facts: Registrant on a LIFO basis of accounting liquidates a substantial portion of its LIFO inventory and as a result includes a material amount of income in its income statement which would not have been recorded had the inventory liquidation not taken place.

Question: Is disclosure required of the amount of income realized as a result of the inventory liquidation?

Interpretive Response: Yes. Such disclosure would be required in order to make the financial statements not misleading. Disclosure may be made either in a footnote or parenthetically on the face of the income statement.

It may be that the gimmickry followed by J&L was not precisely a LIFO liquidation—the implication and impact are precisely the same, however. In short, either an actual penetration of a LIFO pool or maneuvering within the pool to float to the surface in a particular year profits which had been festering over a period of years is definitely dirty pool. And the sooner Ernst & Ernst and my other colleagues comprehend what their role is in the corporate governance and accountability process, the better our profession will be—and the better off our clients will be.

6

Jaws and Star Wars

Robert MacNeil's opening for the March 7, 1979, MacNeil/Lehrer Report on "Mergers Is Big Business" was:

> One dramatic feature of the current business landscape is the stampede to merge. The number of announced takeovers of companies worth more than $100 million doubled last year over 1977, and has accelerated further this year. But in Washington this rush to get bigger has raised fears of too much concentration of economic, social, and political power, and prompted moves to stop it. Existing antitrust law permits the government to stop mergers within one industry, where competition would be reduced—so-called horizontal or vertical mergers. But critics say that present law does not easily cover the most popular kind of merger at present, the conglomerate, where giant corporations can buy up firms doing a different kind of business simply to become bigger. The attempt by American Express to take over McGraw-Hill publishers would be an example.
>
> Those who want to restrict such mergers argue that mere bigness itself can be bad. It's perhaps the most controversial new thesis to surface in the whole field of government regulation. Tomorrow the Senate Judiciary Committee begins hearings to consider legislation based on that thesis. And tonight, with some of the principal actors, we ask, how big is bad, and why?

The star participant in that televised program was Senator Edward M. Kennedy, who, as Chairman of the U.S. Senate's Committee on the Judiciary, was proposing legislation to ban giant mergers and to limit those of lesser size. He stated his objectives in this regard as follows:

90

I think it's important to understand that there isn't any sense of feeling about bigness being badness per se; there isn't any real sense of objection to mergers generally in the United States if it's going to mean more and better business efficiency, better service to the consumer, cheaper prices to the consumer, better products to the consumer. But the real concern that the members of the Congress and the Senate and the American people have is the artificial growth of major economic units in the United States that have really no redeeming value in terms of our free enterprise system and about competition within the free enterprise system.

As to his objections to conglomerate mergers, the Senator observed:

Well, obviously one of the factors would be the general trend towards absentee ownership; travel to Youngstown, Ohio, and meet the 6,000 families there that have been thrown out of work, or travel to Clinton, Massachusetts, and see where the Colonial Press is successful—both of these companies successful independent companies—were merged primarily for tax reasons, not to provide better competition in a particular industry, not to provide better services to the consumers, not to provide lower prices. And the principal concern is to see about the acquisition of these companies and corporations which have no real redeeming value in terms of a free and open and competitive system. . . .

This is not a new issue; it was a concern about the concentrations of power from Thomas Jefferson to Teddy Roosevelt to Franklin Roosevelt, to Learned Hand in the Alcoa decision; and what we are seeing now is the increasing concentrations of economic power and growth in a free and a democratic system, the results of which, I think, will either be new regulation of these large economic units or it will mean some kind of form of nationalization. You can't have the major sources of economic power and growth concentrated, as they're increasingly concentrated, in a free, open, competitive system and expect the free system to survive, and that is the issue that we're dealing with.

Insofar as accounting is concerned, this is not a new issue. According to the November 28, 1973, Financial Accounting Standards Board Status Report, Chairman Marshall Armstrong reported ". . . The letters of comment indicated that the overall subject of business combinations is the one that most urgently required the Board's attention."

This strident note notwithstanding, the FASB some six years later is still trying to get its thoughts together on this critical accounting problem; in the meantime, "Mergers Is Big Business,". . . with all of the fueling and fooling provided by the permissive accounting precepts.

Maybe the FASB, in this area at least, has determined to move with discretion—having learned from history that this was a critical issue which caused the downfall of its predecessor, the Accounting Principles Board. Probably most observers of the accounting scene have some familiarity, however vicarious, with the two Ps in the pod, i.e., "pooling-of-interests" and "purchase" accountings. Nonetheless, a brief overview might be appropriate.

The Poolings Purchase Dichotomy

Pooling-of-interests accounting implies that two entities merge—neither is submerged—and the genetic constituents of the two merging partners are then intertwined and interlinked without any substantive change. Corporation A might give up a billion dollars' worth of its shares for Corporation B, whose shares are traded in the marketplace for an aggregate of but $600 million. If B's book value for its properties (net of liabilities) amounted to $100 million, under this method of accounting the only figure that Corporation A puts on its books as its cost of acquiring Corporation B is $100 million. The $1 billion and the $600 million figures are lost to posterity, like leaves from the trees of yesteryear.

But since matter, we are told, is indestructible, the values impacted in Corporation B aggregate $1 billion (unless Corporation A's executive suite is inhabited by knaves, fools, or madmen). Consequently, Corporation A has acquired $1 billion in value for a bookkeeping cost of but $100 million. Ultimately these suppressed values will flow through A's revenue stream, producing profits far in excess of those predicated on a set of books that reflected the costs of acquiring properties at the amounts for which they were bargained.

Just how quickly these suppressed values will be fed into A's earnings stream will, of course, depend on A's management and economic factors—but when they are injected into the stream, A's management will be made to look better than they deserve.

Because corporate managements enjoy just this pretentiousness they have, at least throughout the decade of the 1970s, succeeded in getting their faithful accountants to resist any movement to abort this absurdity. And if history repeats, the FASB can look back and know its fate by what befell its predecessor when it grabbed this pooling-of-interests nettle.

The other "p" in the pod, "purchase accounting," does tackle the billion-dollar problem head on. There are no suppressed values in the aggregate; the whole billion dollars would go into A's books if A were to apply purchase rather than pooling accounting. But, and this is an enormous but, the critical question comes down to which assets are to be charged with that billion dollars.

Thus, and I am being simplistic, if the billion were charged to inventories, it might flow into costs in the relatively near future (unless A were on the last-in–first-out basis, in which case the billion might stay in inventories in perpetuity). On the other hand, if the billion were charged to plant and equipment, it would be subject to depreciation over a limited period; if it were charged to land, we would once again have the possibility of a perpetual deferral (unless, of course, we had a land developer, in which case this charge would be a charge to inventory generally).

But as luck would have it, the 1970 promulgation by the ill-fated Accounting Principles Board (in its Opinion 17) gave to managements and their independent auditors an extraordinary "deep pocket." In effect, that opinion asserted that after all is said and done and all the necessary allocations and apportionments are made to the various assets (net of liabilities), there is still a remainder—that overplus, that excess, is put on the books as an asset and thereafter amortized over an appropriate period not to exceed forty years. Sadly, in practice this "not to exceed forty years" has been applied generally to mean forty years—thereby producing the least possible charge to income account.

Clearly, whether the choice is "dirty pooling" or "polluted purchase," the potentially good doctrine of accountancy is being perverted in practice. Let us turn to some recent instances of business combinations to see the mode of accounting and to consider the fairness of that accounting.

GE Pools with Utah International

For the first real-life study we turn to the December, 1976, takeover by the giant General Electric Company of the no-slouch Utah International, Inc. (UI). This acquisition was effected by GE's issuance of 41 million of its shares for all the outstanding stock of Utah International. These shares, valued as of the date, when the merger plan became a matter of public knowledge, were worth over $1.9 billion. (The shares were worth over $2 billion at the time the nuptials were sealed.)

How much of that $1.9 billion entered GE's books as its cost for UI? Precisely $547.8 million—hence a cost-suppression of about $1.4 billion. Almost three-quarters of the cost evaporates—not even leaving the smile like that of the Cheshire cat.

How did that $547.8 million find its way into GE's books? Again, you will find that the debits meticulously equal the credits—even if both equal the absurd.

	Debits	Credits
	(in millions)	
Deficit in Working Capital (excluding Inventories)		$102.7
Inventories	$ 88.0	
Investments	106.5	
Plant and Equipment	618.5	
Other Assets	67.9	
Long-term debt		201.3
Other liabilities (including Minority Interest)		29.1
Subtotals	$880.9	$333.1
Shareholders' Equity		547.8
	$880.9	$880.9

The Shareholders' Equity credit was divided among the common stock, paid-in surplus, and retained earnings amounts—but, do take my word for it, the aggregate was precisely $547.8 million, thereby making the arithmetic balance exactly.

So what's so important about the $1.4 billion suppression insofar as GE was concerned? To begin with, while its books might reflect a reasonably salubrious return on the UI investment, if we figure that subsidiary's earnings for 1976 at, say, the $180 million indicated for 1978 related to the $547.8 million booked for the deal, the true yield when related to the $1.9 billion actual cost is very much less felicitous.

By how much would the GE earnings for 1978 have been depressed had it, in fact, booked the true cost incurred on the merger?

Here one must conjecture since the facts are privy to the GE-UI managements. Let us assume that the real assets GE acquired were UI's natural resources—uranium, coal, copper, oil, real estate, and the like. Therefore the suppressed sum of $1.4 billion would be added to plant and equipment so that asset would be booked at $2 billion instead of the $600+ million vestigial figure "inherited" from UI's books. This means that the $600 million would be grossed up by a multiplier of 3.3 to bring it to $2 billion. Let us use as the surrogate for our extrapolation the $77.8 million shown on GE's form 10-K as the 1978 depreciation of mineral property, plant, and equipment. This $77.8 million amount was predicated on the historical UI cost. If we were to multiply this amount by 3.3 (the grossing-up factor), the depreciation of these properties for 1978 would become $260 million—or about $180 million more than the amount booked following the pooling-fooling.

To provide something of a margin for depreciation, etc., relative to additions subsequent to the pooling, I will assume the differential attributable to the accounting suppression to be but $140 million.

Nor could GE assuage the bruising wrought by such a $140 million subtraction for depreciation by presuming a tax-reduction factor of 40 percent or more. Since the merger was effected on a taxfree exchange basis, the acquiring company (GE) does not become entitled to a stepped-up basis.

Had GE's 1978 bottom line reflected that $140 million minus, there would have been a reduction of about 11 percent.

Note that I have at times openly expressed commendation for the GE accountings. I have pointed out that GE resisted the two-sets-of-books syndrome—it deducted depreciation on its shareholders' books on the same accelerated basis as that given to the tax collector, and the company eschews the flabbiness afforded by percentage-of-completion and similar accounting practices.

But even the most virtuous among us might not be able to resist the temptation to put a $1.4 billion shot in the locker—to help sustain an earnings trajectory.

Kennecott Purchases Carborundum

As the first purchase illustration, let us consider the acquisition by Kennecott Copper of almost all of the shares of the Carborundum Company. This was accomplished through a November, 1977, tender offer at a price of $66 a share (at a time when Carborundum stock had been selling at about $22, but it did manage to move to about $40 when an accumulation of the shares was undertaken by the Eaton Corporation). Kennecott bought in over 97 percent of the Carborundum shares for an aggregate cost of about $571.5 million.

The funds for this acquisition might be seen to have been derived by Kennecott from the disposition of its interest in Peabody Coal. In late 1977, $571.5 million loomed as an enormous sum. But in the light of the bankrolls invested in mergers and acquisitions over the succeeding two years, the Kennecott-Carborundum takeover is hardly noteworthy. Nevertheless, if only as a footnote to history, it should be recorded that pursuant to APB 16 Kennecott adjusted the net book value shown by Carborundum prior to the merger ($309 million) to the $571.5 million cost of Kennecott's investment. Of the "step-up" in carrying values, $40.3 million was charged to the goodwill hopper. This intangible is being amortized on a straight-line basis over forty years.

At first blush we might consider ourselves grateful for small favors. After all, the goodwill factor represented only about 7 percent of the aggregate price paid for the Carborundum Company; and then, too, Kennecott did allocate $222.2 million of the excess of the $571.5 million total cost over Carborundum's book value to the fair values assigned to the various net assets of the newly acquired subsidiary. It did not brush the entire overplus into the goodwill account. But if one were to ask the auditors just where is there goodwill in this acquisition, they would be hard pressed to answer except to say they needed a $40.3 million debit to balance the ledger.

Taking Carborundum's earnings for 1978 of $26.7 million as revealed by Kennecott's form 10-K for that year, we see that the company subsidiary earned about 5 percent of Kennecott's investment—surely this is not a rate of return which warrants a determination of excess earnings potential, i.e., the presumptive basis for a determination that goodwill exists. To spread this amorphous differential on a straight line over forty years intensifies the strain on the credibility of the accountants' numbers collage. But let no one doubt this categoric conclusion: The company and its auditors balanced the debits with the credits.

R. J. Reynolds–Del Monte

On the day after Christmas, 1978, R. J. Reynolds Industries, Inc., proclaimed that the tobacco giant was going to swallow up the Del Monte Corporation. This was to be accomplished by Reynolds buying up approximately 45 percent of Del Monte's stock for cash (paying $48.50 a share), the remaining 55 percent to be acquired by the issuance of a new Reynolds cumulative preferred stock. The nuptials were sealed in early 1979—*sic transit* Del Monte!

On the swap, the cash and preferred stock payable on the exchange was estimated by Reynolds to aggregate $618.9 million. Since this amount exceeded Del Monte's shareholders' equity of $434.2 million by $184.7 million, it became necessary to allocate that overplus. This Reynolds did, most meticulously. It added to Del Monte's asset values (in millions):

Inventories	$ 86.5
Growing crops	3.2
Property, plant, and equipment	77.3
Other assets	37.7
Total assets	$204.7

It adjusted Del Monte's liabilities (in millions):

By eliminating its deferred taxes $23.0
Other liabilities were increased by $37.5   (14.5)
                                    $190.2

Increase in net assets
Excess of cost over Del Monte's
    shareholders' equity   184.7
"Negative Goodwill" $ 5.5

That's how R. J. Reynolds determined a negative goodwill factor of $5.5 million. Ironically, looking at the Del Monte track record might indicate the existence of positive goodwill, even when related to the $618.9 million price paid by Reynolds. The food grower and processor had been earning more than $50 million annually over the recent past—just about 8 percent of the Reynolds price package. But then R. J. Reynolds does not appear to require "earnings inflators."

There is a traditional accountants' axiom to the effect that: Those who might well show goodwill on their balance sheets do not; those who should not do so, will.

These Kennecott and Reynolds purchase accountings are relatively innocuous; let us turn to several which are far more flamboyant and, as a consequence, exhilarating.

United Technologies–AMBAC (A July, 1978, Acquisition)

AMBAC is the acronym for American Bosch Magneto Corporation, which traced its history back to 1906 (and was taken over by the Alien Property Custodian in 1918).

By 1977 this venerable corporation had accumulated a book value for its shareholders' equity of almost $100 million and was toting up about $235 million in sales (with a net of $16 million). Along comes United Technologies Corporation and offers to buy up 49 percent of AMBAC's shares for cash at $48 each and to swap a new preferred stock for the remaining 51 percent. United Technologies' total cost was about $220 million, an amount which exceeded AMBAC's book value by $122 million. How did this differential get allocated? According to a pro forma balance sheet included in the proxy material which announced the anticipated nuptials to AMBAC shareholders, the spread went like this (in millions):

Increases in assets:	
Inventories	$ 1.3
Fixed assets	27.8
Decreases in liabilities:	
Long-term debt	7.5
Other (representing a net reduction in assets)	(2.1)
Subtotal	$34.5

There is still $87.5 million to be accounted for—dumped into the accounting hopper as "goodwill." Since AMBAC already had $5.1 million on the books for that intangible, it meant that United Technologies put a total goodwill price tag on AMBAC of $92.6 million. This is a hefty sum to be allocated to goodwill—representing almost half of the total cost for the AMBAC acquisition.

To judge the implications of this accounting configuration, imagine what would have happened if AMBAC had unilaterally put on its books another $87.5 million in goodwill crediting some "whatchamacallit"; I can see the Securities and Exchange Commission sending the Justice Department down to the company to put manacles on the corporate executives who had watered the stock.

Query: Should United Technologies' auditors permit the company to inject the same amount of water into its statements without disclosing just where and how they justified the inclusion of a putative asset with a $92.6 million price tag? Where is the excess earnings justifying that kind of a valuation?

A review of the AMBAC financial statements for the years preceding the UT takeover discloses income as follows (in millions):

1971	$ 2.0
1972	2.6
1973	7.4
1974	8.1
1975	9.4
1976	12.6
1977	16.7
3 months ended 4/2/78	4.8

Even if we were to extrapolate the latest quarterly figure to make it $20 million on an annual basis, we have a paltry 9 percent based on the $222 million aggregate cost to UT (and 15.4 percent of the $130 million allocated to real assets).

That the $20 million annualized income amount is something of an exaggeration might be inferred from some data provided by UT's 1978 annual report. We are told that for the six months subsequent to the acquisition, AMBAC experienced $12.4 million in operating profits. Since this item represents the results for the period before deducting income taxes, interest, and general corporate expenses, the bottom line for AMBAC's six months under UT's aegis might have been about $6 million (since UT's net income was less than half of the consolidated operating profit).

What is so good about a 9 or 15.4 percent yield to warrant the booking of an enormous $92 million blob of goodwill? Maybe the management of United Technologies saw more than meets the eye; it may even be that the UT auditors were let in on that peep show. But then the public generally should be informed of the presumed-to-be-sequestered intangible assets so that the numbers would not appear, as they do to me, to be absurd on their face.

What I also found disconcerting was the fact that United Technologies had heretofore been amortizing its acquired goodwill (e.g., $5 million on the Otis Elevator acquisition) over a ten-year span. Without fanfare UT moved the AMBAC amortization to a 25-year span—thereby reducing the annual amortization by 60 percent.

United Technologies–Carrier Corp.

It now appears that United Technologies has determined to join the Acquisition of the Year Club—with each succeeding year's coup on a plane of greater exhilaration.

In 1976 it was Otis Elevator; in 1978 it was AMBAC. In 1979, having first acquired an almost 49 percent interest in the Carrier Corporation for cash in late 1978, United Technologies moved to merge by the issuance of a new preferred stock for the remainder.

The aggregate cost for the acquisition of the air conditioning and special chemical producer was slightly over $1 billion. Of this amount United Technologies determined to assign a whopping $270 million to goodwill (apparently to be spread evenly over the next quarter of a century).

On what did United predicate this $270 million of goodwill—representing, one must presume, "excess earnings potential"? Let's look at the record.

Carrier's five-year earnings history, included in the call for the July, 1979, meeting to vote on the merger, was as follows (in millions):

1974	$ 9.2
1975	13.9
1976	34.7
1977	57.1
1978	100.0
5-year average	43.0
3-year average	63.9

In view of the fact that United Technologies is booking some $760 million in net identifiable assets (i.e., its cost for the Carrier acquisition exclusive of the $270 million booked as goodwill), I fail to see any excess earnings even if I were to take the peak numerator for the rate of return ratio.

If I were to use the three-year average, the Carrier earnings would come close to paying the dividends required by the preferred stock issued on the acquisition, and there would then be nothing (probably less than nothing) left over to pay for the interest cost (actual or imputed) incurred on the $459 million paid to acquire the 49 percent interest bought for cash.

There is little doubt that United Technologies' management sees things differently from the way I did when I put these numbers together.

UT–Mostek

The foregoing observation about the "acquisition of the year club" was written in late 1979. UT's 1979 annual report confirmed my "prophecy," thus:

> The Corporation acquired approximately 91% of the outstanding common stock of Mostek Corporation (Mostek) for approximately $314,000,000 pursuant to a private purchase and a cash tender offer which closed on November 13, 1979. Mostek's products include integrated circuits and sub-systems for the data processing and telecommunications industries.
>
> The acquisition of Mostek has been accounted for as a purchase. The results of Mostek's operations have been included in the Corporation's consolidated statement of income from November 1, 1979 . . . Based on preliminary accounting studies and appraisals, the total purchase price of the common stock acquired is expected to exceed the Corporation's share of the values assigned to the underlying net assets of Mostek by approximately $214,000,000; such excess is included in deferred charges and is being amortized over 25 years. Mostek became a wholly-owned subsidiary pursuant to a merger on January 11, 1980, which had

the effect of increasing the excess over the underlying net assets of Mostek
by approximately $25,000,000.

So it is that out of $314 million paid for Mostek, UT determined
that a whopping $214 million was for goodwill. To this is to be added
the $25 million counted as goodwill when the remaining 9 percent was
acquired—hence, a total cost for goodwill of $239 million. That kind
of bookkeeping should imply that UT has acquired an earnings bonanza,
insofar as earnings potential is concerned. But when one looks at a
little table of pro forma numbers that followed this acquisition's footnote,
I find it literally impossible to see even a glimmer of this presumptive
bonanza.

Thus, we find that during 1978 Mostek lost $19 million; during the
ten months of 1979 prior to the UT takeover Mostek lost only $11
million (both amounts on a pro forma basis).

Undoubtedly United Technologies and its auditors, Price Waterhouse, must have seen things in the Mostek crystal ball to warrant such
an enormous assignment to goodwill. For myself, based on the numbers
discernible in the 1979 UT report, it would appear that the company
and its auditors were playing with silly putty rather than $239 million
real dollars (assuming, of course, that dollars still have a modicum of
reality).

A quick look at UT's balance sheets included in its 1979 annual
report produces some rather disconcerting relationships. Thus, as of
the end of 1978, the company's common shareholders' equity stood
at $1,430 million, of which $103 million (or 7.2 percent) was represented
by the "Costs in excess of net assets of acquired companies." At the
end of 1979, when the equity was $1,639 million, the goodwill sum
was $530 million, or 32.3 percent.

The question undoubtedly never arose for Archimedes, but it does
for me, to wit: How much water can a balance sheet hold before it
sinks?

Those who may be intrigued by United Technologies' mergers and
acquisitions proclivities should be reminded that the company's chief
executive officer, Harry J. Gray, came to its employ (when it was just
plain United Aircraft) from Litton Industries. He there served as a principal executive when that entity was pursuing its expansionist bent (developing a most creative catalog of accounting and financing practices as
an incident thereto).

And let those who are thus mesmerized be forewarned by Santayana:
"Those who do not remember their past are condemned to relive it."

An Intriguing Bargain Purchase

We are all undoubtedly familiar with the Emersonian wisdom: "A foolish consistency is the hobgoblin of little minds." My colleagues in the accounting profession cannot be accused of having such minds, as evidenced by the accountings for the 1974 acquisition by Sheller-Globe Corporation of all the outstanding shares of the VLN Corporation.

This takeover is not in the same league as the others discussed in this chapter. In fact, it would not be here were it not for the fact that John Eastman, Sheller-Globe's chief executive, followed me at the September, 1978, Senate Antitrust Committee hearings. His role was to justify to the members of the Committee his company's decision to jettison a VLN subsidiary, Colonial Press, a few years after the takeover—thereby causing substantial unemployment in the Massachusetts community where the establishment had existed and prospered for many years. This was the takeover alluded to by Senator Kennedy in the course of the MacNeil/Lehrer Report cited at the beginning of this chapter.

In the course of his testimony Mr. Eastman engaged in the following colloquy with Senator Howard Metzenbaum:

> Senator Metzenbaum: How much did VLN carry this company [Colonial] for on its books and how much did you carry it on your books for?
> Mr. Eastman: I was interested in Professor Briloff's written statement, because the Colonial Press, as I recall it, had a book value of somewhere around $10 million to VLN.
>
> VLN's total assets were $41 million. But because we were forced by the Accounting Principle Board opinion 16 and the Securities and Exchange Commission to account for this as a purchase, even though we exchanged our common stock for VLN's common stock, nevertheless because VLN had bought some shares on the open market, this accounting requirement said that they had to be treated as a purchase and we had to value the assets at the market price on the day of closing of the stock we issued, even though there was no cash changing hands. At that time, in late 1974, the market was in severe decline. VLN stock was down, and so was ours. It was still a fair exchange in terms of market value, but using that $20 million of book value, VLN disappeared in our consolidation.
>
> We got what we called negative goodwill. Instead of having goodwill on the books, we had a deficit in the acquisition, with the result that our corporate balance sheet looked much more highly leveraged than it would have been had we been permitted to take that in. This occurred in consolidation only. The subsidiary books were never changed. The

tax base never changed. The assets of Colonial Press at the time of merger were somewhere around $9.5 to $10 million for the tax basis. Because of this accounting treatment and consolidation, they appeared on the consolidated Sheller-Globe Corp. books as $6 or $7 million less than that.

This, of course, quickened my curiosity and, sure enough, Sheller-Globe did deliver a bundle of its stock valued at the time at $21.6 million and acquired VLN which had a shareholders' equity of $43.0 million.

I do not know precisely why the Sheller-Globe auditors called the takeover a purchase rather than a pooling; Mr. Eastman's recollection is as good a reason as any. Suffice it to say that had the independent auditors permitted the merger to go through under circumstances requiring it to be dubbed a pooling, they would probably have been fired out of hand. Just what maneuvers were pursued to make it a purchase are now merely academic—purchase accounting was implemented for the acquisition.

As a consequence the $43.0 million net book value was cut neatly in half—essentially by reducing the carrying value of VLN's property, plant, and equipment by $20.8 million—from $23.8 million down to $3.0 million. That was quite a haircut. (There were several other debits and credits to make up the aggregate of the book value adjustments to the $21.5 million aggregate reduction in carrying values.)

As a consequence of astute accountings, the Sheller-Globe management was not constrained to swallow year-to-year depreciation predicated on a VLN property, plant, and equipment base of $23.8 million; instead, subsequent profits and losses were to be based on a mere $3 million figure.

What made this arithmetic especially intriguing was the following dialogue between Mr. Eastman and Senator Metzenbaum (but it might have been something out of a Lewis Carroll creation):

Mr. Eastman: . . . We had a curious result. . . . The sale of the assets produced a tax loss because we were valued for tax purposes and shown on the subsidiary's books, but because of the absorption of this asset disappearance factor, the negative goodwill, on our consolidated statements it showed a book gain.

The best way I have been able to explain it to any shareholder is like this. A lot of shareholders don't understand it either. Suppose you bought a car for $5,000. For some reason you had to take it into your accounting system at $2,000. For tax purposes, you have a $5,000 base on it, but your books only show $2,000. Now if you sell it tomorrow for $3,000, you show a book gain. But what has actually happened?

You have lost $2,000 of the $5,000 you paid for it, and that's what happened here.

Senator Metzenbaum: What happened—Give me the numbers, if you would please, . . .

*   *   *

Senator Metzenbaum: Let me get the numbers then. You were carrying it on Sheller-Globe's books at about $6.5 to $7 million?

Mr. Eastman: No; it was included in our plants, property, and equipment accounts at a value of $6.5 million less than the original purchase price depreciated, which was on Colonial Press's books.

Senator Metzenbaum: What was that figure?

Mr. Eastman: About $9.5 million, as I recall.

Senator Metzenbaum: You were carrying it at about $9.5 million?

Mr. Eastman: On the Colonial books.

Senator Metzenbaum: I am not interested in Colonial books; I am interested in the Sheller-Globe books. I would like to know what happened to Sheller-Globe as a consequence of this transaction.

I am not quite clear on that; I understand the automobile transaction, but I don't understand the Sheller-Globe/Colonial Press transaction.

Poor Senator Metzenbaum (like Poor Alice) could not comprehend such apparent contradictions. But assuming that the Internal Revenue Service did not find a catch 22 in the Internal Revenue Code, Sheller-Globe did get away with a neat tax maneuver. But by now you should not be surprised to hear that the books kept for the tax collector may diverge dramatically from those given to the shareholders. The tax collector's loss is the Sheller-Globe shareholders' gain.

It might, however, be of interest for the Senator and my readers to know that sophisticated B-school students learn that frequently a profitable business may be scuttled because the cash inflow from the sale plus the cash inflow generated by the tax loss may exceed the discounted value of the net cash inflows anticipated from the profitable operation of the business.

And what if the employees of that profitable business are thrown out of work and the community is made to sustain an enormous burden? It is sad to say, but the B-school students' computerized game plans do not allow for such externalities nor for any sentimentalities. Everything is reckoned in binaries, and the student would fail dismally if he permitted his conscience to intervene.

As I cut through this convoluted rhetoric it appears that on Sheller-Globe's books, Colonial cost about $3 million but for tax purposes Colonial assets were carried at $9 million, and as a consequence if they were sold at $7 million there would be a tax loss of $2 million but Sheller-Globe would be reporting a profit of $4 million. The cash inflow for Sheller-Globe would be counted as the $4 million that it got for the Colonial assets plus the $1 million of tax benefit resulting from the tax loss of $2 million.

Gelco–International Couriers Corporation

Let us examine another small but intriguing manifestation of purchase accounting involving Gelco Corporation's 1977 acquisition of International Couriers Corporation (ICC)—a service business engaged in providing specialized courier services of electronic data processing materials, bank checks, and other high-priority items, principally in the Midwest and Canada.

For this corporation Gelco parted with approximately $53 million in cash. Since ICC's book value—ICC's shareholders' equity disclosed by its balance sheet—amounted to about $25 million, there remained a gap of about $28 million to be allocated. Possibly because of the enormity of this hole, Gelco enlisted the services of an appraisal company to do the necessary.

I have over the years stood in awe at the ways in which my accounting colleagues are entirely capable of making 2 plus 2 equal almost anything; I must now include appraisers for co-equal status on that pedestal.

In any event, the appraisers did a little fussing with ICC's real estate; they accepted unquestioningly ICC's numbers for all other depreciable property and then with remarkable rhetoric fixed a value for the intangibles at $25 million. That is, of course, a figure—about 50 percent of the aggregate cost. Whereupon the appraisers allocated the numbers (in millions):

To Operating Rights	$21.0
To ICC's name and reputation	2.5
To work force	1.5
Subtotal	$25.0
Other, presumably plain ordinary goodwill	2.6
A total of	$27.6

Gelco's auditors accepted this conclusion (at least they permitted that $27.6 million, more or less, to be incorporated into Gelco's certified statements). The auditors might have had some misgivings regarding the value of the intangibles. Despite the high valuation put on ICC's name and reputation, the title was soon changed to Gelco Courier Corporation and its base of operations was moved from Chicago to Minneapolis.

The valuation put on the labor force might well have been the subject of further probing by the independent auditors when they recognized that there was an almost complete turnover in the administrative staff and a serious coming apart in the ICC control systems.

But let's not quibble over whether the $2.5 million or $1.5 million number was appropriately perpetuated; let us put the entire $27.6 million intangible into a single hopper and consider it as a unit.

At the outset you should know that the company and its auditors determined to amortize this relatively enormous sum over a forty-year period and on a straight-line basis, no less. Hence, give or take a few dollars, Gelco and its auditors are apparently satisfied with a write-off of a paltry $700,000 annually.

What can Gelco expect for this $27.6 million in intangibles? What kind of earnings might be expected? If I could see those presumptive earnings "excess" (or something even remotely approaching that sum), then, at least, I might accept the judgment of Gelco, *et al.*

A review of the 1976 form 10-K indicates that ICC enjoyed income of just about $4 million. Based on the Gelco offering circular of August, 1977, promulgated for the ICC acquisition, that earnings pattern continued through mid-1977. And based on Gelco's form 10-K for its July 31, 1978, fiscal year, there was no change for the better subsequent to the takeover.

If Gelco and its auditors had only taken a few moments to examine dispassionately the decision to spread the $27.6 million equally over the forty-year span, I cannot help but conclude that they, too, would have recognized the absurdity implicit in their determinations.

ICC is a service business; it may well be a specialized service business with some special connections at airports and the like. But forty years is a very long time to presume the continuity of any service enterprise (including that of certified public accountancy, it might be noted). How long can ICC count on its connections? Can they give any assurance that within the forty years there will not be technological advances so that all that ICC is now transporting will be relayed electronically? Or is it not conceivable that some Armageddon will cause a reversion to carrier pigeons as the ultimate courier?

As noted earlier, the ICC acquisition was relatively minor in amount, a mere $50 million ploy. It nevertheless served as an intriguing precursor to a whopping quarter-of-a-billion-dollar acquisition in late 1979—an acquisition considered in some detail in the following chapter.

Proposals to a Senate Committee

All this might be taken as the frame of reference for my September, 1978, presentation before the Subcommittee on Antitrust and Monopoly of the U.S. Senate's Committee on the Judiciary. After considering with the Senators the ways in which the prevailing accounting and tax rules were aiding and abetting the accelerating merger movement, I concluded with a bevy of interrelated recommendations, including:

First, procedures which pertain to the tax law and its administration:

1. Prohibit the use of preferred stock as the catalyst for effecting a tax-free exchange for common stock of an acquired corporation. At the least preferred stock of the "transient preferred" variety should be characterized for what it is, i.e., a debt instrument for all purposes. (This would also imply that the receipt of "dividends" thereon by corporate shareholders would not qualify for the 85 percent exclusion.)

   Significantly, the Tax Reform Act of 1969 gave the Commissioner of Internal Revenue the authority to promulgate regulations to distinguish between indebtedness and stockholders' equity. This the Congress did by adding Section 385 to the Internal Revenue Code captioned "Treatment of Certain Interests in Corporations as Stock or Indebtedness."

It took the Commissioner of Internal Revenue more than a decade just to develop the proposed regulations under this section of the Internal Revenue Code. And then, insofar as preferred stock is concerned, the promulgation provides us with two illustrations (which may be seen as being at opposite poles):

Example (1). On July 7, 1985, corporation C issues 500 shares of $100 par value, 5-percent preferred stock. Dividends on the stock must be paid if earned. The par value of the stock and accumulated dividends are "absolutely and unconditionally" payable on July 15, 2005. If the holders of the preferred stock are not paid $100 plus accumulated dividends on July 15, 2005, they have the right to require the dissolution of corporation C and the application of its assets (after payment of all liabilities) to the payment of their claims. Based on these facts, the preferred stock provides for fixed payments in the nature of principal and interest and therefore is treated as an instrument. Accordingly, the preferred stock may be treated as indebtedness under §1.385-4(a) (relating to instruments generally).

Example (2). On August 8, 1985, corporation D issues 500 shares of $100 par value, 6-percent preferred stock. Dividends on the preferred stock are cumulative, and D may not pay dividends on its common stock so long as dividends on the preferred stock are in arrears. However, dividends on the preferred stock are payable only if declared by D's board of directors. In addition, the preferred stock is callable for $105 a share at the discretion of D's board of directors. Based on these facts, the preferred stock does not provide for fixed payments in the nature of principal or interest. Therefore, the preferred stock is not treated as an instrument.

Regrettably, the Commissioner did not see fit to grab the nettle and provide us with his considered views regarding transient preferred stock, i.e., that required to be redeemed and which provide for adverse consequences to the corporation and/or incumbent management for the failure of the corporation to meet its obligations under the indenture.

2. Give full force and effect to the continuity-of-interest concept implicit in the reorganization provisions of our tax statutes.
3. Where shareholders of a target company are given the option to take cash or stock on the exchange, the transaction should, *ipso facto*, be denied taxfree status. Similarly, where such shareholders are given the option to take cash on the barrelhead or over an attenuated period, the installment method of reporting the gain should be proscribed.
4. Prohibit absolutely the deduction for interest paid by an acquiring corporation for debt incurred to acquire or carry more than a, say, 10 percent interest in acquired corporations.
5. Implement the accumulated earnings tax so as to make it operational against publicly owned corporations as well as to those closely held. Especially in point: It should be a prima facie case of unreasonable accumulation where a corporation is capable of effecting a major acquisition wholly or significantly from internally generated funds.
6. At the very least the Commissioner of Internal Revenue should declare a moratorium on the issuance of ruling letters holding exchanges to be taxfree except in those instances where there are no entangling alliances nor deviations from the traditional concepts for such exchanges.

Thus, the prevailing process of negotiated "declaratory judgments" are leading to a Greshamizing of these concepts.

I urge that the corporations' counsel make the determinations predicated on their best judgments. Let the various parties then proceed at their own risks, permitting the Internal Revenue Serivce to review the transactions in fuller and broader perspective.

Experience informs us that prudent counsel will urge a margin of safety, to avoid the clever and the contrived—which in turn should preserve the prevailing standards, even if it does not raise them.

Second, as to recommendations in the area of corporate regulations by the various regulatory agencies of the United States government:

1. All takeovers involving a consideration in excess of, say, $100 million (and/or cumulatively by an acquisitive acquirer in excess of $250 million) should require the *prior* approval of the Federal Trade Commission and the Justice Department. It should be noted that I urge the prior approval—not merely prior notification on a courtesy basis.
2. The Securities and Exchange Commission should:
   (a) Proscribe pooling-of-interests accounting and then insist that any amount designed as goodwill be justified by the company's auditors to be an asset possessed of corresponding value. In short, it should not be a mere number to balance the debits and credits.
   (b) For a period of, say, five years following all major takeovers, the acquired company's accounts and reporting practices should be maintained essentially consistent with those which prevailed previously. This would permit the evaluation of the acquirer's competence in the management of the resources of the acquired entity. This proposal, if implemented, would also have a salutary effect on segment and line-of-business reporting which is so vital to potential investors and competitors.
   (c) Require that in all proxy and/or prospectus material promulgated as an incident to a takeover, there be a disclosure of all acquisitions consummated by the acquiring corporation during the five preceding years, with a clear, comprehensive summary of the success experienced in the subsequent operations.

Third, some existing agency or, if necessary, a newly created commission should:

1. Forbid public accounting firms, banks, and possibly also management consulting firms from engaging as corporate matchmakers. Each of these professional groups is charged with a significant public interest; as an incident to their professional services each develops an extensive and highly sophisticated data bank—that resource should not be used except as an incident to their primary legitimate objectives, hence, not to serve as a marriage broker.

2. Prohibit the continuance in (or entry into) high corporate office of those convicted of criminal behavior. (Consent decrees, for this purpose, should be construed as such a conviction subject to an effective rebuttal by the defendant.) Most certainly, executives thus convicted should not be permitted to expand their spheres of influence through acquisitions— and thereby to be responsible for even larger pools of other people's money.

Based upon these hearings, Senator Edward M. Kennedy, as Chairman of the Committee on the Judiciary, proposed S.600, a Bill to Preserve the Diversity and Independence of American Business. If enacted the legislation would affect the country's 500 largest corporations. Companies with $2 billion or more in assets or $2.5 billion in sales could not merge with any other entity (unless they divest themselves of a corresponding segment). Companies with $200 million in assets or $350 million in sales could not merge unless they agreed to at least an equivalent divestment or, alternatively, demonstrate an advantage for the consumer.

In his March, 1979, floor speech introducing S.600, Senator Kennedy sketched some of the recent trends in conglomerate merger activity, pointing out that the dollar value of all corporate mergers and acquisitions rose from almost $12 billion in 1975, to $20 billion in 1976, to almost $22 billion in 1977, to $34 billion in 1978. Moreover, the Senator said, the number of large mergers is increasing: In 1975 there were only 14 mergers involving a purchase price of $100 million or more. That number rose to 39 in 1976, 41 in 1977, and 80 in 1978.

It should by now be abundantly clear that I join the Senator in seeing the merger movement as going far beyond the mere aggregation of numbers. I see the accounting implications and ramifications as extending far deeper and further than the mere balancing of debits and credits.

In short, I see the challenge consistent with the stated objective of S.600: Will we succeed in preserving the diversity, dignity, integrity, and independence of American business?

7

Fiddlers on the Road

The communications network of a major Wall Street brokerage firm carried the following glad tidings to the firm's account executives on the morning of January 24, 1980 (marked "For Internal Use Only"):

> Gelco—Price of the stock has been down for the past several days because of a rumor that *Barron's* Dr. Briloff could be writing on the company. We do not know if the rumor is correct or what the thrust of the article could be, from an accounting standpoint the one area that could be hit is that the acquisitions the company made in the past three to four years including its most recent one has resulted in a significant amount of goodwill. Otherwise we do not see too much in the way of accounting gimmickry at the company with the exception of a change to flowing through investment tax credits effective this year. In the past Gelco's tax rate has always been a full one. We believe the company has always had an ability to manage their earnings, which they have done very well over the past 15 years, plus their basic subsidiary companies are leaders in their various markets.

The gnomes of Wall Street did not have to wait long to see just what *Barron's* was going to publish on the company; the February 4th issue carried the article under the caption "Great Asset Play: But Gelco Had a Lot of Help From Its Accountants."

The Gelco "Great Asset" Saga

The article as published in *Barron's* read as follows:

> On the final day of 1979, Gelco Corp., the Eden Prairie, Minn., lessor of autos and trucks, paid a cool $250 million to Reliance Group Inc., for

its CTI International Inc. subsidiary, the global cargo container leasing operation. The deal was Gelco's most ambitious, catapulting revenues to almost
$570 million (on a pro forma basis) from $30 million in fiscal 1974 (its
fiscal year ends July) and total assets to $1.6 billion, from $271 million six
years earlier.

As such deals go, the CTI purchase went off relatively smoothly. To
pay for it, Gelco borrowed $120 million from a group of banks (at ½%
over prime and payable from 1982 to 1987); it also floated $85 million of
14⅝%, 20-year subordinated bonds; and it issued to Reliance $50 million
in mandatorially redeemable 11% preferred stock. But there were snags.
One was a tussle with the enforcement division of the Securities and Exchange
Commission, which took exception to an aspect of Gelco's past accounting.
Gelco settled the case in December, just prior to the bond financing, by
consenting to an administrative order that bars the use of such accounting;
Gelco did not admit or deny the Commission's findings. A second [snag]
related to CTI itself, focusing on the size of the transaction and, as detailed
in the bond offering prospectus, its impact on Gelco's already highly leveraged
balance sheet.

Both, in my view, warrant further discussion, at least in the accounting
realm. Additional documents which provide new insight into the role the
auditors played in applying the accounting principles the SEC questioned
also are worthy of note. And how the CTI transaction was entered on Gelco's
books is worth considering, too.

Efforts to discuss both issues with partners of Touche Ross & Co., Gelco's
independent auditors, were unsuccessful. They simply refused to do so. Nor
would Gelco officials approve such a discussion. "We are not in a position
to comment on Touche Ross's accounting methods," explained Gelco executives.

In a telephone conversation with the latter—specifically, Executive Vice
President Richard W. McFerran, and Vice Presidents Charles R. Schmidt
and Dennis B. McGrath—I was told that the SEC had taken exception to
an accounting approach in use for years and which never before had been
questioned. Moreover, the Gelco executives said, Touche Ross itself never
raised an objection. As for CTI, they commented: "We stand on our business
sense. CTI has a crackerjack management, and a good cash flow. From our
viewpoint, it was seriously undervalued."

SEC Challenges UTA

The circumstances that gave rise to the accounting dispute with the
SEC are spelled out in the Dec. 13, 1979, prospectus (the same date on
which the SEC promulgated the administrative order). The argument centered on a so-called used truck allowance (UTA), which Gelco's Feld Truck

Leasing Division received from its truck suppliers, principally International Harvester, when it purchased new equipment. (Feld is a truck leasing operation which Gelco took over in October 1974.) While it booked the UTA as income immediately, Feld apparently was not required to turn over to Harvester, nor to sell elsewhere, its used vehicles at the time of the purchase of the new trucks.

The SEC questions centered on when—and how—the UTA ought to have been included in Gelco's results from operations. Gelco had followed the practice, begun back when Feld was an independent entity, of including the UTA in income in the period in which the company billed Harvester for the allowance, ostensibly as additional proceeds from the sales of used trucks. The SEC contended that Gelco's treatment of the UTA as additional proceeds was "in error." Rather, it held, the allowance should have been accounted for as a reduction of the purchase price of the new equipment.

In consenting to the administrative order, Gelco was required to restate its prior earnings going back to fiscal 1975. The early retroactive per-share adjustments were not especially significant, amounting to, fully diluted, five cents, 10 cents and one cent, respectively, in the three years through fiscal 1977. However, the rollback hit harder in subsequent years. It reduced fiscal '78 earnings by almost $2 million, or 29 cents a share, fully diluted, and lowered fiscal 1979 by $1.1 million, or 17 cents a share—years when Gelco originally reported net per share of $2.74 and $3.39, respectively. (According to the SEC calculations, the most recent two-year overstatements amounted to 11.9% and 5.2%, respectively.)

A footnote in the prospectus also contained a statement to the effect that Touche Ross "presently agrees that the Commission's accounting method described in the order is an acceptable one." In a preliminary prospectus the corresponding footnote included an assertion that "The company has been advised by its independent auditors, Touche Ross & Co, and believes, that its method of accounting for these allowances was an accepted method." A reader, otherwise uninformed, might conclude this was nothing more than a dispute between two accounting alternatives—one "acceptable," the other "accepted." But I believe that Touche Ross's original accounting was tenuous at best and, under the circumstances, improper.

The SEC's promulgation recites that "The term 'used truck allowance' arose because it was Supplier's (Harvester's) original practice to pay a UTA to Feld with respect to Feld's purchase of a new truck from (Harvester) only if Feld traded in a used truck to (Harvester) at the time of the purchase of the new truck. For many years, however, and certainly by the time Gelco acquired Feld in 1974, (Harvester) had ceased to tie the UTA to any trade-in, but rather granted the UTA to Feld *solely* upon the purchase of a new truck by Feld" (emphasis supplied).

The SEC order went on: "Under Feld's arrangement with (Harvester),

Feld paid for new trucks without reduction for the amount of UTA. Thereafter, at Feld's discretion, Feld requested and received payment of the unre-
mitted UTA. Feld recorded these amounts not when earned, but only when
it requested payment of the UTA."

Audit Supervisor's Misgivings

Let us study how Touche Ross wound up concluding that Gelco's UTA
accounting method was appropriate for its fiscal year ended July 31, 1978.
(This is the year when these allowances shot up to $5.5 million from $600,000
the year before.) We begin with a memorandum dated Sept. 19, 1978, in
which a Touche Ross audit supervisor comments:

Based on our knowledge of the circumstances, we indicated that UTA
may be more applicable to the new vehicle as a purchase discount since
a new vehicle must be purchased. Gelco stated this is just not true, as
evidenced by the fact that they must sell or trade in a truck at the time
of purchase in order to get the UTA. Touche and Gelco both decided
to think on the dilemma more.

Tax Considerations

The auditor then added:

Another alternative brought up by Touche was to amortize the UTA
over three or more years as Ryder (Systems) does. Gelco strongly opposed
this, as they thought it would again appear somewhat as a purchased
discount. The reason for concern on this treatment is that they would
lose the ITC (investment tax credit) related to what is not UTA if it
was considered a purchase discount. Further thought was to be given
on this matter also.

In another memo a month later, although concluding that Feld's method
was acceptable, the same audit supervisor, after again discussing the pros
and cons, observed: "I believe the purchase discount method is preferable
from a purely theoretical point of view and looking at true substance over
form it is also more conservative."

Audit Partner's Rationalization

A Touche Ross partner concurred with the audit supervisor's conclusion.
While also sanctioning Gelco's practice, he noted (in an Oct. 26, 1978, memo):

Two arguments appeared convincing to us as it related to the appropriateness of this allowance being associated with used vehicles. One of those was that it would appear to be in violation of certain laws to give this kind of a special discount to selected purchasers of new vehicles (an apparent reference to an earlier comment by the audit supervisor that such allowances if not really under the UTA guise might run afoul of the antitrust laws). . . . The other argument was that it appears to be industry practice to record these in income upon receipt or upon disposition of the used vehicle.

Yet, earlier in the same document he indicates misgivings:

The question that arose was whether or not this used truck allowance applied to the new units purchased or applied to the old units that had been disposed of. The reason that this is significant is that if it did apply to the used units, it would be appropriate to take into income upon the disposition of the used units or when the amount is known. If it attaches to the new units, it is more proper to spread over the estimated life of the new units at least while they are under rental or lease. Our concern that it might be attached to the new units was that that was the basic method that it was paid.

TR's Think Tank Digs Deep

The issue refused to go away. From a Touche Ross Central Technical Center memorandum (dated Nov. 2, 1978), we learn that "engagement management (that is, of Touche Ross) has rechallenged" the determination that permitted Gelco to account for the UTA as an immediate flow-through to its income statement. The Central "think tank," however, saw things Gelco's way:

From a theoretical standpoint, it could be argued that this allowance should apply against the purchase price of the new unit. The allowance, however, requires the sale of the old unit as well as the purchase of the new. When the company expands its fleet, adding (rather than replacing) units, it does not get this credit. It could therefore also be argued that the sale of the old as well as the purchase of the new is required to realize the credit, so attaching the credit to the sale is just as correct as attaching it to the purchase.

On the subject of industry practice on which the auditors and Gelco's management appear to have relied so implicitly to rationalize the income-injection approach to the UTA allowance, here is the way the Central Technical Center tackled it:

To get a handle on practice, we reviewed 10-Ks for truck leasing companies to see whether they spoke to this question. Not surprisingly, none spoke directly. However, several companies implied that this sort of allowance was credited to income upon the sale of used units. For example, Saunders Leasing says, "The extent to which the Registrant's earnings may be affected in the future by disposition of used revenue equipment depends on a number of factors, including the market for such equipment, the *purchase of new equipment.* . ." [emphasis supplied].

Several other companies including Ryder System Inc. and Hertz indicate that profit on sale of used vehicles is at least in part a function of the purchase of new vehicles. This leads us to the inference that Gelco's accounting has support within the industry, which Gelco has represented to us.

The "think tank" reached into its data bank of 10Ks and from some ambiguous language "inferred" the answer for which the client was arguing.

Improper Income Management

But there was another aspect of the UTA accountings which was the subject of SEC criticism. This concerned the deferral until fiscal 1978 of $1.6 million in allowances which Gelco, said the Commission, could have billed and recorded in fiscal 1977. As the SEC's administrative order alleged: ". . . in its 1977 fiscal year Feld was able to shift approximately $1.6 million of pre-tax income into fiscal year 1978. Feld accomplished this by deliberately not billing for this amount until 1978."

In the same document, the SEC found: "Even assuming Gelco's original accounting treatment for UTA could be justified, its practice of recording UTA when payment was requested violated principles of accrual accounting and allowed Gelco to improperly manage income. The recordation of approximately $1.6 million of UTA in 1978 which was deferred from 1977 was clearly improper. . . ."

Of course, the restated financial statements corrected for this impropriety—thereby apparently satisfying the SEC. But I am far from satisfied. My dissatisfaction is exacerbated by an assertion in footnote Q to Gelco's financial statements in the prospectus that the aberration came to the attention of the independent auditors only "recently." For me, this is hard to believe.

As is evident from the extensive internal Touche Ross documents, the UTA was subjected to careful scrutiny. Nor were the auditors dealing with hundreds of thousands of nickel and dime transactions which somehow got themselves dispersed in Gelco's system. Instead, there was essentially a single source with a correspondingly limited number of documents which had to be studied in order to fight the figures and get the facts (to adopt a phrase suggested by one of our great forebears of the accounting profession). There is reason to believe that Touche Ross might well have determined to defer certification of the 1978 financial statements while the auditors fully satisfied themselves on the substantial amount passed into 1978 income.

When 2 Times 2 Doesn't Equal 4

Thus, starting with the aforementioned Sept. 19, 1978, audit supervisor's memo, mention was made of Feld's UTA climbing from $600,000 on approximately 1,000 units purchased in 1977 to $5.5 million on approximately 1,600 units purchased in 1978. As he stated, ". . . we have been unable to audit why such a significant change." Addressing himself to a request for the document that would indicate the basis for the UTA, the supervisor comments: "Management is somewhat reluctant to produce this since it is located in St. Louis and problems exist as far as antitrust violations by the truck companies."

Subsequently, both the audit supervisor and a Touche Ross partner, the documents show, were satisfied, on the basis of Gelco's explanation and some documentation, for the huge jump in UTA—namely, the greater number of units (from 1,000 to 1,600) and a rise in the average UTA per vehicle (from $600 to $1,500).

I have difficulty with their arithmetic. My handy calculator informs me that even the 1,600 units at $1,500 each would aggregate but $2.4 million—how could they possibly have been complacent about $5.5 million? In fact, even today, knowing that $1.6 million of the $5.5 million was improperly deferred from 1977, I remain stymied. After subtracting that infusion from the $5.5 million I come up with $3.9 million, still $1.5 million above the product of the 1978 units multiplied by the presumptive 1978 average UTA.

As noted, I tried to obtain response from Gelco on how Touche Ross went about their audit of the 1978 UTA. They passed the buck to Touche Ross, who previously declined to discuss any aspect of the Gelco controversy with me (except to direct me to the public files). I would, of course, welcome the "new math" which permits 1,600 times $1,500 to equal $5.5 million, or even $3.9 million.

The "Great Asset" Acquisition

Let's now direct our attention to Gelco's acquisition of CTI Corp. And for our initial frame of reference we turn to the prospectus promulgated by Gelco on Dec. 13, 1979, covering issuance of $85 million in 14¼ % subordinated debenture bonds, due 1999. The issue was underwritten by Drexel

Burnham and Paine Webber. The CTI balance sheet (as of June 30, 1979) included in the prospectus may be summarized as follows (in millions):

Cash and Receivables	$ 50.2
Less Accounts Payable and Accruals	25.4
	$ 24.8
Container Rental equipment (net of depreciation)	305.6
Other	3.1
Total	$333.5
Notes Payable	239.3
Equity of Reliance Group (including subordinated notes payable)	$ 94.2

As noted, Gelco paid $250 million for CTI. The excess of $155.8 million over the $94.2 million of Reliance's old equity was spread as follows—a net of $22.4 million to the container rental equipment, and $133.4 million to "Excess of investment over net assets of businesses acquired"—presumptively goodwill.

Search for the Good in Goodwill

The final valuation, to be sure, awaits detailed procedures. But, be that as it may, when Gelco finished with the "ups" and "downs" to CTI's balance sheet, it determined (at least for the time being) that CTI's goodwill was worth a tidy $133.4 million, and, not unexpectedly, management determined that this item was going to be good for two score years, the outer limit permitted by the Accounting Principles Board. And, of course, that it was going to be thus good on a straight-line basis.

According to the prospectus, the container company's pre-tax income worked out as follows:

Calendar Years	Total Revs. (millions)	Pre-tax Income (millions)	%
'74	$ 36.3	$ 4.8	13.2
'75	37.4	(2.8)	
'76	48.2	10.3	21.4
'77	75.7	28.6	37.8
'78	111.5	36.8	33.0
Nine months ended Sept. 30:			
'78	80.6	28.0	34.7
'79	103.4	26.5	25.6

Gelco figures its annual financing cost for CTI at $36.9 million (interest on the bank loan and bonds amounting to $31.4 million, plus dividends on the redeemable preferred of $5.5 million). On a pro forma basis, its coverage—the ratio of earnings to fixed charges—including preferred dividends—is a rather thin 1.26.

So far so good—Gelco might appear to have $4 million left out of a presumptive $40 million of historical CTI pre-tax earnings. But that is before factoring in the additional depreciation which results from the introduction of another cost layer over the CTI historical basis.

If, as I believe it should, Gelco were to add the bulk of the $155.8 million excess over Reliance's old historical cost to the rental equipment account and then to depreciate that additional cost layer over a 10-year period (as CTI has done historically for its newly acquired equipment), there would be an added annual depreciation charge of possibly $15 million. That would be far more than the $4 million left over after deducting the annual cost for financing the acquisition.

During our telephone conversation, Gelco's officials pointed out that as part of the CTI deal, Gelco also acquired computers, computer software, a customer list, service organization and the like. Granted they did—but is it worth $133.4 million, even on a tentative basis? And will that software, etc., be good for 40 years on a straight-line basis?

Who's Kidding Whom?

Gelco has made its pro forma debits equal the credits; the company may even be able to rationalize its bookkeeping by pointing to Accounting Principles Board Opinions 16 and 17. But such interpretation of accounting precepts may "kid" the reader and possibly even themselves.

Moreover, Gelco has added $133.4 million to its intangibles (goodwill) account, thereby heavily waterlogging its balance sheet. Thus, the pro forma balance sheet bound into the prospectus indicates that upon completion of the CTI acquisition—and after all the debits and credits have been put through—Gelco's common shareholders' equity would stand at $123.3 million, of which a total of $164.7 million would be in that amorphous intangible "excess" account.

Gelco's management, of course, regards the acquisition most felicitously. As they informed me in our phone interview, with each of the nearly 250,000 of 20-foot container equivalent units having an estimated replacement value of $2,000 to $3,000 each, they contend the purchase was a "great asset play."

Now, it should be noted, Touche Ross is not only Gelco's independent auditor, but has been also throughout the period that CTI was under Reliance's wing the independent auditor for CTI. The pro forma statements showing the allocation of the $155.8 million excess over CTI's book value were presented as unaudited; nonetheless, it would have been most informative if Gelco had taken advantage of Touche Ross's familiarity with the CTI earnings history and other factors surrounding the company to determine just where and how they could discern the excess earnings to support a substantive goodwill factor predicated on a $250 million purchase price.

In short, there should be an end to the prevailing practice of making the "excess" account a catch basin to absorb whatever numbers cannot be, or in any event are not, assigned elsewhere.

The Ultimate Question

This has been an essay revolving about Gelco's accounting and accountability. There is, however, a second central theme: the accountability on the part of the accounting profession. Thus, insofar as the accounting for the CTI acquisition is concerned, it should be evident that the accounting for business combinations (both pooling-of-interests and purchase alternatives) remains in a state of disarray.

The Financial Accounting Standards Board in the initial stages of its existence set how to properly account in mergers and acquisitions as the problem of greatest urgency. Seven years later the item is not even on its agenda.

So ended the *Barron's* essay; but there are other serious questions remaining to be explored—even if they are not yet capable of being answered.

Swallowing an Enormous Tax Bite

First among the themes for this epilogue is the matter of the very substantial hidden cost which Gelco's management imposed upon the corporation's shareholders by the way it structured the CTI acquisition. Gelco bought the CTI stock from Reliance Group for $250 million— an amount which appears to have exceeded Reliance's basis by about $156 million. Because Gelco bought CTI *stock* and not CTI's *assets,* Gelco is presumed to be constrained to perpetuate the old tax bases for the container equipment and other assets included on the CTI balance sheet. (This is very much like what happens when shareholder A sells his General Motors shares to shareholder B—GM's tax basis for its assets remains entirely unaffected.)

If, then, we were to assume a 50 percent tax rate, Gelco was made to swallow an added tax cost of about $78 million because the excess over the CTI carrying values is not available to Gelco for subsequent tax depreciation; this $78 million of added cost implicit in the deal will never find its way into the subsequent income statements promulgated by Gelco's management pursuant to GAAP excepting, possibly, and only indirectly, as an incident to the forty-year amortization of the goodwill blob.

As I recall it, during our telephone interview I inquired of the Gelco executives as to why they did not buy CTI's assets and thereby get a stepped-up tax basis by reference to the full amount actually paid on the acquisition. The response was to the effect that Reliance wanted to get a capital gain on the entire amount of its gain on the transaction. This, it should be noted, would indicate that it was the seller that was in the driver's seat in these negotiations. Charles R. Schmidt, a Gelco vice-president, has denied making this statement, but then has refused to respond to the question *de novo*, i.e., whether Gelco had discussed an asset deal with CTI and, if so, what was that company's response. Accordingly, at least for the present, I shall rely on my recollection of that aspect of the January, 1980, telephone conversation.

It is true that by structuring the deal as a stock acquisition, Reliance got itself a capital gain on the entire profit—so that if one accepts the statements at face value, the entire $156 million profit is taxable at 28 percent; on the other hand, if the transaction were an asset deal, then *part* of that gain (possibly half) would be taxed at 46 percent, under the so-called "depreciation recapture" provisions of the Internal Revenue Code. In addition there would be some "investment tax credit recapture"—in an amount which I cannot presently estimate.

My experience informs me that if the parties were really negotiating as equals (and where neither was more so), the objectives of the seller and buyer might be reconcilable. Gelco might have budged somewhat to accommodate the 18 percentage point spread (46 versus 28) on the portion of the Reliance gain which would be subject to depreciation recapture—such an addition could then be added to the basis for the container equipment.

But if Gelco had, in fact, negotiated an asset deal, management could not logically turn around and say that almost all of the overplus above the old book values is attributable to goodwill—and thereby permit that grotesque amount to be spread over two score years. An asset deal would have mandated the actual cost to be depreciated over the decade, or less, consistent with the schedule appropriate for the container equipment.

It should be noted in passing that Gelco might yet be able to salvage the tax benefits which were sacrificed initially through the stock acquisition. This could be accomplished by Gelco liquidating CTI's assets into a new subsidiary (or into itself) under circumstances where Internal Revenue Code section 334(b)(2) was applied. The added tax would then be somewhat greater than if the assets, per se, were acquired—but yet, in all likelihood, the overall tax consequences should be salutary to Gelco and its shareholders. However, once again, Gelco's management would be hard pressed to rationalize an accounting ploy which shoved most of the excess over old book values into goodwill.

Significantly, there is verbiage in Accounting Principles Board Opinion No. 16 (re Business Combinations) which, in a situation like this one, can turn reality on its head. Let us go back to the *Barron's* piece and take note of the fact that Gelco did allocate $22.4 million to the container rental equipment item. That number was the result of an intriguing calculus, to wit (in millions):

It began with an addition for upward revaluation of that equipment in the amount of	$100.0
Then, to reflect the fact that the aforementioned sum was not available for a tax deduction there was subtracted	50.0
So that the net upward revaluation became	$ 50.0
From this amount there was subtracted a number representing the "reclassification of CTI estimated deferred income taxes"	27.6
Leaving the net *plus* of	$ 22.4

Take note of the fact that the $50 million haircut for the non-tax-deductibility of the assumed $100 million adjustment added $50 million to the goodwill blob. (How else would the debits equal the credits?)

Here, Gelco can undoubtedly point to paragraph 89 of APB 16 which reads as follows:

> The market or appraisal values of specific assets and liabilities . . . may differ from the income tax bases of those items. Estimated future tax effects of differences between the tax bases and amounts otherwise appropriate to assign to an asset or a liability are one of the variables in estimating fair value. Amounts assigned to identifiable assets and liabilities should, for example, recognize that the fair value of an asset to an acquirer is less than its market or appraisal value if all or a portion of the market or appraisal value is not deductible for income taxes. . . .

Theoretically the rule makes sense. If, for example, you contemplate buying property which you plan to sell for $100 and you are required to pay a 50 percent income tax on any taxable gain, and assuming that you are told the tax basis to you will be zero regardless of what you might pay, then the most you can logically and prudently pay for the property is $50; anything you might pay in excess of $50 is destined to represent your net-after-tax loss.

Consequently, had you paid $90 for the property and resold it for $100, you would be constrained to pay a tax of $50 (since your tax basis was zero), leaving you with a cool loss of $40 (i.e., proceeds $100, cost $90, plus a tax of $50, aggregate outflow $140).

But supposing you were a corporation and bought for $90 the shares of a corporation which owned the aforementioned property with its associated tax basis of zero. Your hot-shot accountants could proceed in the manner of Gelco, putting no more than $50 into the property or inventory account; the remaining $40 would be shoved into the "excess cost" ("goodwill") account and then amortized to income at the rate of $1 a year for forty years—so that at worst the $40 managerial goof would show up in the bottom line as $1 a year. Mind you, I could play with these numbers (all consistent with GAAP) to come up with an actual profit—but as I said I wanted to portray "a conservative" picture that would confront management under the prevailing book of rules.

To repeat: The precepts of APB 16 can be seen to be fair and logical—if fairly and logically implemented. But as we have seen in so many contexts, Gelco included, the essentially good doctrine of GAAP is all too often forsaken in practice.

An Affront to the SEC

Let us move on now to another facet of the Gelco–SEC proceedings which has fascinated me. The Commission's Administrative Order, after reciting a catechism of factual allegations, rises to its ultimate majestic heights by providing: "It is hereby ordered that . . . 2. Gelco will not assert in any future filings that the prior accounting for UTA was an accepted method."

The ink was undoubtedly still wet on this decree when Gelco proceeded to violate it. Thus, at pages 21–22 of the bond prospectus there is set down the saga of the "SEC Administrative Order"; included in that discourse we are informed that:

> . . . Touche Ross & Co. has advised the Company and the staff of the Division of Enforcement that, while Touche Ross & Co. presently agrees that the Commission's accounting method described in the order is an acceptable one, Touche Ross & Co. does not believe that retroactive application as mandated in the order is permitted in accordance with generally accepted accounting principles. . . .

To comprehend the violation alleged by me, it is necessary for us to refer to Accounting Principles Board Opinion No. 20. That deals with "accounting changes" and provides that in the usual case a change in the accounting principles applicable to a particular entity does not permit retroactive restatement; instead, the change from one such principle to another is to be implemented by a so-called "cumulative effect" adjustment. That is, the entire net difference of all of the prior years' divergences is determined and that cumulative aggregate net difference goes into the current statements as a single figure. For example, the cumulative effect as of July 31, 1978, of Gelco's misuse of the UTA accountings was but $2.9 million. And, according to Gelco's accountants, this is the way the accounting change to conform to the new precepts should be handled. Instead, the SEC, over the protestations of Gelco's accountants, ordained the retroactive restatement of Gelco's accountings for the five years included in the prospectus.

Here you might fairly ask, what's so fascinating about an essentially "plumbing" problem, i.e., cumulative effect versus retroactive restatement? But ah! The difference is almost as great as the classic argument over the shape of the globe (or the center of the solar system).

This is because APB 20 provides that the cumulative-effect directive applies, with some specific exceptions, only when the change ". . . results from adoption of a generally accepted accounting principle different from the one used previously for reporting purposes. . . ." The opinion then goes on to make clear that: "A characteristic of a change in accounting principle is that it concerns a choice from among two or more generally accepted accounting principles. . . ."

On the other hand, where the accounting change is necessitated to correct an error in prior misapplications of accounting principles, then, according to the APB (paragraph 13), ". . . A change from an accounting principle that is not generally accepted to one that is generally accepted is a correction of an error for purposes of applying this section."

Subsequently, paragraph 36 states: "The Board concludes that correction of an error in the financial statements of a prior period discovered subsequently to their issuance (paragraph 13) should be reported as a prior period adjustment. . . ."

Therefore when Gelco insinuated into its prospectus the assertion that ". . . Touche Ross & Co. does not believe that retroactive application as mandated in the order is permitted in accordance with generally accepted accounting principles," it was, in effect, saying that the UTA-accounting switch was nothing but a change from one generally accepted accounting principle to another generally accepted accounting principle (like switching from chocolate to vanilla ice cream). By this assertion,

I maintain, the prospectus violated the direct decree of the SEC that "Gelco will not assert in any future filings that the prior accounting for UTA was an accepted method."

My fascination led me to inquire of the SEC accounting staff person who was involved in the negotiations leading to the administrative order as to whether the Commission was thus finessed or flim-flammed knowingly or unwittingly. It turned out that the SEC sensed what was happening but, proceeding with its prevailing pragmatism, determined to close its eyes. How to rationalize this? According to the staff person, the order was directed against Gelco and *not* against its auditors. And, he said, if I carefully read the wording in the prospectus, Gelco is merely reporting what its auditors had informed the SEC—in short, it was not Gelco *qua* Gelco saying anything.

This kind of sophistry might be entirely appropriate to a lawyer defending a client caught with the smoking gun in hand. It is entirely unworthy of a great agency of the United States government given to full and fair and truthful disclosure in the securities marketplace.

My special indignation in this chapter is directed at Touche Ross, Gelco's independent certified public accountants. It may well be that Touche Ross did little, if anything, other than what some other accounting firm might do to help its client achieve a particular end result. But remember that at the time when Touche Ross was making critical judgments in behalf of Gelco, it was "on probation" as a consequence of its misdeeds in the U.S. Financial mess; it was awaiting the special peer review mandated by ASR 153 (see Chapter 3)—a review put on a back burner pending the completion of the SEC's investigation into the firm's allegedly perverse conduct in the Ampex–Giant Stores audits. These latter proceedings were, in turn, held in abeyance while the courts were being importuned by Touche Ross to prevent the SEC from proceeding with its investigation.

One might expect that a firm which was on the griddle would be particularly committed to insuring that its current practices met the highest standards dictated by our profession—and to avoiding the race for the bottom evidenced by the Gelco record.

Great "Asset Play" or "Numbers Ploy"?

As we saw, Gelco's management assured us that the CTI acquisition was "a great asset play"; it might appear from subsequent developments that if it did not quite work out that way then Gelco would make it into a great numbers ploy.

Thus, the company's form I0–Q for the quarter ended January 31,

1980 (one month after the acquisition), informed us that: ". . . In the second quarter of fiscal year 1980, the Company changed the estimated useful lives of its containers from 10 years to 12½–15 years and increased such equipment's estimated salvage value from 10% to 15% . . ."

This maneuver was commented on by *Business Week* in its April 21, 1980, "Inside Wall Street" column, as follows:

> The company . . . lengthened the depreciation periods of container equipment made by CTI Corp., which it acquired last Dec. 31 from Reliance Group Inc. Reliance's chairman is Saul P. Steinberg, who has gained notoriety for, among other things, aggressive accounting. . . . "Gelco liberalized Saul's accounting," marvels one analyst.

The magnitude and seriousness of the change can be better discerned by looking at an item in the company's press release covering the April 30 quarter, i.e., the one that reflected CTI's operations for the first full quarter under Gelco's hegemony. There we are informed that "We changed depreciation lives on CTI equipment, and this increased our earnings by 37 cents a share." This extrapolated out to at least $3.6 million on a pre-tax basis for but a single quarter—a boost of $14.4 million, at least, on an annualized basis.

For the April 30 quarter the great asset play produced a loss of 55 cents a share for Gelco, figured before the depreciation stretchout.

And, mind you, this is a "numbers ploy" above and beyond those described by the *Barron's* article. If that's the stuff $133.4 million in goodwill is made of, then words and numbers have lost their meaning.

But the study of the January 10–Q revealed something else—to my mind even more serious than the depreciation caper. Thus footnote E states, in part:

> In the second quarter of fiscal year 1980, the Company changed its method of income recognition for income earned on vehicles purchased for lease by the Fleet Management, Leasing and Related Services segment. Under the new method, which more closely matches revenues with related costs, a portion of the income earned is deferred and recognized over the anticipated lease term and at the time of the sale of the used vehicle rather than at the time of delivery of the vehicle. The $3,500,000 or $.51 per share cumulative effect at July 31, 1979 (after reduction for income taxes of $3,497,000), was charged to income for the six months ended January 31, 1980.

Despite several requests Gelco's management refuses to flesh out the nature of the Fleet Management change, i.e., refuses to describe just what they were "front-end loading" into income and were now attenuating. I am, therefore, constrained to provide a scenario predicated on the aphorism, "Let the past be prologue."

With that as the lead, I proceed to the inference that in Gelco's Fleet Management accounting calculus there lay a "used car allowance" corresponding to the used truck allowance discerned and struck down by the SEC in its December, 1979, Administrative Order. If the Commission neglected to inquire about, and Gelco, therefore, determined not to reveal, the existence of a parallel allowance in the automobile-leasing operations—well, then, there would be something of an internal contradiction that Gelco could not long keep to itself.

Whereupon, according to my scenario, Gelco determined to "bite the bullet" and "go straight."

Now really straight would mean to restate the prior years' statements to correct the wrong accounting treatment accorded to the automobile discounts. Nevertheless, taking the lead from what the independent auditors were saying about not restating the prior years' figures under APB Opinion 20, Gelco determined to slide the switch through the "cumulative effect" process (thereby implying a mere switch from one GAAP to another).

And here now the scenario takes on another intriguing twist. Under the SEC's Accounting Series Release No. 177 (relating to changes in rules regarding filings of quarterly forms 10–Q, September 10, 1975):

> In connection with accounting changes, a letter from the registrant's independent public accountant is required to be filed in which the accountant states whether or not the change is to an alternative principle which in his judgment is preferable under the circumstances. A number of accountants objected to this requirement on the grounds that no standards exist for judging preferability among generally accepted accounting principles and that authoritative accounting principles only require that management justify that a change is to a preferable method. The Commission believes that professional accounting judgment can be applied to determine whether an alternative accounting principle is preferable in a particular set of circumstances. Since a substantial burden of proof falls upon management to justify a change, the Commission believes that the burden has not been met unless the justification is sufficiently persuasive to convince an independent professional accounting expert that in his judgment the new method represents an improved method of measuring business operations in the particular circumstances involved.

How did Touche Ross meet this burden? Here's the whole letter just as it was reproduced in its client's January, 1980, 10–Q:

As stated in Note E to the financial statements for the three months and six months ended January 31, 1980, the Company changed its method of income recognition relating to certain vehicles and states that the newly adopted accounting method is preferable in the circumstances in order to more closely match revenue and related costs. At your request, we have reviewed and discussed with you the circumstances and the business judgment and planning which formulated your basis to make this change in accounting principle.

It should be understood that criteria have not been established by the Financial Accounting Standards Board of selecting from among the alternative accounting principles that exist in this area. Further, the American Institute of Certified Public Accountants has not established the standards by which an auditor can evaluate the preferability of one accounting principle among a series of alternatives. We understand that this subject is actively being considered by the appropriate authoritative bodies. However, for purposes of the Company's compliance with the requirements of the Securities and Exchange Commission, we are furnishing this letter. At the time authoritative literature is promulgated, containing a different form of response than that contained in the following paragraph, we will withdraw this letter and will substitute the response sanctioned by the AICPA, for submission to the SEC on a Form 8 amendment.

Based on our review and discussion, we concur with management's judgment that the newly adopted accounting principle described in Note E is preferable in the circumstances. In formulating this position, we are relying on management's business planning and judgment, which we do not find to be unreasonable. Because we have not audited any financial statements of the Company as of any date or for any period subsequent to July 31, 1979, we express no opinion on the financial statements for the three months and six months ended January 31, 1980.

This is for me déjà vu! I saw it (or something like it) in the writings of Lewis Carroll and/or in Orwell's *Nineteen Eighty-Four*. Mind you, this is my scenario. Undoubtedly in time the truth will out—at which time I will determine upon a correction if one is needed or lodge a formal complaint against those who may have again determined to play fast and loose with our standards of accounting and accountability.*

* See note on page 272.

8

Write-Offs or Rip-Offs

After a full-term, nine-month period of gestation, the Financial Accounting Standards Board, in September, 1979, gave birth to a grotesque monstrosity—its Statement numbered 33, "Financial Reporting and Changing Prices." As a consequence of this promulgation, the financial statements of about 1,300 of America's largest corporations began sporting some new appendixes in 1979, and will be adding some others starting with the 1980 crop.

These appendixes are designed to add credibility to the financial reporting process during periods of "changing prices" (which is, of course, a euphemism for inflation). This added credibility will be induced by telling shareholders, for example (see the illustration below, provided by the FASB), that their company's profit from continuing operations was $9,000 during a particular year—unless it was a loss of $2,514. On the other hand, the shareholders might prefer to opt for the other bottom line, i.e., a loss of $8,908.

While the FASB must bear the blame for this act of creation, the monster might have been aborted had it not been for persistent prodding from SEC Chairman Harold M. Williams. In speech after speech around the country, like Chicken Little he exclaimed that the sky was falling on corporate America, and the FASB must do something about inflation accounting—and so it did in the form of Statement 33.

When and if this FASB edict becomes fully operational, American corporations with (1) total assets in excess of $1 billion or (2) inventories, property plant, and equipment costing in excess of $125 million will be required to provide certain information supplementary to their financial statements, to wit: restatements of the cost of goods sold and depreciation and amortization expense on the basis of (1) "Historical cost/ Constant dollar" conversion (applying a general purchasing power index) and (2) "Current cost" basis.

There would also be footnotes to these appendixes to disclose, for example, the gain (or loss) from having net monetary liabilities (or holding net monetary assets) during periods of declining purchasing power. Also, the gains or losses from holding the inventories, property plant, and equipment.

The consequences of the mathematical manipulations decreed by the FASB may take the following format:

Hodge Podge Concoctions, Inc.

STATEMENT OF INCOME FROM CONTINUING OPERATIONS
ADJUSTED FOR CHANGING PRICES

For the Year Ended December 31, 1980

	As Reported in the Primary Statements	Adjusted for General Inflation	Adjusted for Changes in Specific Prices (Current Costs)
Net sales and other operating revenues	$253,000	$253,000	$253,000
Cost of goods sold	197,000	204,384 *(A)*	205,408 *(B)*
Depreciation and amortization expense	10,000	14,130 *(C)*	19,500 *(D)*
Other operating expense	20,835	20,835	20,835
Interest expense	7,165	7,165	7,165
Provision for income taxes	9,000	9,000	9,000
	$244,000	$255,514	$261,908
Income (loss) from continuing operations	$ 9,000	$ (2,514)	$ (8,908)

Let us zero in on the four transmutative computations.

Cost of Goods Sold (*A* and *B* References)

A. *To Restate to "Constant Dollar" Amount*

B. *To Restate to "Current Cost"*

The "average current cost" per unit sold was figured at $65.50; this figure multiplied by the 3,136 units sold produces the $205,408 figure inserted into the hypothetical income statements.

	Historical Cost	Constant Dollars
Inventory 1/1/80	$ 56,000	$ 58,907[a]
Purchases during 1980	204,000	204,000
Subtotal	$260,000	$262,907
Inventory 12/31/78	63,000	58,523[b]
Cost of Goods Sold	$197,000	$204,384

[a] Conversion effected by multiplying the historical cost of $56,000 by 105.2 percent (i.e., the average 1980 price index in relation to that of the fourth quarter of 1979, when the inventory was acquired).

[b] Obtained by multiplying the $63,000 closing inventory by 92.9 percent, i.e., the ratio of average 1980 price levels to those prevailing during the fourth quarter of 1980, when these inventories were deemed acquired.

Depreciation (C and D References)

C. To Restate to "Constant Dollars"

This will delight the heart of every "number-cruncher." The book-keeper digs into the corporate entrails to determine the year-by-year build up of the plant and equipment pools. And then, year-by-year he applies the price index conversion of that year's prices to the 1980 price levels. I will not burden this narrative with the clinical details, but the bookkeeper concluded that at 1980 price levels the $100,000 historical cost becomes $141,300. As a consequence, at 10 percent per annum the depreciation is recomputed to be $14,130—rather than $10,000.

D. To Restate to "Current Cost"

Management has measured the "current cost" of the plant and equip-ment as of December 31, 1979, and 1980, to be $170,000 and $220,000, respectively. Take the sum and divide by two and you have an arithmetic average of $195,000—take 10 percent of that average and, whiz bang, you have the $19,500 being plugged into the new model.

PuPU and Baloney

All of these reckonings are designed to add credibility and confidence to the accountant's artistry—to give the readers of the statements more meaningful information. By this act FASB has enshrined two highly ques-tionable and even frequently rejected procedures: On the one hand it decrees PuPU (purchasing-power-unit accounting) effective peremptorily, and on the other hand, what can be seen as "Replacement Cost" accounting for implementation presently.

The argument against PuPU accounting (that inspired acronym was coined by Dr. John C. "Sandy" Burton when he was the SEC's Chief Accountant) is rooted in the lack of relevance of the general consumer price level for the data being subjected to the transmutative process. There is little question that the method can be applied with expedition— put the historical cost data and the price indices into a computer and out will come the new numbers, all balanced precisely to the penny.

But what has the computer wrought? After all, the sins of historical cost accounting are perpetuated in this system; what is added is the artificial multiplier, the consumer price index. This PuPU process simply exacerbates any existing defects in the accounting process by their multiplication. Moreover, the user of the financial statements is being led to believe that he is being presented with an improved model. This is deception squared.

What about the current-cost alternative? This might be analogized with the replacement-cost concepts with which the accounting profession has been conjuring since the Securities and Exchange Commission promulgated Accounting Series Release No. 190 in March, 1976.

The companies affected by that SEC edict developed a remarkable art style—a lengthy exposition running to page after page of verbiage tightly packed into the annual forms 10-K (sometimes also in shareholder reports), generously sprinkled with caveats that should warn the statement users to treat these data the way they would an exotic perfume— smell but do not swallow. Typically, in its 1979 report submitted to the SEC, U.S. Steel states:

> Investors and analysts are cautioned against simplistic use of the data. The disclosure requirements were not designed to provide a basis for adjusting net income and balance sheet values. In addition, due to widely varying subjective judgments and assumptions, as well as different factual circumstances involved, the data are not comparable among companies and are inherently subject to errors of estimation.

Big Steel was not alone in expressing disapprobation of the SEC's disclosure requirement. An Arthur Andersen and Co. survey concluded that "a great majority of the affected registrants developed footnotes that included a number of caveats in an effort to mitigate the possibility that financial statement users would interpret the data in a way that might be misleading."

Specious Cash Flow Data

Yet, despite the entirely justified opprobrium for both the PuPU and replacement-cost alternatives, the FASB determined to push on with this nonsense. In doing so it relied for its authority on a foundation of quicksand. The FASB statement (paragraph 2) reads:

> This Statement is based on the objectives set out in FASB Concepts Statement No. 1, Objectives of Financial Reporting by Business Enterprises. That Statement concludes that financial reporting should provide information to help investors, creditors, and others assess the *amounts, timing,* and *uncertainty* of prospective *net cash inflows* to the enterprise (paragraph 37). It also calls for the provision of information about the economic resources of an enterprise in a manner that provides direct and indirect evidence of cash flow potential (paragraphs 40 and 41) and it concludes that management is accountable to the owners for "protecting them to the extent possible from unfavorable economic impacts of factors in the economy such as inflation or deflation" (paragraph 50) [emphasis mine].

The FASB thus proceeds to justify these new-fangled measurements—its new math—on the repeated assertion that it would give users of the financial statements better insights into an enterprise's cash flows. This obsession is evidenced in many other contexts in the FASB promulgation. For example, an entire section of the "Basis for Conclusions" appendix to the statement is devoted to "The Assessment of Future Cash Flows" (paragraphs 116–123). The term "cash flow" is used in those eight paragraphs no fewer than fifteen times—as though FASB Statement 33 really provided the users of the financial statements of the affected companies with a *meaningful,* as contrasted with a *specious,* basis for any assessment of the net cash inflows.

Possibly of greater import is the implication that the FASB, in its frantic endeavor to promulgate a statement, has turned its back on some traditional, sound wisdom of accountancy. In 1963 the Accounting Principles Board asserted, as a part of its Opinion No. 3, Statement of Sources and Application of Funds:

> 6. In recent years a new concept (or more correctly an old concept with a new name) has become increasingly important in the analysis of the flow of funds. The term "cash flow" has been used to refer to a variety of concepts, but its most common meaning in financial literature, and to a lesser extent in accounting literature, is the same as "funds derived from

operations" in a statement of source and application of funds. It is often
defined as "net income plus depreciation" or "net income before deducting depreciation, depletion, amortization, etc." Synonyms which are sometimes used include "cash earnings," "cash income," and "cash throw-
off."

7. Many of the comments made in connection with "cash flow" analysis leave
the reader with the erroneous impression that "cash flow" or "cash earnings" is superior to net income as a measure of a company's real earning
power. . . .

The Accounting Principles Board Opinion concluded as follows:

15. The amount of funds derived from operations cannot be considered as
a substitute for or an improvement upon properly determined net income
as a measure of results of operations and the consequent effect on financial position. Misleading implications can result from isolated statistics
in annual reports of "cash flow" which are not placed in proper perspective to net income figures *and to a complete analysis of source and application
of funds.* "Cash flow" and related terms should not be used in annual
reports in such a way that the significance of net income is impaired,
and "cash earnings" or other terms with a similar connotation should
be avoided. The Board regards computations of "cash flow per share"
as misleading since they ignore the impact of cash expenditures for re-
newal and replacement of facilities and tend to downgrade the significant
economic statistic of "earnings per share" [emphasis mine].

This APB Opinion 3 was superseded in 1971 by Opinion 19 (Reporting Changes in Financial Position). This later promulgation made mandatory the presentation of a statement of sources and applications of funds;
the concepts enunciated in Opinion 3, especially the enjoinder against
the irresponsible use of the phrase "cash flow," remained unchanged.

The FASB has done the accounting profession a grave injustice by
loosely bandying about the term "cash flow." The Board undoubtedly
is aware that depreciation, *per se,* is *not* a source (nor deployment) of
cash. Every capital budgeting treatise makes clear that depreciation impacts on cash flow only indirectly—through the amount and timing of
the liability for income taxes.

Accordingly FASB Statement No. 33 meddles with the depreciation
amount by pretending that this surgery is required to provide improved
insights into the cash flow projections. This is spreading a canard.

I added emphasis to the following words and phrases in the FASB
and APB announcements: "amounts," "timing," "uncertainty," "net
cash inflows," and "a complete analysis of source and application of

funds." I have done so to point up the speciousness in the FASB's Statement 33 whereby the Board pretends (there is no other term) that by its machinations it has given the users of the financial statements a better insight into when, if at all, the enterprise will be compelled to incur an actual cash outflow for the replacement of plant and the like.

But most important, the FASB has done actual violence to its predecessor's repeated demand for a *complete analysis* of the net inflow of funds. To the extent the present Board does wish to use hypothetical data, it should factor in the hypothetical projected revenues contemplated in an economy characterized by inflationary pressures—in addition to the hypothesizing of the future possible cost counted in currently as the depreciation cost. In short, if the Board is determined to provide readers of financial statements a meaningful insight into the "cash flow" implications of a potential investment (replacement or otherwise), let the Board direct the disclosure of the capital budgeting models used by the particular business enterprises.

Meaningful Cash Flow Data

The following is intended to illustrate what factors would be involved in such a configuration.

Let us assume that a widget manufacturer is considering the purchase of an automated extruder costing $30,000. This machine is expected to last ten years, and will generate $16,000 in revenues annually (requiring the outlay each year of $6,000 in cash costs). The corporation will purchase this equipment only if it could anticipate its target rate of return, namely, 30 percent on a pre-tax basis.

From compound interest tables we determine that the present value of $1.00 per period for ten periods at a 30 percent discount rate would be $3.0915. In consequence, $10,000 for ten periods would have a present discounted value of $30,915. Since this commuted value is greater than the price tag on the machine, the investment would be made.

Having made the investment, the question might arise as to the after-tax rate of return. This requires the calculation of the tax. Assuming for the moment that the machine is to be depreciated over the decade on the straight-line basis to a zero scrap value, we can come up with a net-after-tax rate of return of somewhere between 17 and 18 percent.

But this is as unrealistic as it is simplistic. The corporation would undoubtedly use an accelerated method for tax depreciation; in addition the company would claim the 10 percent investment credit. The corporation would be enjoying an "internal net-after-tax rate of return" of about 22 percent on this investment. This felicitous result prevails because of the very substantial net-after-tax cash proceeds in the early years. True, this is offset by correspondingly reduced amounts for later years—but since a dollar expected in an early year is worth more, at present, than a dollar due in a later year, the effective rate of return is increased.

Even this capital-budgeting model, felicitous though it might be, is not nearly the ultimate. So far, we have assumed that the entire $30,000 was provided from the corporation's own resources (rather than through some form of external financing). Let us now assume that the corporation borrows 80 percent of the cost, $24,000, and agrees to repay that sum at the rate of $2,400 annually with interest at 12 percent per annum on the unpaid balance. As a consequence, in year one the corporation would repay $2,400 plus $2,880 (12 percent of $24,000) in interest—a total of $5,280. However, the $2,880 of interest would produce a 48 percent* tax saving of $1,382, so that the actual net cash outflow in this first year, by reason of the loan repayment, would be $3,898. In the second year the gross outflows on the financing would be $2,400 in principal and $2,592 (12 percent of the reduced balance of $21,600) in interest. Since the interest effects a reduction in tax of $1,244, the "net-net" debt service cost is $3,748. And so it goes.

The following table sets forth the data (rounded) for the ten-year cash-flow projections for this capital investment. I have yet to find a compound interest table to provide the answers as to the internal rate of return on this deal—one which is certainly not atypical. But the yield is in excess of 80 percent per annum. In fact, the effective internal rate of return might well turn out to be in excess of 100 percent. This would be the case where the corporation is able to utilize the 10 percent ($3,000) investment tax credit at "point zero." This offsets taxes owing at the outset—instead of utilizing that sum to swell the cash inflow as of the close of the first year. Be that as it may, whether it be 80 percent or more than 100 percent, the yield should be beyond most dreams.

The FASB knows full well that cash-flow analysis demands that data be disclosed regarding the timing of the cash outflows (hence the timing of any replacements), the mode of financing, tax consequences, as well as the projections regarding the anticipated revenues and rates of return. Only with this information can users of financial statements obtain an insight into the net cash inflows resulting from a capital budgeting deci-

---

* After the development of the tabulation the maximum corporate tax rate was reduced to 46 percent; inasmuch as this change would have a minimal effect on these data, the tabulation was not revised.

Year	Investment and Borrowing Inflows (Outflows)	Taxable Income	Income Tax	Net-After-Tax Inflows (Outflows)
	(Col. 1)	(Col. 2)	(Col. 3)	(Col. 4)
0	$(30,000)			$ (6,000)
	24,000			
			$ (3,000) Inv. Cr.	
1	(5,300)	$ 1,100	500	7,200
2	(5,000)	2,600	1,300	3,700
3	(4,700)	3,900	1,900	3,400
4	(4,400)	4,900	2,400	3,200
5	(4,100)	5,800	2,700	3,200
6	(3,800)	6,600	3,200	3,000
7	(3,500)	6,900	3,300	3,200
8	(3,300)	7,100	3,400	3,300
9	(3,000)	7,500	3,600	3,400
10	(2,700)	7,800	3,800	3,500
Totals	$(45,800)	$54,200	$23,100	$31,100

Source of Data:

Col. 1: Reflects the investment in the equipment ($30,000) and the related borrowing ($24,000). Then, for years 1 through 10, reflects the payment on account of principal in each year ($2,400) and the interest in reducing amounts for $2,880 to $288.

Col. 2: Reflects the pre-tax proceeds in each year ($10,000) minus the sum of: (1) the interest included in the Column 1 data and (2) the depreciation determined on the basis of the double declining-balance method.

Col. 3: Reflects the tax at 48 percent on the amounts in Column 2 (and the $3,000 investment tax credit).

Col. 4: Reflects net investment after deducting the initial borrowing and then, for years 1 through 10, reflects the pre-tax proceeds of $10,000. Minus the sum of (1) the outflows incidental to the borrowing (Column 1) and (2) the tax (Column 3).

N.B.: All data rounded to nearest $100.

sion, discounted at an appropriate rate of return to the target date for the presumptive investment.

Potential for Tax Rip-Offs

If, as the U.S. Steel form 10-K and the Arthur Andersen study point out, the users of the financial statements are forewarned that ingesting these supplemental data could be injurious to their health, why am I so intensely anxious that the FASB abominations be aborted? I am not especially concerned about the deleterious effect it might have on the accounting process per se. My concern stems from recognition that the pressures for this gimmickry come from those who would use the supplemental statements to generate additional write-offs for business enterprises—thereby producing an even deeper erosion in our tax structure governing corporate and other enterprises.

As my capital budgeting models demonstrate, adjustments of depreciation for replacement cost would actually distort economic reality. Oddly, should we reappraise the net assets on this basis, we would find that business benefits enormously from inflation—in absolute dollars, of course, but even more important, relative to those to whom this sector had incurred dollar obligations expressed in dollar terms.

The FASB, wittingly or otherwise, is perpetrating a deception on the users of financial statements in yet another way. It is axiomatic that there are two ways of deceiving the statement users, namely, to make like situations appear different and to make unlike situations appear similar.

As we recognized from the Hodge Podge configurations, a company which acquired plant and equipment over the preceding seven years (it might well have been scores of years) would be made to appear as though it had acquired the properties in 1980. As a consequence Hodge Podge and its competitor (which *did* acquire its properties in 1980) would be made to look like Siamese twins.

There is a critical distinction between a landlord who bought property for $500,000 now worth a million dollars who sets rents on the basis of that million, and the landlord who actually paid a million and is renting on that basis (the two landlords are deriving identical rents). The first landlord in this simplistic illustration is far more favorably situated than his counterpart. The distinction becomes even more evident if we assume that each landlord has managed to "mortgage-out," i.e., obtained 100 percent financing. The cash flows for the two would be significantly different.

But if we were to go along with the FASB's alternative responses, the landlords would appear identical.

Pressures from the SEC

In all this the Financial Accounting Standards Board has been cast as the villain. However, in my view, the Board has become something of a scapegoat for the Securities and Exchange Commission and especially its incumbent Chairman, Harold M. Williams.

This might be evidenced, first, by the prominence accorded this accounting issue in the Securities and Exchange Commission's July, 1979, Report to the Congress on "The Accounting Profession and the Commission's Oversight Role." Thus, at pages 44–46:

. . . Accounting for the effects of inflation and changing prices is one of the most important issues facing the FASB, the profession, the business community, and the general public. Conflicting reports of record profits on the one hand, inadequate earnings to maintain and expand capacity on the other, serve only to confuse the issue. Further, they raise questions about the integrity of financial reporting. The basic question in a period of inflation and changing prices is how best to report the effects of all economic events, and not only the effects of transactions with outside parties. . . .

Earlier in the Report the Chairman of the SEC wrote to Vice President Mondale (as President of the Senate), as well as to Speaker O'Neill of the House, informing them that:

The FASB's conceptual framework project is quite clearly the most basic and most difficult of the items on the FASB's agenda. Similarly, the Board's exposure draft concerning accounting in an environment of changing prices reflects the pressing need for the profession to address a problem which threatens to undermine the usefulness of historical cost-based accounting. The Commission will continue to monitor the progress of these two projects and regards them as important indicators of the FASB's leadership.

From this Report as well as other utterances emanating from members of the Commission, it is clear that they are going into battle under the banner of "economic reality." Understandably, they do not endeavor to define that phrase. Economic reality and truth, fairness, justice, love, beauty, etc., are transcendents which defy precise definition and can only be discerned from the context used.

Chairman Williams and "Economic Reality"

We should turn to some instances where, for example, Chairman Williams did seek to demonstrate what he had in mind. When addressing a FASB conference on May 31, 1979, SEC Chairman Williams provided what might be an exemplification of his understanding of the elusive phrase:

In 1978, U.S. non-financial corporations reported record earnings of $167.1 billion before taxes and $98.6 billion after. Studies have shown, however, that if depreciation were recomputed based on the current-cost, double declining balance method, in order to charge against revenues a sum which more accurately reflected both the manner in which capital equipment was consumed and the cost, in inflated current dollars of replacing it; and if inventory consumption charges were converted from historical to current costs, the 1978 after-tax profits of non-financial companies would shrink to some $56.5 billion—only about sixty percent of the figure reported. The economic reality of an inflationary environment is that much of American business is not generating and retaining sufficient funds to replace existing capacity and to maintain the present level of operations—let alone expand and invest in improved productivity.

*   *   *

Conflicting reports of record profits on the one hand and inadequate earnings to maintain and expand capacity on the other serve only to confuse the public and political leaders. Further, they raise questions about the integrity of financial reporting. . . . Unfortunately, however, daily press reports of record earnings fail to communicate the effects of changing prices in a meaningful way, and thus the confusion and conflicting claims are likely to continue—with corporations complaining that profits are too low, while the public, labor unions, and some parts of the government respond that profits are excessive. In such a conflict, business, serving up the weapons for its own destruction, is clearly and predictably the loser.

The accounting profession and the business community are running out of time in which to develop meaningful solutions to this problem. . . .

The Chairman was holding the FASB hostage to further his crusade in behalf of economic reality as he sees it.

This May, 1979, speech manifested a remarkable change by the SEC Chairman during the relatively brief period during which he had been developing his Cassandra message to the populace. If we look at the 1978 SEC Report to the Congress on the Accounting Profession, beginning at page 1002, we will note that Chairman Williams had gone through a correspondingly dismal calculus. However, in that earlier presentation he disclaimed responsibility for the methodology by which the corporate earnings for the year 1976 were made to appear illusory. He made clear that he disowned any responsibility but was merely conveying the message from Dr. George Terborgh, the economist for the Machinery and Allied Products Institute. Dr. Terborgh is the traditional spokesman for that constituency, i.e., the producers of and investors in machine tools and other capital-intensive equipment.

In that earlier presentation, in a section captioned "Financial Reporting and Economic Reality," the Chairman presented the Terborgh configurations as follows:

In my view, we are, as a nation, facing a crisis in business's ability to earn the profits necessary to generate capital needed for accomplishing the national goals I have outlined. . . . Without necessarily [adopting] either his conclusions or his methodology in their entirety, I find very thought-provoking the approach to this problem which appears in economist George Terborgh's study prepared under the auspices of the Machinery and Allied Products Institute. . . . Take as an example the year 1976. That year saw the highest corporate earnings in history—reported after-tax profits of $77 billion. Terborgh performed two adjustments in order to convert those earnings to a figure which, he believes, more closely represents the real purchasing power generated from business operations. First, he recomputed earnings based on current-cost, double-declining balance depreciation. The objective of this step was to charge against earnings a figure which, in Terborgh's view, more accurately reflects both the manner in which capital equipment is consumed and the cost, in inflated, current dollars, of replacing it. Second, Terborgh endeavored to convert inventory consumption charges, as reflected in the cost of goods sold, from historical to current costs. Net of these adjustments, 1976 after-tax profits shrank to $43 billion, only a little more than half the $77 billion figure reported.

*   *   *

The effect of this effort to adjust corporate earnings for inflation is even more startling from the perspective of federal tax policy. Terborgh points out that, in 1965, the effective tax rate was about 42 percent, whether computed on the basis of reported profits or on profits as he adjusts them to reflect inflation. In 1974 and 1976, for example, the effective rate on reported earnings—that is, earnings computed on the basis of traditional accounting assumptions—was still essentially the same 42 percent. However, if actual tax liability is compared to pre-tax profits adjusted, as described above, for inflation-based underdepreciation and inventory gains, a much different picture emerges: In 1976, the effective tax was 56 percent, while in 1974 it was a shocking 80 percent. Thus, Terborgh's approach suggests that inflation and the failure of the tax system to recognize its distortion of corporate profits have resulted, in effect, in tax increases which have gyrated as high as nearly 100 percent over the apparent effective rate during the last decade. These increases have, as I have observed in other speeches, been accomplished without Congressional action of any sort and, consequently, with no opportunity for debate over the effects on capital formation—a debate which would certainly occur if a legislative doubling of the corporate tax rate were proposed. Indeed, these figures make a case for the proposition that discussion of adjustments in the legal rate of taxation is almost meaningless if it is not premised on a recognition of the impact of inflation.

Apparently Chairman Williams has now accepted Dr. Terborgh as his guru, or, conceivably, Mr. Williams has repeated the same message so often that he now assumes that the earning-evisceration process is of his own creation. Be that as it may, the Chairman now espouses the Terborgh mathematical mystique.

Responding to "Chicken Little"

Briefly, let me respond to the Chairman's cry that the sky is falling on corporate America—that it is confronting a "capital formation crisis." I don't know where the Chairman is getting his information but certainly not from data generated by his Commission or the Federal Reserve Board or the Department of Commerce.

Two Bankers Trust monographs, *Credit and Money Markets—1979 and 1980,* revealed the following significant relationships (in a table, Sources and Uses of Funds—Business Corporations):

	Funds Provided from Operations (after deducting dividends as paid)	Investment in Plant and Equipment (Amounts in Billions)	Funds Provided by Net New Bond Issues	Funds Provided by Net New Equity Issues
1973	$ 102.4	$ 102.2	$ 9.2	$ 6.9
1974	116.1	113.0	19.7	4.2
1975	119.2	106.9	27.2	10.7
1976	139.9	121.2	22.8	10.0
1977	155.1	143.3	21.0	2.7
1978	174.0	170.0	18.9	2.6
1979 (estimates)	200.2	198.0	20.8	3.0
1980 (projections)	195.0	212.0	28.0	5.4
Totals	$1201.9	$1166.6	$167.6	$45.5

Is this the kind of configuration which should compel the SEC Chairman to importune for new subsidies for business corporations, while he asserts that they are being eaten away by inflation? If any sector is being consumed, it is the sector buying the bonds generated by these entities. It is that sector which is providing "real" dollars, permitting corporate America to acquire the capital resources which, in turn, generate increasing numbers of dollars because of inflation. Corporate America then uses a portion of this augmented hoard of cheap dollars to pay back the bondholders.

Which sectors are generating the new resources (debt and equity) for corporate America? Again the Bankers Trust compilations are informative. Tables captioned Corporate Bonds and Corporate Stocks give data regarding funds raised through new issues by corporations engaged in manufacturing and extractive, transportation, electric, gas and water, communications, finance and real estate, commercial, and other. (These tables reflect all of the foregoing categories, after subtracting the funds raised by "financial intermediaries," i.e., real estate, investment trusts, and commercial banks.)

From those tables the following relationships are discernible (all data in billions):

	BONDS		STOCKS	
	Net New Issues	Funds Provided by Insurance Companies and Pension Funds	Net New Issues	Funds Provided by Insurance Companies and Pension Funds
1973	$ 12.7	$ 11.3	$ 9.1	$ 15.3
1974	25.1	15.8	4.3	6.9
1975	31.9	19.6	10.4	9.0
1976	29.9	23.3	11.1	13.5
1977	30.0	31.8	3.6	12.0
1978	28.2	29.4	4.1	12.1
1979 (estimated)	28.7	27.8	4.4	17.5
1980 (projected)	35.6	34.0	7.1	20.3
Totals	$222.1	$193.0	$54.1	$106.6

No, you are *not* seeing things. The amounts invested over the years by insurance companies and pension funds exceeded by increasing margins the aggregate amounts of new securities (bonds and stocks) issued by corporate America. What has happened is that *individuals*, mass America, the very sinews of our American capitalistic democracy, have been compelled to disinvest in corporate securities. If there is to be a call for a great national debate regarding the sector or sectors entitled to some surcease in their tax burden because of the cruel tax imposed by inflation, I hope the Chairman of the SEC and others committed to the total society will reflect on these data and the many other, even more intimate, data to which they are privy—and not pursue blind prejudice derived from some special interest group.

Going back to the Williams (really Terborgh) calculus, I reject it as a mishmash essentially because it involves nothing but playing with arbitrary numbers applied to other hypothetical assumptions (unless it's vice versa). The Chairman ignores entirely the fact that over the years putative investment in fixed assets was recouped by corporate

America through tax credits and deductions. But of probably greater import, the principal cost of those capital resources was undoubtedly funded by bonds, preferred stock, or other fixed-dollar obligations. Hence, the economically real cost was the actual number of dollars paid out to those who provided the resources—the mere "rentiers."

I speak of this issue admittedly in strident and urgent terms. As Chairman Williams made clear in the speech included as a part of the SEC's 1978 report, an important objective of his proselytizing is to get the Congress to grant some special tax relief to the business corporations for which he and Dr. Terborgh are importuning.

Corporations and the Grim Reaper

A more objective, and to my mind more appropriate, picture was presented to the Congress by Congressman Charles Vanik (*Congressional Record*, June 22, 1979). The Congressman was then presenting his seventh annual report (covering the year 1977) "on the effective Federal tax rate of America's 'Fortune 100' top industrial, banking, transportation, utility and retailing companies."

The report documented "the significant decline in the average effective Federal corporate income tax rate during the 1970's . . . [making] hash of the argument—for large corporations at least—that Federal taxes take too much venture capital and that additional general corporate tax relief is needed."

Among the report's findings:

1. In 1977, 17 of the profitable corporations with pre-tax worldwide earnings of $2.1 billion paid no Federal income taxes.
2. In 1977, 38 corporations with worldwide pre-tax income of $33.8 billion paid 10 percent or less in effective Federal income taxes.
3. The big oil companies paid an average Federal tax rate of 11 percent on worldwide income of $30.1 billion. "This ridiculously low tax rate will be aggravated by decontrol. . . ."
4. The Tax Act of 1976 has virtually removed airlines and railroads from the lists of taxpayers.
5. The nation's big banks paid an effective Federal tax rate of 7.1 percent on $2.5 billion in worldwide pre-tax income.
6. Utilities generally pay little or no Federal corporate income tax.

In late June, 1980, when Congressman Vanik submitted the 1980 report on his committee's analysis of the 1978 tax returns of America's giant corporations, he updated his lament, saying:

. . . The basic trend line of Federal corporate tax rates established in the last 8 years is steadily downward—this year is no exception to that rule. This pattern of tax payments destroys the conservative myth that there is a need for across-the-board corporate tax relief or that corporate tax cuts in the past have resulted in increased tax receipts. Without the impetus of new tax laws, the corporate share of Federal income tax contributions will soon fall to a nominal 5 or 6 percent. There appears to be very little room for corporate capital formation by cutting corporate taxes unless the country moves to refundable tax credits—or a Treasury-taxpayer supported Government dole for business and industry.

*   *   *

Observers already maintain that the corporate tax reductions of 1978 have increased investment, stimulated the economy, created jobs and done everything except cure the common cold. I am skeptical of those who would sell this medicine as the magic potion to cure our sagging economy. A double or triple dose of a useless potion does not improve its curative powers. Across-the-board corporate tax cuts in the past have not produced the desired results and have only contributed to deficits and shifting the tax burden to individuals. . . .

Those for whom Chairman Williams, *et al.*, are importuning are already effectively compensating and even overcompensating for the ravages of inflation. Those whose incomes have not responded *pari passu* with inflation forces do not have the shelters provided by our tax system, sometimes to an obscene extent, to those who own or control capital equipment and natural resources. Mass America, instead, is subjected to increasing tax rates and compelled to pay prices exacted in a noncompetitive marketplace by sellers whose pricing refers to the presumptive cost of replacement (i.e., the amount a potential new competitor would pay).

GE Jumps the Gun

In the forefront of the campaign for the restatement of financial statements to reflect changing prices is the General Electric Company. As we saw, FASB Statement 33 called for the constant-dollar restatement for 1979, deferring to the 1980 restatement to reflect current costs. GE jumped the gun; its 1979 report showed both sets of restated data in the following table in a three-page section captioned "Financial Issues: Impact of Inflation" (data in millions):

For the year ended December 31, 1979	As Reported in the Traditional Statements	Adjusted for General Inflation	Adjusted for Changes in Specific Prices (Current Costs)
Sales of products and services to customers	$22,461	$22,461	$22,461
Cost of goods sold	15,991	16,093	16,074
Selling, general and administrative expenses	3,716	3,716	3,716
Depreciation, depletion and amortization	624	880	980
Interest and other financial charges	258	258	258
Other income	(519)	(519)	(519)
Earnings before income taxes and minority interest	2,391	2,033	1,952
Provision for income taxes	953	953	953
Minority interest in earnings of consolidated affiliates	29	16	13
Net earnings applicable to common stock	$ 1,409	$ 1,064	$ 986
Earnings per common share	$ 6.20	$ 4.68	$ 4.34

So it is that the GE shareholders can "put up their money and take their choice" as to whether their company earned $1,409 million, or $1,064 million, or $986 million. They might well be pardoned if, consistent with the prevailing mood of 1980, they might vote for "none of the above."

The General Electric Company can be seen in this work to be in a somewhat anomalous posture. Thus, in the "Jaws and Star Wars" chapter (Chapter 6) we saw the way in which the company's pooling accounting with Utah International served to suppress an enormous cost—with a corresponding earnings-inflation potential, a potential I conjectured might amount to $140 million annually. And here I am pointing up GE's aggressive pursuit of the downward restatement of earnings to reflect the ravages of inflation.

On reflection, apparently diametrically opposite pursuits might not be contradictory—at least they might both be rationalized on pragmatic grounds. Thus, when it comes to the traditional, historical accounting model, the one on which management's bonuses, perquisites, and very survival in office might depend, management would have a vested interest in the earnings-inflation proclivities of generally accepted accounting principles.

On the other hand, when they turn to the supplementary statements that might serve as the platform for importuning the Congress for "tax relief," or to rationalize price increases or resist demands for increased dividends or wages, it is handy to have the more dismal model provided by FASB 33.

Most assuredly, that FASB promulgation may not give us better accounting, but it will certainly provide doctoral candidates with grist for the mills from which Ph.D. theses are ground.

I will close this chapter by recommending to the accounting profession the precept of Isaac Newton, *"Hypotheses non fingo!"*—deal with facts, not hypotheticals.

9

The Odd Couple

The problem is not new. Over the past fifteen years various research studies have demonstrated the conflicts which may arise when an ostensibly independent audit firm is concurrently performing peripheral services—management advisory and/or tax consultative services. The hierarchy of the accounting establishment has asserted in various contexts that this condition is entirely appropriate and, in fact, "more is better." They have endeavored to pooh-pooh the concern demonstrated by the various studies, hoping that by their omnipotence and frequence of assertion the critics would be subdued, and the controversy would evaporate. Alas, the issue will not die. It raises its head in promulgations of the Congress and the Securities and Exchange Commission, and as a consequence, the leadership of the accounting profession is kept on its guard, and made to respond defensively.

The Stakes Are High

The magnitude of the problem is dramatically demonstrated by a tabulation included in a *New York Times* article of June 25, 1979, which sets forth the following revenues derived by various firms from management consultative services (the asterisks were provided by me to point up the accounting firms included in this "Who's Who in Management Consulting Services"). The top 15 and their 1978 global billings according to the article are:

148

	(Millions)
Arthur D. Little	$121
Booz Allen & Hamilton	115
* Arthur Andersen	114
McKinsey & Co.	100
* Coopers & Lybrand	83
* Touche Ross	72
* Peat, Marwick, Mitchell	70
Towers Perrin Forster & Crosby	60
* Arthur Young & Co.	53
* Ernst & Ernst	51
Reliance Consulting Group	42
Hay Associates	42
* Price Waterhouse	33
A. T. Kearney	30
Boston Consulting Group	27

When the Metcalf Committee released its November, 1977, Report it devoted an entire section to this festering issue. The Committee indicated that the subject had not been adequately considered by the AICPA Commission on Auditors' Responsibilities and asserted that:

> The subcommittee is deeply concerned about improving the professionalism and independence of auditors, and is also committed to fair competition as a basic principle of the Nation's economic system. The benefits derived from professional self-regulation carry with them a corresponding responsibility of self-restraint from engaging in activities which detract from professional ideals. The subcommittee firmly believes the important function of independently auditing publicly owned corporations should be, and is, financially rewarding and personally satisfying in its own right, without any need for engaging in activities which appear to detract from professional responsibilities.

When the Moss Committee introduced H.R. 13175, it alluded to this issue:

> (3) The Organization [National Organization of Securities and Exchange Commission Accountancy] shall also, in conducting individual reviews of independent public accounting firms registered under this Act, examine (A) nonaudit services provided by the independent public accounting firm being reviewed and any potential conflict arising from the provision of such services, (B) the professional training being received by such firm's staff, (C) the adequacy of review within such firm of audit work performed, and (D) any other matter which the Organization considers necessary or appropriate in conducting such review. . . .

Questions from the SEC

The Securities and Exchange Commission in its July, 1978, *Report to the Congress on the Accounting Profession and the Commission's Oversight Role* determined that a critical issue was "the appropriate range of services—other than the performance of the audit itself—which accounting firms should be permitted to offer to their audit clients." In this connection the SEC report posed several questions:

> Are there situations in which the magnitude of the potential fees from management advisory services are so large as to affect adversely an auditor's objectivity in conducting an audit?
>
> Are there some services which are so unrelated to the normal expertise and experience of auditors that it is inconsistent with the concept of being an auditing professional for auditors to perform those services?
>
> Are there, conversely, some services so closely linked to the accounting function that, for the auditor to perform those services for his client . . . the auditor will, in conducting the audit, be in a position of reviewing his own work?

Earlier, in 1977, the Commission issued for comment proposed amendments to its accounting field rules which would have required disclosure of all nonaudit services performed by an independent auditor for audit clients, as well as of the specific fees charged for each nonaudit service. The Commission sought this disclosure to "provide objective evidence of the types and amounts of services being provided by auditors," and to permit shareholders to compare fees paid by similar companies for similar services. At the same time, the Commission solicited comments and information on the scope of services accountants actually provide to their audit clients.

In June, 1978, the SEC, in Accounting Series Release 250, adopted a watered-down rule requiring disclosure in proxy statements of services provided by the registrant's principal independent accountant and disclosure of whether the board of directors or its audit or similar committee had approved each service and considered its possible effect on independence. In ASR 250 the SEC also indicated that it had not yet determined whether it should propose rules to prohibit public accountants from rendering certain types of services to their publicly held audit clients. In this connection the Commission noted that the SEC-Practice Section had asked the Public Oversight Board to consider the matter and stated that the Board should be given an opportunity to present its conclusions before the Commission acted.

The AICPA Takes Cognizance

Even the high priests of the accounting establishment, the Executive Committee of the SEC-Practice Section of the AICPA Division of Firms, took cognizance of the controversy. In its Organizational Document it included as Appendix A a discourse on this controversy and suggested a number of don'ts.

In my view the committee was grievously myopic when it asserted that "In no case have the studies identified instances where the auditor's independence was in fact impaired by the performance of management advisory services." Nonetheless, the fact that a blue-ribbon group from the establishment's hierarchy has condescended to recognize the possibility of a conflict is cause for rejoicing. This recognition contrasts sharply with the aggressive prose contained in an earlier AICPA release, the 1974 Report of its Ad Hoc Committee on Scope and Structure:

> . . . Such a remedy, purchased at such a heavy cost, would be warranted only if adequate evidence could be cited that the performance of consulting services was in fact imperiling the profession's reputation for independence. As noted earlier, the committee has not found any significant objective evidence which would suggest that such an impairment of independence has occurred.
>
> The suggestion has also been advanced that one or more of the "peripheral" management advisory services, i.e., those which may appear to be only marginally related to the traditional accounting function, ought to be proscribed.
>
> This may seem at first to be an inviting course of action.
>
> The challenged services are presently performed by relatively few firms, and none of them constitutes a major part of the practice of any firm. A prohibition against one or more of these services would not inflict much of a hardship on the profession, but it would deprive the business community of convenient access to useful assistance. . . . If any proscription were to be adopted, it ought to be the result of a clear determination, based on solid evidence, that the prohibited service was creating serious questions about the profession's independence in performing its attest function.

The POB Hearings and Response

This leads us to the mid-August, 1978, hearings conducted by the SEC-Practice Section's Public Oversight Board on the scope of services by CPA firms. These proceedings included presentations by representatives from:

Big Eight accounting firms	7
Other accounting firms	6
The American Institute of CPA's	
Accounting academics	2
Non-accounting groups:	
Accounting placement agencies	
and MAS Consultants	4

The presentation by the accounting firms and their organizations had no surprises. The non-accounting firms and their organizations correspondingly advocated the particular interests of their constituents.

After deliberating for more than a half year, the Public Oversight Board (POB) put its thoughts together in its report, *Scope of Services by CPA Firms.* The rhetoric and conclusions varied little, if any, from what one might find in corresponding promulgations of the accounting establishment, e.g., the AICPA's Commission on Auditors' Responsibilities.

The Board did hedge its bets; it did suggest some serious misgivings:

> [Its] conclusions should not be interpreted to mean that the Board views the matter of scope of services with complacency or believes that possible dangers can be avoided solely with general exhortations to the members to preserve independence. The mere fact that so many persons have expressed concern with the subject, both in and out of the government, over an extended period is reason to conclude that it cannot be dismissed as a chimera. The Board believes that there is possibility of damage to the profession and the users of the profession's services in an uncontrolled expansion of MAS to audit clients. Investors and others need a public accounting profession that performs its primary function of auditing financial statements with both the fact and the appearance of competence and independence. Developments which detract from this will surely damage the professional status of CPA firms and lead to suspicions and doubts that will be detrimental to the continued reliance of the public upon the profession without further and more drastic governmental intrusion. Effective measures must be taken to guard against such a development. . . .

The POB believes that such effective measures are at hand, for example: (1) The new proxy disclosures mandated by the SEC in Accounting Series Release 250. (2) The inclusion in the peer review program of a review of the accounting firm's practices in the management advisory service (MAS) area. (3) The expanded role and responsibility of audit committees of boards of directors.

In the Conclusions and Recommendations chapter of the *Scope of Services* report, the Public Oversight Board set forth the following:

The Board generally concludes that mandatory limitations on scope of services should be predicated only on the determination that certain services, or the role of the firm performing certain services, will impair a member's independence in rendering an opinion on the fairness of a client's financial statements or present a strong likelihood of doing so.

Independence is generally defined as the ability to operate with integrity and objectivity. Integrity is an element of character, and objectivity relates to the ability of an auditor to maintain impartiality of attitude and avoid conflicts of interest. All conflicts of interest are not avoidable and some conflicts of interests produce countervailing benefits. Such conflicts are accepted, consistent with the concept of independence, because of practical necessity and the realization of important benefits, coupled with the fact that auditor integrity and various legal incentives provide adequate public protection. This helps explain public acceptance of the fact that auditors can be "independent" even though the client selects them and pays their fee. It also helps explain why there has been public acceptance of accounting firms furnishing a variety of tax advisory services to audit clients. Recognizing, therefore, that independence in an absolute sense cannot be achieved, when evaluating whether certain services should be prohibited, it is necessary to consider the potential benefits derived from the service and balance them against the possible or apparent impairment to the auditor's objectivity.

The POB would put its full faith and confidence in the integrity, self-discipline, and self-restraint of the accounting firm. It is time the Board also looked to the rules of professional ethics and recent SEC releases to provide some further inducement to the firm to pursue the path of righteousness. The report proceeded to its ultimate conclusion: "In general . . . the Board is reluctant to support prohibitions against useful services which are based primarily on appearance without an adequate basis in fact."

The *Scope of Services* report is unquestionably a fine lawyer's brief in behalf of a client. This is, of course, to be expected when one realizes that among the quintet comprising the POB there were at the time four members of the bar who had distinguished themselves over the years as effective advocates for clients. Whether this standard of advocacy is appropriate for a body which came into existence in response to pressures from the Congress and which by its very designation should consider the public as its client is open to serious question.

It should, however, be emphasized that the POB report does not differ from the way in which its distinguished chairman, John McCloy, explained his role in his January, 1978, testimony before the Moss Committee:

Mr. Nelligan [of the Committee's staff]. . . . Did you gentlemen accept positions on the Public Oversight Board because you think reforms in the accounting profession and the public disclosure of its activities are needed?

Mr. McCloy. They came to me and asked me whether I thought I would be prepared to perform this service. I took it as a lawyer who has a client who comes in and says, "I have a need and we would like your services and we would like to use your services in this connection because we believe it is an important aspect and that there is a lack of confidence in the accuracy, in general perhaps, of some of the accounting work that has been done in the last few years and we want to do what we can to not only improve the image but improve the reality and would you be prepared to serve?"

After talking at some length with them and after giving it a good deal of thought, I said that I would "try it on." I said, "If you think that I have the abilities to deal with this, then I will try it."

The AICPA SEC-Practice Section did, in fact, become a valued client of Mr. McCloy's law firm. In addition to the $50,000 stipend for his chairmanship of the POB, his law firm, Milbank, Tweed, Hadley & Mc-Cloy, received $181,500 in fees during the Board's initial year. The late Mr. Garrett, the vice chairman, received a fee of $40,000 and his law firm, Gardner, Carton & Douglas, received $93,000 for services.

The SEC's less than enthusiastic response to the POB's Scope of Services report was evidenced by its Accounting Series Release No. 264. This release was designed as a "sensitivity-training" device, to alert the accounting profession and corporate boards of directors to the potentially inimical consequences that might result from the independent auditor's concurrent rendering of management advisory services.

In this connection the Commission set down a set of standards to help accountants steer an appropriate course, including:

1. Accountants should consider the aggregate amount of revenues generated from MAS and the relationship of those revenues to total firm revenues. Similarly, in considering a particular MAS engagement for a publicly held audit client, the accountant should examine the relationship between the audit fee and the proposed MAS fee.

2. In determining whether to offer nonaudit services to audit clients, accountants must exercise extreme care to assure they serve only in an advisory capacity. They cannot make management decisions and they must avoid situations that will give that appearance.

3. A related problem MAS engagements may raise is that, as the auditor—through an MAS practice—becomes enmeshed, for example, in structuring the client's internal accounting controls or designing its accounting system,

the client loses the benefits that normally result from the outside auditor's dispassionate review of these systems.

4. The broader base of knowledge about, and greater understanding of, the business which often results from the performance of nonaudit services may improve the efficiency and thoroughness of the audit. This broader perspective on the audit is healthy and desirable. In this connection, auditors must recognize that the acceptance of an MAS engagement may well carry with it the corresponding obligation to bring the knowledge gained in the course of the MAS work to bear on the audit. An auditor who failed to act upon information known to his MAS colleagues would, in the judgment of the Commission staff, run a substantial risk.

The SEC then provided the following by way of counsel to the corporate boards:

The Commission . . . believes that audit committees, board of directors, and managements have a responsibility to act in the best interest of their shareholders, and must therefore be concerned about the credibility of their financial reporting. To the extent that the independence, in fact or in appearance, of the entity's auditor may be called into question, the credibility of the financial statements will be similarly questioned. Accordingly, the impact on auditor independence of potential MAS engagements should be of direct concern to the issuer and especially its independent audit committee. . . .

The Public Oversight Board did not accept the SEC's counsel "lying down"; in an October, 1979, letter to the SEC the Board set down the aspects of the Release with which it disagreed (from the POB 1980 Report):

. . . (1) fails to recognize adequately the efforts of the AICPA over the years in addressing problems raised by MAS; (2) fails to give sufficient guidance as to whether adherence to the MAS standards for membership in the Section will be a sufficient defense against a charge that MAS impaired an auditor's independence; and (3) confuses notions of independence and professional image. The Board also commented that ASR 264 may discourage managements and boards of directors from retaining their auditors for MAS engagements in circumstances where it may very well be in the interest of shareholders to do so, and that it incorrectly concluded that the MAS Report recommended no proscriptive rules solely on the basis that there was an absence of empirical evidence showing that MAS impairs independence. Finally, the Board advised the SEC that ASR 264 unnecessarily and unfortunately casts a cloud over the performance of MAS related to internal controls at a time when the Foreign Corrupt Practices Act makes it essential for boards of directors and audit committees to seek assurances of their independent auditors with respect to internal control systems.

The Board believes that audit committees and boards of directors are qualified to make reviews and determinations as to the effect of MAS on independence of their auditors as called for by ASR 250. It regrets the confusion that seems to have resulted among audit committees and boards of directors from the issuance of ASR 264.

While ASR 264 remains on the books, the POB protestations (and those of others) notwithstanding, SEC Chairman Williams did proceed to smoothe the ruffled feathers of critics. Thus, in a January, 1980, address before an AICPA conference, Williams clarified certain aspects of ASR 264. He stated that the Commission, in the release, did not intend to "deprecate the benefits that may accrue from certain MAS activities." He indicated that assisting clients in reviewing internal accounting control systems could be the type of service that would produce enough benefits to more than offset the danger that such assistance might impair the auditing firm's independence.

With respect to whether a firm's dependence on MAS could affect its independence, Chairman Williams indicated that, even though ASR 264 suggested that an auditor's independence might be impaired by the magnitude of the ratio of the firm's nonaudit fees to audit fees for a specific client or for the firm as a whole, the Commission did not mean to suggest that it would, after the fact, question an auditor's independence based solely on a percentage relationship. He did, however, say that the profession cannot ignore the magnitude of MAS on a firm-wide basis since "undue emphasis on MAS could ultimately translate into an effect on the quality of audit work performed."

It is time to set down my considered view regarding this controversy. It would appear that the POB's response is rooted in the belief that:

1. The several studies by various scholars in this field are, at best, inconclusive and would not demonstrate that informed statement users would see the rendering of the management advisory and tax consultative services as being inimical to the independence of the auditor in the performance of the critical audit function for publicly owned corporations.

2. Any proscription of these peripheral services might well deny to the clients the benefits which might be derived from having an independent auditing firm render these peripheral services in tandem.

3. The professional firms are to be trusted "to do good"; besides, there are certain ethical constraints imposed by the profession's Code of Professional Ethics and the administration thereof.

4. And this above all! The record is devoid of any situations where the auditor's independence has, in fact, been impaired by the concurrent rendering of these peripheral services. This is, of course, consistent with the conclusion reached by the Cohen Commission.

Responding to the POB

Let us take up each of these deeply held beliefs of the venerable gentlemen who comprise the Public Oversight Board of the American Institute of Certified Public Accountants.

As to the various scholarly studies, it appears that the POB has swallowed the line advanced by the accounting establishment, to wit, that they are inconclusive or indeterminate. What would it take to convince the Board, *et al.*, to concede that the public which ultimately foots the bill for the independent audit function is not willing to accept the risks inherent in the conflict of interests?

In this connection, in June, 1975, Professor Seymour Eisenman at Baruch College completed his study on *Attest Independence and Management Advisory Services;* this study was undertaken to reconcile the conclusions reached by the Schulte and Briloff studies (the financial community would find a conflict between the two areas of services if rendered concurrently), and the Titard and Hartley-Ross studies (which appeared to conclude otherwise).

Among the Eisenman determinations:

(1) Due to the fact that all of the researchers appeared to be unaware that they were performing behavioral accounting research, they used the most unsophisticated technique which is available for assessing attitudes—the so-called "single-question" technique. While it is true that behavioral accounting research is only about five years old, it must nonetheless be recognized that the psychological literature warns that only minimal reliance should be placed on this single-question approach.

None of the surveys presented any evidence regarding either the *validity* or *reliability* of their test instruments. This shortcoming proved to be particularly crucial with respect to the Titard and Hartley and Ross studies. Based on the results of our research specifically related to these two later studies, we significantly demonstrated that these researchers had employed test items that were not entirely valid for a proper assessment of attitudes toward the MAS question. In both of these studies, the selected research vehicles were biased in the direction of producing findings that would tend to support the AICPA's position on the MAS controversy.

In general, the prior research studies relied upon intuitive rather than statistical analysis for determining the significance of percentage differences. This lack of statistical analysis appears to have been an important factor contributing to the kind of conclusions rendered in the Titard and Hartley and Ross studies. Based on our statistical analyses of the data, we concluded that the *findings* as opposed to the *conclusions* of the later Titard and Hartley and Ross studies, in spite of their biased research designs, were essentially in agreement with the findings of the earlier Schulte and Briloff studies [emphasis mine].

In short, a significant number of informed observers would identify MAS as being incompatible with auditor independence. If a researcher requires an absolute majority to convince him of the conflict, he might not be *absolutely* convinced. But the conflict is there, just as there is an energy crisis even though a majority asserted that it was a hoax when questioned during a spring, 1979, Associated Press–National Broadcasting survey.

What the advocates of MAS appear to believe is that it requires an absolute majority of the public to put a particular conflict of interests into sufficient question so as to decree the elimination of the roots of such conflict.

I venture to say that it would be difficult to demonstrate that an actual majority of the public would hold Bert Lance's involvements as really evil; just as it is likely that an actual majority might agree with our former President that he was "no crook."

Nor did Caesar determine that an actual majority was suspicious of his wife.

An obsession with statistical data—whether 49 percent or 51 percent of the public would consider the auditor's independence compromised— is nonsense. It is abundantly clear that a significant portion of the public which is using and paying for the independent audit function is disdainful of the potential contamination of the auditor's independence and his ultimate product.

Now we turn to the second justification by the POB of the audit service: Proscription of the audit firm's performance of peripheral services might deny to the client certain valuable services which the firm is capable of performing, or require the client to obtain such services elsewhere at a greater cost.

To begin with, let it be clear that we are considering the conflict only insofar as publicly owned entities are concerned. This limit is appropriate since it is in these circumstances that the POB is concerned, and independence in fact and in appearance is the *sine qua non* of the audit function. Further, in closely held enterprises it is likely that all users and potential users of the financial statements are capable of determining exactly what services other than the independent audit function were performed and to judge accordingly.

Independence (and the appearance of independence) may require the client to make some sacrifice. I maintain that this is a price, an opportunity cost, which the client and our total society must be prepared to accept for the sake of a higher or greater good.

Surely, the four lawyers on the POB would respond with horror at the suggestion that an attorney who had engaged in the development of his client's actions, and who was actively advocating that client's position, should be permitted to grace the bench as judge in a controversy surrounding those actions. Surely one might say the attorney is in a position to comprehend the facts better than any judge; surely the attorney would know best where justice lies; surely controversy could be resolved with greater expedition and much less cost than the present system calling for an independent judiciary. Yet society is ready and willing to absorb the cost for the sake of a transcendent objective.

A parallel relationship describes the independent, objective historian, as distinguished from the statesman-political-decision-maker; and the independent journalist, as distinguished from the public relations representative.

In fact, the constitutional process of checks and balances and separation of powers imposes a major cost in money and efficiency on our society; but who would be willing to sacrifice that safeguard of our confidence in the process of government? In short, the POB, *et al.*, emphasis on this score is painfully remindful of Oscar Wilde's definition of a cynic, someone who "knows the price of everything and the value of nothing."

Regarding the Public Oversight Board's confidence in the accounting profession's inherent integrity, I urge the reader to recall the Godfather chapter, where the ways were presented in which the profession's standard-setting and self-regulatory bodies become obsequious to the power structure within the profession, i.e., to those committed to the expansion of these peripheral services in issue here.

The Ethics Division of the AICPA has evidenced its propinquity with the acquisitive and expansionist proclivities of the major firms comprising the profession's hierarchy.

If the POB had taken but a moment to reflect on the circumstances which brought it into existence it would have recognized that the implicit confidence expressed in its *Scope of Services* report was naive. Insofar as the Board's reliance on ASR 250 is concerned, it should be noted that this watered-down disclosure requirement comes more than a decade after a stricter proposal, but in the same vein, was urged upon the Commission in my earlier work, *The Effectiveness of Accounting Communication.*

This leaves us with the ultimate argument of the upholders of the status quo and those who have ambitions regarding the peripheral services here under consideration: that there are no cases actually demonstrating that the performance of management advisory services affected the auditor's independence.

Under the caption Actual Independence, the Public Oversight Board states (footnote references omitted):

> From the voluminous record before the Board, it is apparent that documented evidence of MAS abuses or impairment of independence through the use of MAS is virtually nonexistent . . . no one can counter the demonstrated benefits of MAS with some proof that specific practices lead to actual impairment. . . .

> Despite more than fifteen years of research—much of which conducted by persons, however sincere their motives, with an apparent preconception about the impropriety of MAS—the record of MAS practice as it relates to audit independence is unblemished: *Not a single compromising instance has been presented.* Both equity and reason would seem to suggest that the question has been answered adequately.

> The two special committees established by the AICPA to study this problem failed to find any evidence of actual impairment of independence after years of performance of MAS for audit clients. . . .

> Finally, one mechanism which potentially could reveal whether the independence of auditors has actually been impaired is our legal system. Research conducted by the Cohen Commission, however, produced only one case that could arguably have involved an actual impairment of independence on the part of auditors. One commentator cited a few other cases which were considered by the Cohen Commission before reaching its conclusion, but, otherwise, there have been no instances of litigation concerning this issue.

Having stated its case so categorically, the paragraph which follows appears strange indeed:

> While the available empirical evidence does not reveal any actual instances where the furnishing of MAS has impaired independence, the Board recognizes that the nonexistence of such evidence does not necessarily mean that there have not been instances where independence may have been impaired. Not all situations where an auditor's objectivity is compromised will

result in a lawsuit. Accordingly, the absence of any known cases, while com-
forting, does not serve to prove conclusively that independence has not been,
or will not be, impaired due to the furnishing of MAS to audit clients.

Is the Board seeking to hedge its previously stated conclusion (which
led to its ultimate *laissez-faire* recommendation)? If the Board had a reasonable doubt regarding this critical point, it should have pursued its
own independent investigation—possibly using its presumptive right to
demand documentary evidence beyond that produced in open court.

Most certainly the four lawyers on the Board must have been aware
of the all-too-frequently employed rules of confidentiality imposed on
evidence developed in pre-trial depositions and other discovery proceedings. Surely these lawyers must know of the numerous instances where
after such extensive discovery the parties agree that discretion is the
better part of valor and agree to terminate the litigation by settlement.
In fact, the accounting firm's vulnerability to having its independence
put into question may serve as an important incentive for its conceding
a more liberal judgment.

The Board's reference to the commentator who cited violations sup-
posedly refuted by the Cohen Commission is to me. In *Unaccountable
Accounting* and *More Debits than Credits,* I pointed the finger accusingly
at the contamination of the auditor's independence in, *inter alia,* Yale
Express, Westec, National Student Marketing, Wall Street's Back Office,
Penn Central. In each instance I set forth the basis on which I concluded
that the rendering of the MAS function contaminated the auditor's independence.

Relying on an AICPA Committee Report

In reaching its conclusions on this score, the Public Oversight Board
gave full faith and credit to the *Report, Conclusions, and Recommendations*
released in early 1978 by the American Institute of Certified Public
Accounts' Commission on Auditors' Responsibilities (the Cohen Commission).

The Commission in the report and in news releases flaunted its independence. After describing the extensive involvement of the AICPA in
the Commission's activities, I challenged these protestations of virtue
on the part of this AICPA group.

After the Cohen Commission's presumptive rebuttal of allegations
that the auditor's independence has been adversely impacted by performance of peripheral services, the Public Oversight Board might have

sought to determine who carried out the investigative responsibility. Had the POB done so, it would have read the following at page XV of the final (1978) report:

> The Commission's research related to auditing practice required staff with extensive, current auditing experience. The analysis was performed by members of the staffs of public accounting firms on assignment to the Commission, principally Alan N. Certain, a manager in Price Waterhouse & Co., Eugene F. De Mark, a manager with Peat, Marwick, Mitchell & Co., and Ann Gabriel, a manager with Coopers & Lybrand. Wenona Waldo of Alexander Grant & Co. and Jerald Folk of Haskins & Sells also assisted.

This paragraph is a truncated version of the far more revealing one which appeared at page XIV of the Cohen Commission's 1977 *Report on Tentative Conclusions,* which read:

> The Commission's *analysis of significant cases* against auditors and other research related to auditing practice required staff with extensive, current auditing experience. The analysis was performed by members of the staffs of public accounting firms on assignment to the Commission, principally Alan N. Certain, a manager in Price Waterhouse & Co., Eugene F. De Mark, a manager with Peat, Marwick, Mitchell & Co., and Ann Gabriel, a supervisor with Coopers & Lybrand. Wenona Waldo of Alexander Grant & Co. and Jerald Folk of Haskins & Sells also assisted [emphasis supplied].

It may be that the research people at the Cohen Commission were thus endeavoring to respond to the comments of one critic that in this aspect, at least, the commission's investigative practices were analogous to sending a fox to guard the hen house.

The POB might want to reconsider its abject reliance on the report of the Cohen Commission, at least insofar as its conclusion that there were no cases in the record which would demonstrate the adverse consequences of the multiplicity of services under consideration.

Let me now repeat my assertion that only a deliberate myopia would preclude an investigator from discerning the contamination of an auditor's independence in fact, as well as in appearance.

Some Specific Cases in Point

Herewith I present a series of particular cases where there were overt manifestations of a loss of auditor independence *in fact.*

Item: In mid-1975 I served as the expert accounting witness in behalf of the Federal Trade Commission in its divestiture proceedings against Retail Credit Corporation (now dubbed "Equifax"). This proceeding, before an administrative law judge, stemmed from Retail Credit's acquisition in 1970 of Credit Bureaus Inc. of Oregon. The thrust of my testimony was to the effect that the involvement of RCC's auditors, Arthur Andersen & Co., in the pre-merger negotiations and other activities leading up to the takeover so seriously contaminated Arthur Andersen's independence that its accountings for Credit Bureaus should not be accepted as indicative of that company's financial condition or results from operations.

My arguments in this vein were persuasive with the administrative law judge; he ruled for the government and ordered the divestiture. His determination was subsequently upheld by the Commission.

My assertions were made in open court and were subjected to cross examination. Members of the accounting firm were present throughout the proceedings and undoubtedly were providing RCC's counsel with arguments to refute my assertions.

Item: In my *Unaccountable Accounting* I questioned the independence of Haskins & Sells as the auditor of record of a number of major Wall Street brokerage firms which went "belly up" during the early 1970s. I did so on the ground that the firm was the one which had been intimately involved in the development of data-processing systems for their many brokerage clients, and as a consequence developing and piloting the systems of internal control intended to protect the enormous quantities of cash, securities, and other liquid resources of these brokerage clients.

I also alluded to H&S's involvement in Orvis Brothers—an involvement which caused the New York Stock Exchange to bring suit against the accounting firm (a lawsuit settled out of court). In that connection, I said:

> Now what does all this have to do with the two-hats syndrome? Simply, Haskins & Sells has for the past several years been the recognized leader in the development of the data-processing systems for stock brokerage firms and in offering the services of their management-consultative services division to these firms for the introduction and implementation of their systems. The auditing arm of an accounting firm would be hard-pressed to condemn the accounting system designed, installed, and "piloted" by their own management-consultative division.

In a more recent situation, H&S moves front and center; this is the case of Samuel F. du Pont against Haskins & Sells, a partnership, in Federal District Court in Manhattan. This action stemmed from the Francis I. du Pont (FID) fiasco, in which Samuel F. du Pont had invested substantial sums in late 1969.

Mr. du Pont asserted that he was misled into making his investment by H&S's failure to set forth in its September, 1969, audited statements for FID the serious contingencies which threatened the viability of the brokerage firm—contingencies of which the accountants were intimately aware.

In early 1979 United States District Judge Charles E. Stewart, Jr., dismissed the action on the ground that it was outlawed by the statute of limitations. The Circuit Court of Appeals for the Second Circuit affirmed the decision of the District Court.

In the development of its case, plaintiff's counsel engaged the services of Gustav A. Gomprecht, CPA, a retired partner of the firm of Main, Lafrentz & Co., who had, over the years, been an important member of audit committees of the New York State Society of CPA's as well as the American Institute of Certified Public Accountants. His findings, comprising 21 tightly packed pages (exclusive of exhibits), set forth an extensive catalog of errors of commission and omission on the part of Haskins & Sells in connection, principally, with its 1969 FID audit and reports. Especially to the point is Gomprecht's conclusionary statement numbered 2:

> Haskins & Sells' opinion on the Statement of Financial Condition of Francis I. du Pont & Co. as of September 28, 1969, included in the scope paragraph a reference to the review of the accounting system, internal accounting control and procedures for safeguarding securities. In view of the fact that there were material inadequacies in the accounting system, internal accounting control and procedures for safeguarding securities and also material unreconciled differences in the accounting for securities and dividends receivable and payable, Haskins & Sells should:
>
> (1) Have required proper treatment of the reserve for securities count differences and dividend accounts in that there should have been a liability reserve for possible losses in connection with security count differences, dividend accounts and bad debts and the reserve should have had an explanatory note to the Statement of Financial Condition, and because of the material violation of Rule 325 of the New York Stock Exchange as of September 28, 1969, as determined by both Haskins & Sells and the New York Stock Exchange, Haskins & Sells should have required a note to the statement of financial condition disclosing the violation and the factors and/or steps taken to bring the firm within the limits prescribed by Rule 325. . . .

The Stock Exchange Rule sets forth the critical standard whereby member firms are prohibited from incurring indebtedness which would, in the aggregate, exceed 2,000 percent (hence 20 times) the brokerage firm's net capital.

The record discloses absolutely and categorically that H&S found the ratio to be 3,242 percent in September, 1969, and failed to disclose that critical fact (among others) in the certified financial statements disseminated to the public. Even more intriguing, the Gomprecht report cites a 1970 memorandum compiled by the Advisory Committee of the Department of Member Firms of the NYSE on the subject, *Francis I. du Pont & Co.—Possible Violation of Exchange Rule 325 (Capital Requirements)*. The ratio in November, 1969, was a staggering 76,128 percent.

To add insult to injury, H&S's counsel, in resisting Mr. du Pont's claims, asserted that he could have found out H&S's misgivings if he had only gone to the SEC and NYSE files. As quoted by Gomprecht:

> Haskins & Sells' 1969 audit of FID, the reports of which were filed with the SEC and the New York Stock Exchange and were available to plaintiffs, revealed and disclosed the following as set forth in such reports:
>
> (i) FID was in violation of Rule 325 of the Exchange as of September 28, 1969. . . .
>
> (iii) FID had "material inadequacies" in its accounting system, internal accounting control, and procedures for safeguarding securities;
>
> (iv) FID had "fails" to receive of approximately $44,451,000 and "fails" to deliver of approximately $27,662,000. . . .

In its brief on appeal, plaintiff's counsel responded to Haskins & Sells' *caveat emptor* assertion, as part of paragraph numbered 10:

> (ii) [The H&S brief] failed to apprehend the nature and form of the Answers to Financial Questionnaire and the degree of expertise and sophistication which would have been necessary to understand and relate this report to the 1969 Statement of Financial Condition;
>
> (iii) [It] overlooked the fact that the most critical of the H&S reports (the 1969 letter of Comments on Conditions . . .) was filed with the SEC in "confidential files" not available for public inspection;
>
> (iv) [It] held, without ever seeing these documents, that had plaintiffs examined them, they would have discovered the Haskins fraud; and
>
> (v) [It] failed to discern that even the report on the Memorandum of Net Capital prepared by H&S and filed with the SEC was materially false and misleading and would not have put a reasonable investor on notice of the astonishing magnitude of FID's capital violation in the fall of 1969, but would simply have lulled the investor to believe that that capital violation was transitory and had been cured by ordinary means.

A Senator's Commentary

The POB's *Scope of Services* report evoked the following comment from Senator Thomas Eagleton (who succeeded the late Senator Metcalf as the accounting profession's senatorial gadfly):

To no one's surprise, it [the report] found that management services are not a serious problem and that disclosure of the types of services performed by accountants is sufficient to remedy any problems.

The oversight board rejected what was called the "more extreme view" of the Metcalf subcommittee with the following conclusion: "Such a draconian measure would not only deprive audit clients of services that they obviously deem valuable but also would cause a substantial reduction in revenues for many CPA firms. . . ."

We in Congress are giving the accounting profession every reasonable opportunity to put its house in order. If the profession cannot or will not look beyond its immediate self-interest, then we will be forced to consider other alternatives to protect those who don't share its privilege of self regulation. I certainly don't regard reasonable action to prevent abuse of legally protected markets as draconian, and I think the burden of proof rests upon those who take advantage of their special position in our economy.

My Draconian Solution

What, then, would I decree if I were endowed with the authority vested in the Public Oversight Board?

The recommendation with which I concluded the chapter on peripheral services in *The Effectiveness of Accounting Communication* a dozen years ago was: strict separation of the independent audit function from management advisory services for the same client. A CPA firm should be barred from performing the two functions concurrently.

The passage of time has emphasized the importance of the independent *qua* independent audit function for publicly owned corporate enterprises. I would now absolutely prohibit rendering management advisory or tax consultative services for any business enterprise (whether or not it is an audit client) by any accounting firm which derives, say, more than 50 percent of its revenues from the independent audit function for publicly owned entities.

It is to be noted that I would proscribe the rendering of these services only by firms whose principal commitment is, or should be, to the independent audit function essentially for the benefit of third parties—which I assert is the circumstance where such service to a publicly owned enterprise is inappropriately involved. It is now believed that such a proscription would, at most, affect a dozen accounting firms—the giants in the profession.

Why such a rule which at first blush might appear to be draconian?

First: I believe it would clarify the objectives of such accounting firms and their partners and personnel. Such firms would be made to understand their primary, transcending, pervasive commitment, i.e., that their clients are *not* the entities or corporate managements which happen to pay their bills; instead, all of society is to be recognized as the client of such firms.

The POB appears to have been oblivious of the tensions within the firms to give proper recognition to the stellar performers and producers in the MAS area who happen not to be CPA's. The firms have been constrained to create special designations and subsidiary enclaves for these non-CPA's in order to recognize their talents and to afford them the stature and compensations their egos demand. And the AICPA's ethics apparatus has accepted this condition and provided rules and interpretations to permit end runs around the requirement that only CPA's are to be partners of a certified public accounting firm.

The tensions within the profession on this score surfaced dramatically in the *Report of the Committee on Scope and Structure* of the AICPA. Thus, the *ad hoc* committee recommended that the Institute develop specialty groups involving examinations and experience standards.

> . . . As mentioned earlier, firms have been forced to look beyond the ranks of CPAs to those trained in other disciplines. It is estimated, for example, that nearly three-quarters of the approximately 5,000 individuals who perform management advisory services on a full-time basis within the larger accounting firms and who contribute their expertise in such fields as computer sciences and statistical sampling to the conduct of audit engagements are not certified public accountants. These are men and women of stature, with outstanding academic credentials in terms of their own special fields of knowledge; and they are a vital factor in the ability of their firms to render the wide range of services being sought from them.
>
> It might be argued that the only appropriate way for them to achieve recognition within the profession is to become certified public accountants. But this would be asking more than can be reasonably expected of them. . . .

Having thus agonized over the plight of the 5,000 or so indispensable non-CPA specialists, the committee proposed:

> In view of these factors, it seems highly desirable that the non-CPA specialists employed by public accounting firms should be allowed to participate in any institute program for the recognition of specialists.
>
> The exclusion of them would have the serious defect of failing to recognize the realities of present-day practice.
>
> This could lead to two results, neither of which is pleasant to contemplate. It could deprive accounting firms of the valuable skills of non-CPAs by discouraging them from pursuing their specialties within the profession, and

it could impel the non-CPAs to seek recognition elsewhere and thus impede efforts to nurture unity within the profession.

This splintering was not implemented by the Institute; nevertheless, the very fact that such important consideration was afforded to this relatively tiny component of the major accounting firms should have demonstrated to the POB the internal tensions which prevail within these firms as a consequence of their harboring these stellar performers and producers.

By imposing the strict divorce and divestiture of the MAS–tax consultative services, these distractions would be exorcised; all within the firm would fully comprehend their unitary and primary commitment to the independent audit function.

Second: This is probably implicit in the foregoing; nevertheless, it bears emphasis. It is my view that the present education of potential CPA's is sorely deficient in that there is such a compelling obsession with technique that there is little room for courses in the philosophy of accounting and of the social implications and ramifications of the independent audit function.

It is hoped that by the divorce suggested here and the consequent unitary commitment, the affected firms would be able to devote increasing resources and energies to filling this philosophic void. And then, because demand creates the commensurate supply in the academic marketplace, course offerings in this realm would become generally available—and then required of all who aspire to the public accounting profession.

Third: I would be less than candid if I did not also refer to another salutary consequence of my bill of divorcement. It would put some restraint on the expansionist proclivities of the affected giant firms. Such a restriction should contribute to the survival of second-tier and smaller accounting firms—thereby contributing to the broadening of the availability of services and improving the competitive environment.

It should be emphasized that the divestiture of the peripheral service as independent engagements should not imply that the affected accounting firms would lose their talents in these areas. To the contrary, recognizing the complexity of the corporate enterprises for which they are rendering the independent audit function, I would expect the firms to have the full panoply of marketing and quality expertise (to help in making evaluations); actuaries (re pension and insurance funds); engineers (safety and other); legal and tax (to determine the liabilities to be reflected); etc., etc. The critical difference is that all of this expertise would be overtly subsumed to the independent attest function.

As the POB noted in its report (influenced by the pleadings of the two academicians who testified at its hearings), such a proscription might discourage some whiz-kids from pursuing a public accounting program. As a consequence we would lose some of the presumably best and brightest who know how to play the computer games to win. These people would be lost to the hard-sell, more aggressive management consulting firms. This is a price which the profession might have to pay but if as a consequence the independent audit firms are able to attract those who have a fuller understanding of and commitment to their third-party responsibility to society, I would consider the opportunity cost (the disaffection of the whiz-kids) a relatively cheap price to pay.

10

Grease

In 1975, Senator William Proxmire, speaking before the U.S. Senate Committee on Banking, Housing and Urban Affairs, said that close to a hundred publicly held corporations had made disclosures to the SEC of literally hundreds of millions of dollars paid over the years as bribes to foreign officials and political parties.

By 1978 the one hundred number cited by Senator Proxmire swelled to more than four hundred "voluntary" disclosures to the SEC by corporations which had made contaminated payments.

A Catalog of Accounting Perversion

The Charles E. Simon Company, a Washington-based consulting firm, had undertaken the responsibility of analyzing these disclosure filings in great detail. Mr. Simon, in association with Tom Kennedy, published the results of the analysis insofar as the cases related to corporations based in the tri-state area of New York, New Jersey, and Connecticut. That compendium, *An Examination of Questionable Payments and Practices,* included as Part VI the following configuration:

Questionable Accounting Practices

A. Questionable Accounting Practices Which Appear Not to Have Involved Third Parties
   1. Improper Bookkeeping (General)
   2. Improper Expense Account Vouchers
   3. Funds or Assets Questionably Transferred

    4. Separate Set of Official Books
    5. Non-Deductible (or Questionable) Expense Treated as a Deductible Expense
    6. Improper Reporting of Revenues
- B. Questionable Accounting Practices Which Appear to Have Involved the Collusion of Customers, Suppliers or Others
    1. Overbilling and Underbilling Transactions
    2. Questionable Rebates or Discounts, Granted or Received
    3. Payments Disbursed for Goods or Services not Received or Received Only in Part
    4. Payments Received for Goods or Services not Provided or Provided Only in Part
    5. Improper Invoicing
- C. Questionable Accounting Practices Which Appear to Have Involved Employees' Salaries
    1. Unrecorded Supplemental Salaries
    2. Taxed Employee Compensation to be Used for Questionable Purposes as Directed by the Company
- D. Other Questionable Practices
    1. Off-Book Cash Funds
    2. Off-Book Accounts (Either Bank Accounts or Not Specified as Cash or Bank Accounts)
    3. Creative Bookkeeping
    4. Companies Improving Audit Procedure
    5. Detailed Review of Investigative Procedures

These patterns of creative accounting were not contrived by accountants operating in the penumbra of our business sector; all of this related to publicly owned corporations required to file reports with the SEC. Nor were the companies audited by accountants who function in the interstices of the profession; instead, we find that the books of the reporting corporations were audited by those who are presumed to be the best and the most skilled among us—principally by firms comprising the accounting establishment.

A number of the disclosing entities were constrained by the Securities and Exchange Commission to create special investigative committees of their boards of directors, who were then required to file reports of their investigations with the Commission. The matter was the subject of a number of consent decrees as well.

Four such reports deserve special comment, namely, those relating to Gulf Oil, Lockheed Aircraft, Northrop, and International Telephone and Telegraph Corporations. I will not be especially concerned with to whom or for what the payments were made. I will consider the critical manifestations of disintegration in the control and audit process in the entities.

Gulf Oil Exploits

First as to the Gulf Oil Corporation: Under John J. McCloy (later the chairman of the Public Oversight Board—see the preceding chapter), the Special Review Committee of Gulf's board rendered its report on December 30, 1976. This committee was mandated by the settlement of the legal proceeding instituted by the Securities and Exchange Commission in the United States District Court for the District of Columbia.

The broad outlines of Gulf Oil's machinations had been exposed previously before various congressional committees and in other proceedings which were reported by the press. These earlier disclosures had attracted the interest of the Justice Department and the Internal Revenue Service—in addition to the SEC. So it came as no surprise that the Special Review Committee (sometimes referred to as the McCloy Committee) determined that the domestic and foreign skullduggery was perpetrated through an offshore subsidiary, Bahamas Exploration, Limited (referred to as Bahamas Ex).

The idea was conceived in 1959 by William K. Whiteford, the dynamic and colorful chairman of Gulf's board and its chief executive officer. He wanted an available source of funds to grease the company's expansionist objectives at home and abroad. Following a strategy meeting between Whiteford and Gulf's counsel, it was determined to utilize a Gulf subsidiary which had no direct U.S. involvement so that the contemplated mischief would not run afoul of the Internal Revenue Service. Bahamas Ex, the chosen instrument, was organized in 1944 to undertake oil exploration in the Bahamas; however, from 1944 to 1960 it did little more than hold some exploration licenses and operated on an annual budget of about $10,000 to $12,000. During this period this subsidiary reported to Gulf's Exploration Division based in New York, but in 1960 there were two dramatic developments: Bahamas Ex was henceforth to report directly to home base in Pittsburgh, and William C. Viglia, an assistant controller in the Tulsa operations, was moved to Nassau to take charge of Bahamas Ex's finances.

Thereafter a trail of checks was issued by Gulf-Pittsburgh to the Bank of Nova Scotia in the Bahamas, and the money disappeared from Good Gulf's books. Pittsburgh appears to have debited the millions of dollars to some deferred exploration cost on its books, while Bahamas Ex wrote them off as operating expenses.

Viglia is described in the McCloy report as the trusted courier delivering packages of loose folding money to Claude C. Wild, Jr., Gulf's Vice President for Government Relations, and to certain other highly positioned persons in the Gulf hierarchy. The whole relationship, extending over a fifteen-year period, raises some questions, none satisfactorily answered:

1. Where was Gulf's internal control system and where were the company's internal auditors? The McCloy Report does indicate that certain of these internal auditors did request permission to go to Nassau to audit that contaminated subsidiary; but their suggestions were invariably vetoed by persons higher up.

2. What about Price Waterhouse, Gulf's independent auditors? Should they not sometime during the fifteen-year period of this illicit operation have audited Bahamas Ex and discerned that the subsidiary's books were not symmetrical with those of the parent? A dormant offshore subsidiary which suddenly springs to life with enormous fervor, demanding increasing funds without demonstrating any revenues, is an entity deserving review at some time over an extended period.

3. What could possibly have induced God-fearing, highly respected persons like chairmen and chief counsel for a giant multinational corporation to engage in a *modus operandi* generally presumed to be exclusively within the domain of organized crime?

A clue might lie in the following colloquy between Bob Rawls Dorsey (who was Chairman of the Board and Chief Executive Officer when the scheme was exposed) and the McCloy Committee regarding a $3 million payment to Korean government officials:

> Mr. Dorsey: So you really are there at the mercy of the government and you are there at the sufferance of the government; if you're going to prosper and do well, you need the government on your side. You need that kind of an environment, unlike any Western country.
>
> Mr. Jackson (for the Committee): Did you fear that if you didn't make the contribution there might be nationalization of assets of your company?
>
> Mr. Dorsey: No. I don't think I—I don't think I thought that, at all. I just thought that the opportunity to continue a profitable business, without unwarranted and inhibiting government interference, required it. I think that I felt that there were further opportunities to—or, for further investment to expand and to do other things there. And that our ability to do, then, again depended on ministers and government officials that really made the decisions in the end.

This is a deplorable attitude—transcending the particular circumstances and deception. It is significant that, according to the McCloy Report, Whiteford specifically excluded Dorsey from the inner ring of executives who were to be apprised of the Bahamas Ex scheme because Dorsey was one of the "boy scouts."

A Rube Goldberg Apparatus

An intriguing Appendix E to the McCloy Report is labeled Viglia's Outline of Procedures for the Establishment of a Successor to Bahamas Ex. When it became clear in mid-1972 that the old order could no longer function, Gulf's trusted courier developed a remarkable labyrinth of accounting entries to be made on Gulf's books which would continue to obfuscate the off-the-books cash accounts. After one works through the maze of entries, he will come to the ultimate entry: Debit Miscellaneous Expenses and Credit Cash.

Just what games Viglia thought he was playing is beyond me; nor can I tell you how well he slept at night. He must have felt, though, that such manifestations of creative bookkeeping would endear him to those responsible for handing out brownie points.

The McCloy Report is a remarkable document disclosing corporate transgressions at the highest levels; I was nevertheless surprised and disappointed on reading the following:

> It should be borne in mind that the Committee, its counsel, and its accountants, whether in investigating in the United States or abroad or in examining into the distribution or receipt of corporate funds, has had no power to compel testimony under oath, to subpoena documents, or to impose any of the sanctions for contumacy or perjury usually available to courts, legislative committees, or administrative agencies. . . .

Could Mr. McCloy have obtained the power of subpoena and the right to take testimony under oath had he requested such powers from the federal district court under whose aegis the investigation was undertaken? In view of the fact that counsel in simple negligence cases (for example) can subpoena documents *en masse* and take testimony under oath, the court probably would have accommodated the committee's request. The McCloy Committee may have had its reasons for undertaking this probe in what appears to be a nonadversary atmosphere.

Are We *In Pari Delicto?*

It is of interest to note that the committee's report would have each of us share a portion of Gulf's guilt. In the Preliminary Overview we are told:

It is common knowledge that enforcement over the years since the passage of the Corrupt Practices Act has been marked by great slackness on the part of federal authorities. Indeed, enforcement by both federal and state authorities until the Watergate prosecutions has been practically nonexistent. Nor is there much doubt that political contributions and payments have been induced in large part by strong importunities on the part of expectant recipients and their representatives as much as by a calculated effort on the part of contributors to induce governmental favors from elected officials. Nonetheless, the fact remains that well-known laws were honored in the breach rather than the observance by both donors and donees. It is hard to escape the conclusion that a sort of "shut-eye sentry" attitude prevailed upon the part of both the responsible corporate officials and the recipients as well as on the part of those charged with enforcement responsibilities.

If Mr. McCloy and the committee's counsel (his law firm) had the "common knowledge" that statutes were not being enforced, then, independent of any particular client representation and as officers of the law sworn to its upholding and uplifting, they had the responsibility for blowing the whistle. Then, at least, Congress and the executive and judiciary branches of our government would have been challenged to either enforce the statutes or, by their repeal, put an end to the fiction of the laws.

The Lockheed Aircraft Perversity

The bitter fruit of Lockheed Aircraft Corporation's perversity has been strewn far and wide and extensively reported on in the general and financial press. We know that in Italy a former defense minister and President Giovanni Leone were forced to resign in the wake of disclosures of their corruption by Lockheed. In the Netherlands the disclosure that Prince Bernhard was the beneficiary of a $1 million gift from Lockheed necessitated his resignation as inspector general of the air force. And in Japan former Prime Minister Kakuei Tanaka and two other officials stood trial for being beneficiaries of Lockheed's generosity. I will comment briefly on the failure of the internal and outside independent auditors to blow the whistle on Lockheed's illicit intrigue in the foreign bribery realm.

For this expedition I will be relying on the May 16, 1977, report (and related volume of exhibits) released by the Special Review Committee of the Board of Directors of the Lockheed Aircraft Corporation. The committee was comprised of seven board members and was assisted by Shearman and Sterling as counsel and Arthur Andersen and Co. as accountants. According to the report, tens of millions of dollars of corporate moneys were illicitly diverted; the objectives and patterns of diversion were summarized by the following litany, which brings to mind the Kennedy-Simon compilation. The committee developed substantial evidence confirming these patterns of questionable payments or conduct in connection with foreign sales during the period under investigation:

Direct payments to, or for the benefit of, government and military officials and employees.

Direct payments to government officials and employees which were intended or viewed by Lockheed as political contributions.

Direct payments to employees of commercial customers—often government-owned commercial airlines.

Direct payments to third parties, e.g., consultants, where the Company understood, or the third party represented, that all or a portion of the payment was intended to be passed on to [politically connected] persons.

Direct payments to consultants who had been retained at the suggestion of [such] persons.

Increases in amounts previously agreed to be paid to consultants based on representations by a consultant during a sales campaign that the previously agreed amount was insufficient to meet necessary in-country commitments to third parties.

Acceleration of standard consultant payment schedules, sometimes when the consultant represented that the amounts accelerated were required to be paid to third parties in order to obtain a sale.

Payments to third parties in cash, bearer instrument form or under other unusual circumstances.

Backdating of consultant agreements.

Execution of multiple agreements with the same consultant to assist in creating the appearance that commission payments in a given year were significantly less than the amounts actually paid.

Possible failure by Lockheed employees to comply with United States laws relating to the reporting of currency and negotiable instrument import and export transactions.

Possible failure to comply with foreign exchange control, foreign government procurement, and other laws.

Accumulation and disbursement of funds outside normal financial controls.

*   *   *

Direct hiring of foreign governmental officials as consultants.

Utilization of "shell" corporations to enter into consultant agreements which served as a screen for questionable payments or to provide false receipts for payments actually made to other third parties, such as customer employees.

Assistance to customer employees in converting their employer's funds to their personal benefit.

Issuance of false invoices to a consultant for unsold and undelivered goods to facilitate the transfer of funds by the consultant from one country to another.

Arrangements whereby a domestic supplier overinvoiced Lockheed (and simultaneously issued Lockheed a credit for the overinvoiced amount) for equipment resold by Lockheed abroad to a foreign government customer at a price based on the overinvoiced amount.

Payment to a commercial customer of amounts characterized as public relations funds where Lockheed believed that the customer would utilize the funds to influence foreign government regulatory decisions.

Possible failure to disclose information to the United States government with respect to applications for government approvals of various aspects of foreign sales.

The committee noted that in 1973 internal auditors did discern certain irregularities in the payment practices involving foreign commissions; somehow, these findings were never communicated to the Lockheed executive suite.

Lockheed's Outside Auditors Develop Anxieties

The section of the report on Lockheed's outside independent auditors (Arthur Young & Co., since 1933) gives some intriguing insights into the way things happen when the military-industrial complex interfaces with the accounting establishment. For example, W. G. Findley, an Arthur Young partner, told the Committee that in 1971, he learned of assignments of commissions from a Lockheed consultant to a third party. It was his understanding this was a means of "diverting" money to the head of a foreign air force. Findley told the Committee he was advised the arrangement was a private matter between the consultant and the military official, having nothing to do with Lockheed. Findley stated that he insisted that Anderson, chief financial officer, be advised. Anderson told the Committee he does not recall the matter.

In connection with the 1972 audit of Lockheed Aircraft International Limited (LAIL), Arthur Young's Hong Kong office learned of a $100,000 bank transfer to the account of an undisclosed party and a payment of $200,000 for an unspecified purpose. A schedule from the work papers of Arthur Young's Hong Kong office states that the former payment was discussed with LAIL's director of financial operations, F. J. Andrew, and that it "might have been paid under the counter" in connection with a contract then under negotiation; the schedule further states that the nature and purpose of the second item "was not known or if known, not disclosed," and bears a notation: "OK, Mr. C. R. Warman is aware of this item." Warman, who was then the partner in charge of Arthur Young's Hong Kong office, has since died. The Committee has found no evidence that the information shown on the schedule was communicated to Arthur Young personnel in Los Angeles, and Findley and W. J. Mayhugh, also an Arthur Young partner, could not recall having been advised about it.

The report further observed that subsequent to February, 1973, [Findley] continued to review yen payments and to examine receipts. There is no documentation of such review or examination in Arthur Young's working papers, and there is no indication of any subsequent confirmation by the president of Lockheed Asia, J. W. Clutter, of the currency in his possession, even though the balance apparently in his possession at year-end 1973 was Y116,000,000 (approximately $387,000).

What makes this information remarkable (aside from the substantive aspects) is the clear indication that Arthur Young's communication and/ or working papers and/or recollections are anything but optimal. This is, of course, an especially grievous condition in view of the fact that it was Arthur Young to whom Peat, Marwick, Mitchell turned in 1975 to obtain an expensive peer review of the latter's audit procedures. If Arthur Young's house was in the state of disarray indicated above, could they be counted on to criticize meaningfully the practices and procedures of a fellow member of the accounting establishment?

We are also informed by the Special Committee's report of how Arthur Young determined to proceed with the integrity and intrepidity fitting its responsibilities as Lockheed's outside independent auditors. On February 25, 1973, near the completion of the 1972 audit, Arthur Young met with Haughton and Kotchian (Lockheed's chief executives) and expressed concern regarding the substantial cash payments in Japan. Over the objections of Haughton and Kotchian, who were apprehensive that any disclosure would jeopardize Lockheed's position in Japan, Arthur Young insisted on bringing the matter to the attention of the audit committee.

Arthur Young's representatives (Mayhugh and Findley) expressed their concern to the audit committee at a meeting on March 4, 1973, stating that the currency and bearer check payments aggregated approximately $4.6 million in 1972 and were supported only by receipts. They also indicated that there was no written contract with the consultant to whom the payments were purportedly made. The audit committee members at the time were J. K. Horton, a Lockheed director, L. J. Hector and D. M. Cochran. Haughton and Kotchian were also present at the meeting.

After Mayhugh and Findley described the payments to the audit committee, it was recalled by one or more of those present that Haughton and/or Kotchian stated it was necessary to make these kinds of payments in order to do business in many countries and that it was most important that such matters be maintained in the strictest confidence since any public knowledge of the payments and relationships could have a significant adverse effect on the Company's ability to do business overseas. It was also recalled by most of those present that Kotchian specifically stated he did not know what the consultant did with the money, but indicated that part of it might be used for political campaign purposes in the foreign country.

Horton recalled the audit committee concluded that, considering Haughton's and Kotchian's comments and the information at hand, the payments were "proper sales costs" and that it was not necessary to make a report to the entire board. Horton also told the Committee, "We asked the auditors to continue to pursue this matter and report anything else they considered significant in future meetings . . . and we asked that (a consulting) agreement be obtained."

Some time later in 1973, Arthur Young was shown a copy of a signed agreement with the consultant dated "as of" 1969. . . .

Have auditors become so naive and guileless that they believe that an important contract which was not in existence in February, 1973, could sprout full-blown like the goddess Athene from the forehead of Zeus later in 1973 bearing a 1969 dating?

Anxiety in the AY Hierarchy

But there is more, much more, that the Special Committee disclosed about the anxious meetings between the Arthur Young people and Lockheed's audit committee; for these intimate details we must turn to a separate volume of exhibits promulgated by the committee.

Exhibit 9, devoted to Additional Information Concerning the Audit Process, provides the following tidbits:

> After the meeting of the 26th [of February, 1973, between certain Arthur Young partners and principal executives of Lockheed] Arthur Young personnel continued to consider the matter and their responsibilities to the board of directors. The matter was discussed with C. G. Gillette, a senior technical partner in the firm's New York office and formerly the partner in charge of

the Lockheed engagement; R. E. Kent, then the firm's managing partner; and T. D. Flynn, then the number two partner in the firm. In addition, White & Case, Arthur Young's outside counsel, was consulted. It was Arthur Young's conclusion that the matter had to be discussed with the audit committee at its regularly scheduled meeting on Sunday, March 4, 1973. Mayhugh told the Special Review Committee that upon being informed of Arthur Young's decision, Haughton commented to the effect that:

> you have spoken to your counsel and if you go to the audit committee they will speak to their counsel and their counsel will tell them to tell the board. Why don't you just go put it in the Los Angeles Times? You will destroy our ability to do business there.

Haughton requested permission of Horton to attend the meeting of the audit committee together with Kotchian.

*   *   *

At the conclusion of regular business at the audit committee meeting of March 4, 1973, Haughton asked that there be an "executive session" and the secretary of the Company was excused. Therefore, no minutes were kept of this session and the only information available to the Special Review Committee regarding what took place is the recollections of those present and notes prepared by Arthur Young (Mayhugh and Findley) in advance of the meeting for their use thereat. The practice of meeting in "executive session," with no minutes or notes being kept, was continued by the audit committee at subsequent meetings whenever commissions or currency payments were discussed.

. . . Mayhugh told the audit committee that there had been "large, unusual and partially unauditable transactions" and referred to the currency and bearer check payments in Japan. He also stated that Arthur Young was not in a position to pass judgment on the "legality or morality" of the payments. He then described the procedures Arthur Young had followed in gathering information and described the receipts they had examined. He further stated to the audit committee, "(W)e have no hard evidence as to (the) ultimate disposition of the funds (and) have no reason to believe that the transactions were not as represented by the Company."

The following further assertion, contained in Exhibit 10 relating to the March 4, 1973, meeting, is devastating:

> Notes prepared for the meeting by Findley state that, with respect to the Japanese currency payments "(t)hese are material amounts of money and subject the Company to . . . incalculable consequences with respect to the L-1011 program." Such notes also make reference to $200,000 being given to another consultant and $400,000 in currency being disbursed by

Clutter to unknown parties. In addition, reference is made to the need to obtain a final accounting for a disbursement of $100,000. While Findley recalled reading his notes to the audit committee, the others present stated they did not specifically recall these statements.

The Auditors Make Everything "Crystal Clear"

What about the "incalculable consequences" with respect to the L-1011 program? This is explained away by a footnote reference:

> Concerning the potential "incalculable consequences with respect to the L-1011 program," Findley subsequently stated that this concern was adequately covered by Arthur Young's qualification of their opinion with respect to Lockheed's financial statements as to the ultimate realization of the Company's investment in the L-1011 program. They did, however, have the Company add language to a footnote to the financial statements, which described the status of the program, to indicate that orders on hand could be canceled.

So Mr. Findley said he blew the whistle with the rhetoric in the 1972 auditor's certificate and relevant footnote. I had read the 1972 footnote most carefully years ago and it never dawned on me that lurking in there was even a veiled reference to Arthur Young's anxious soul-searching regarding its client's nefarious sales practices.

But Mr. Findley said that his early 1973 discoveries were reflected in his firm's certificate as Lockheed's independent auditors. This caused me to exhume Arthur Young's opinion on its 1972 as well as 1971 Lockheed audits. I maintain that excepting for the dates there is no change in the verbiage for the two years; as a consequence that certificate carries no new forebodings prompted by the early 1973 discoveries attendant on the 1972 audit.

But then there is the footnote to which Mr. Findley referred—the one which, he said, he made the company revise to include the special contingencies resulting from his discovery regarding the payments to Lockheed's "constituents." I have carefully reviewed the lengthy footnote 4 to the company's 1972 report; that footnote referred to the L-1011 inventories. It provided some description of the composition of the inventories, and some facts regarding the Rolls Royce bankruptcy and the implications for the program. The only reference to a cancellation contingency is included in the concluding paragraph of that footnote and reads, ". . . Recovery of the TriStar inventory is dependent on the number of aircraft ultimately sold (orders on hand, plus additional orders, less cancellations, if any), and the actual costs and selling prices. . . ."

Once again I put the challenge directly to Mr. Findley and his partners at Arthur Young; precisely where in the subject footnote is there even a soupçon of the anxiety which you manifested during the course of your meetings in New York and Los Angeles at the time when you were "putting the 1972 audit report to bed"? I also challenge Arthur Andersen and Co. and Shearman and Sterling, as the special accountants and counsel to the Special Review Committee, to inform us regarding their independent investigative procedures and practices in the fulfill- ment of the responsibilities vested in them. Were they so willing to be flim-flammed that they determined to accept all statements at face value apparently without even a modicum of probing?

This leads to the general question as to why this special committee did not obtain subpoena power and the right to interrogate under oath (or if it had such powers, why it did not exercise them). The committee's charge was not to act as Lockheed's advocate—but to proceed with maximum diligence in behalf of the country, since Lockheed is a key member of the military-industrial establishment.

Because I found these questions vexing, I wrote to Arthur Andersen and Co. to put the question to them; its managing partner responded, first, that the partner who handled the Lockheed engagement had retired and, second, my inquiry ought better to be directed to the corporation.

I followed Arthur Andersen's counsel and did receive a reply dated October 2, 1979:

> As I am sure you are aware, the Committee's report has been thoroughly reviewed by the appropriate government and private authorities and consider- able time and effort has been devoted by the management and the Board of Directors to consideration of the report. We therefore do not feel it appro- priate to respond to the matters raised in your letters.

Compounding my sense of outrage at this performance is my aware- ness that at the time the Arthur Young managing partner, R. E. Kent, was agonizing over the payments problem, he was sitting at the head of the Financial Accounting Foundation, thereby identifying those in our midst whose standards were of such high quality that they should be put at the apex of the profession insofar as its precepts and practices are concerned.

Criminal Proceedings Against Lockheed

Lockheed's activities received the attention of the Fraud Section of the Department of Justice. In the post-Watergate era of born-again vir- tue, they filed an "Information" on June 1, 1979, accusing Lockheed of felonious activity in ten separate counts. The essential facts alleged by the United States Attorney were:

Lockheed entered into contracts with All-Nippon Airlines (ANA) of Japan for 21 L-1011s. The purchase price of the 11th through 21st such aircraft was financed by loans (or guarantees) by the Export-Import Bank.

During the years 1974–75 Lockheed devised a "scheme and artifice to defraud . . . Ex-Im. . . ." This scheme involved the concealment and disguise on Lockheed's books and records that it had agreed to pay . . . in connection with the sale of 21 L-1011 aircraft to ANA: (a) approximately $1.8 million to the office of Prime Minister Tanaka of Japan; (b) $50,000 for each of the first L-1011s to the officials of ANA; and (c) $100,000 to six Japanese political officials.

Paragraph 6 of the Information read as follows:

6. It was further part of the scheme that the defendant would conceal and disguise and caused to be concealed and disguised from Arthur Young & Co., its independent certified public accountants, that it had made and agreed to make the payments referred to in paragraph five above by the following practices:

(A) Lockheed would direct and cause false entries to be made on its books and records and the books and records of its affiliates and subsidiaries which did not reflect the true nature, purpose, and description of the aforementioned payments and intended recipients of monies.

(B) Lockheed would and did cause the execution of a back-dated consultant agreement with ID Corporation, a Cayman Island company, in order to provide documentation in its books and records of the aforementioned payments.

(C) Lockheed would and did cause the obtaining of false receipts from ID Corporation in order to provide documentation for the aforementioned payments indicating that ID Corporation received monies from Lockheed when in truth and in fact the monies had not been disbursed or agreed to be disbursed to ID Corporation.

(D) Lockheed would and did cause the use of an off-the-books Swiss bank account containing monies which were not recorded as assets on the books and records of Lockheed, its affiliates, and subsidiaries, and which account was intended to be used for paying the principal of ID Corporation for the issuance of the false and fraudulent receipts.

The fraud perpetrated against the Export-Import Bank involved Lockheed's representation to the bank that Lockheed "had not granted or paid . . . any discount, allowance, rebate, commission, fee, or other payment in connection with the sale. . . ."

What was the punishment for the crimes alleged by the Department of Justice? Did the perpetrators go to jail? Not so! Instead, pursuant to the bargained arrangement, Lockheed agreed to pay about $600,000 in fines, and thence justice was done! Once again, street crime will get you into jail; executive suite crime will get you into the social register!

Look again at paragraph 6, where Arthur Young & Co. is described as an innocent victim of its client's nefarious machinations. Maybe the firm did not know that the documents involved in the particular transactions were contaminated. But were they not aware that insofar as Lockheed's L-1011 program was concerned, they were caught in a mare's nest, so that as *independent* auditors, committed to the public interest, they should have been especially alert in the audit of all commission payments? Their experiences in 1972 and 1973 should have alerted them, and they should have prevented this monstrous fraud perpetrated on the Export-Import Bank, and the nation.

The firm knew what should have been done as far back as 1973, I maintain. As the Special Review Committee Report pointed out, when the lid blew off foreign corrupt practices during testimony by Northrop Corporation before a Senate committee:

> . . . Arthur Young requested that Kotchian, D. O. Wood, president of Lockheed California, J. H. Martin, chief counsel, and L. T. Barrow, vice president-international finance, sign a letter which, among other things, stated that to the best of their knowledge and belief:
>
> > All payments (by the Company to consultants or agents) are made in accordance with (written) agreements and are duly recorded on the books of Lockheed. . . .
> >
> > No employee or official of any foreign government, or any director, officer, or employee of a customer is a party to any of the (consulting or commission) agreements.
> >
> > No director, officer, agent, or managerial employee of Lockheed or an affected subsidiary has knowledge of the disposition of the payments made to the consultants.
>
> On June 11, 1975, Arthur Young was notified that these officers would not sign the letter. Haughton told the Committee he would not allow them to sign it. This refusal led to the joint investigation of commissions and questionable payments by the Company and Arthur Young, and to the disclosures to the board of directors on June 23 and July 7, 1975.

Northrop Flies High

For the Northrop Corporation saga it might be best to begin with the statement with which Senator Frank Church opened the June 9,

1975, hearings of his committee; after alluding to a volume of documents in the committee's possession, he continued:

The message contained in the 530 pages of documents pertaining to the Northrop Corporation released by the subcommittee on Friday can be summed up in a single phrase. Frank DeFrancis, one of Northrop's consultants, said it: "I don't know a damn thing about an airplane except the nose and the tail." But DeFrancis knew the "right" people and that is really what the Northrop case is all about: How to get the "right people" in foreign governments to make the "right" decisions about which airplane to purchase. The propriety with which this was to be done seems not to matter.

The documents lay out in excruciating detail a sordid tale of bribery, and of shadowy figures operating behind the scenes whose activities are vaguely alluded to but never explicitly stated; in short, a cast of characters out of a novel of international intrigue.

However, here we are not dealing with fiction but with real life; deliberate deception, . . . The documents show payments made by Northrop to agents and business partners in a way that would permit the company to disclaim knowledge or responsibility for the uses to which it was put. They relate the formation of foreign corporations funded by Northrop designed to insulate from public view individuals working "behind the scenes" for Northrop but who did not wish to be known to be associated with the company. We are shown military officers of the highest rank and members of parliament of foreign governments on the Northrop payroll as "consultants" under arrangements which permitted them to keep their Northrop connection concealed.

We are told that as a result of the activities of one such consultant, Northrop has had an unusual visibility in the highest councils of NATO, the Common Market community, and the many official and unofficial discussions between the highest officials in Europe as they affect the sale of Northrop aircraft.

A way of life, a necessary evil, is the phrase used again and again by Northrop executives to describe this use of secret agents to promote the sales of arms to foreign governments. But that is precisely the issue. Is this pattern of behavior an acceptable way of life?

As the *Wall Street Journal* put it: "At the very least, the head office ought to know what is going on in its foreign branches. The most immoral position of all is to perform, and we don't want to know how."

The vehicle created by Northrop to fulfill its illicit objectives was the Economic and Development Corporation (EDC), a Swiss corporation established in early 1971. According to the documents disclosed by the Senate committee:

One of the underlying factors and conditions that was a prerequisite in the organization of the Economic and Development Corporation was that it remain a separate and independent organization. As a consequence, the methods and utilization of personnel on behalf of the corporation are so structured that it is able to advance the cause of Northrop in the sale of the International Fighter not only on the basis of confidentiality, but also uniquely independent of any Northrop connection. This principle provides a wide degree of flexibility in procuring the best people for the particular assignment at hand and, in many instances, enables the securing of persons who otherwise could not be directly involved for variant reasons with Northrop as such.

Frank J. DeFrancis, to whom Senator Church referred, was the key figure in making EDC operational. The *modus operandi* to achieve the desired "deniability" was the subject of the following dialogue between the Senator and Thomas Jones, Northrop's chief executive:

Senator Church: In other words, the actual agents who were hired to promote the sale of the F-5 aircraft were to be hired by this corporation. You would not even know who they were, would you, necessarily?

Mr. Jones: Right. And that was a great weakness. At the time we set this up you have to remember the situation. I was expecting a relatively low number of sales of the F-5 extension. I was not expecting it to be a big thing. This was a mechanism that would allow us to pay individuals of high quality that would represent our interest.

In any new structure we have I will insist that ahead of any activity in any country we approve of the individuals.

I counted on Mr. DeFrancis' judgment in this case.

Senator Church: Well, the document suggests that you knew just what you were doing, and I would think with a commitment on the part of the company to pay such a large potential fee to this corporation, that you understood fully the arrangement and why you were entering into it.

For instance, on page 231 of the documents you state in a letter to Crim, EDC is so structured that, and I quote, "It is able to advance the cause of Northrop in the sale of the International Fighter, not only on the basis of confidentiality but also uniquely independent of any Northrop connection. This principle provides a wide degree of flexibility in procuring the best people for the particular assignment at hand and, in many instances, enables the securing of persons who otherwise could not be directly involved for variant reasons with Northrop as such."

Now, did you not design this arrangement to provide an opportunity for Northrop to indirectly employ either government officials, or highly placed private citizens of foreign governments who would be in position to influence the decision of their respective governments?

Mr. Jones: Certainly not government officials in the sense of someone in a procurement process or bribery or anything of that nature. It was to be able to have the services of individuals who liked to remain independent. . . .

*   *   *

Senator Case: And so it was incorporated under Swiss laws?

Mr. Jones: Yes sir.

Senator Case: And shares of stock were held by whom?

Mr. Jones: I can not give you the precise—

Senator Case: What was your general understanding? How many shares were issued?

Mr. Jones: I do not know.

Senator Case: Was it just a dummy? Was it just an entity created for various purposes of the kind that you have been talking about to the chairman?

Mr. Jones: In a sense it was, as I understand it to be, an office through which the contract could be held and the services would then be performed by individuals who would either be consultants to this organization, they could be owners—.

Further questioning made clear that EDC was a dummy corporation— organized with but a nominal capitalization, with shares owned by persons not known to Northrop's hierarchy. They also cared little about who the directors were of that Northrop subsidiary.

After a thousand pages of Senate hearings, the details of Northrop's debasement and its prostitution of civilian and military officials around the globe are laid bare.

Crimes and Punishments

Chief Executive Jones was convicted of felonies in connection with his handling of Northrop's slush funds and submitting falsified documents to federal officials. He was severely punished by the law: a fine of $5,000. His punishment by the shareholders of his corporation and the financial community was even more ludicrous. According to Northrop's proxy materials, Jones's 1974 salary (i.e., before the Senate disclosures) was $286,000; thereafter he was compelled to accept the following amounts:

1975	$354,000
1976	438,333
1977	620,349
1978	790,777*

* Excludes "securities or property, insurance benefits or reimbursement, personal benefits." First disclosed for 1978 in the amount of $598,830.

These then are the wages of sin in this era of born-again morality.

The ITT Horror Stories

We turn next to another horror story—this one involving International Telephone and Telegraph Corporation. In Chapter 3 we saw the way in which, in October, 1977, ITT and its financial mentor, Lazard Freres, negotiated a remarkable deal to terminate the SEC's probe of the Byzantine deception of the Internal Revenue Service, incident to the takeover of the Hartford Insurance Company in 1970.

The SEC initiated a Rule 2(e) inquiry into the actions by ITT and Lazard Freres, but simultaneously terminated proceedings. However, the Commission was given permission to expose the tortured web woven by the respondents; further, ITT agreed to make known to interested persons the existence of this SEC release and Lazard Freres agreed to tighten up its internal control procedures so that it would recognize more effectively who pays them for what—thereby permitting the financial conglomerate to avoid conflicts of interest.

But that *entente cordiale* did not end ITT's problems with the Securities and Exchange Commission. In 1978 the SEC initiated a civil action in the U.S. District Court for the District of Columbia (File No. 78–0807) describing in some detail ITT's perfidious conduct around the globe. Included in the court filings were allegations by the SEC which should make an ordinary defendant blush. Strewn through the complaint we find such phrases as:

> ITT . . . has employed and is employing devices, schemes, and artifices to defraud, has obtained money and property by means of untrue statements of material fact. . . .
>
> ITT has made illegal, improper, corrupt, and questionable payments aggregating many millions of dollars to foreign governmental officials and employees of nongovernmental commercial customers of ITT. . . . Among the numerous countries in which the aforesaid payments were made are Indonesia, Iran, the Philippines, Algeria, Nigeria, Mexico, Italy, Turkey, and Chile. . . .

ITT facilitated the making of certain of the aforesaid payments by arranging for such payments to be made through the use of numbered bank accounts in countries other than those in which the contract or transaction related to such payments was entered into or performed.

False and fictitious entries were made on the books of ITT and its subsidiaries and affiliates.

ITT made payments of at least $400,000 to certain bank accounts controlled by Chilean political interests that were opposed to Salvador Allende's presidency. The payments were made on the instructions of senior officials at ITT world headquarters in New York.

Italian subsidiaries of ITT made improper payments totaling more than $385,000 between 1971 and 1975 in connection with negotiations for settlement of taxes levied on the ITT subsidiaries. The payments were made from "unofficial" funds, which were not recorded in the official financial books and records of the subsidiaries. Such unofficial funds were generated through the use of fictitious invoices from purported suppliers of the ITT subsidiaries.

Were ITT's Lawyers *In Pari Delicto?*

There was another aspect to this SEC complaint which warrants consideration. In December, 1975, after the SEC had become aware of certain ITT practices regarding questionable payments, ITT's board of directors designated a special review panel to investigate. The investigation was to be conducted jointly by the office of the ITT general counsel and by independent counsel to the board of directors. These investigators did not review documents but instead relied on interviews with ITT executives at various levels during the following months. Upon completion of the investigation, no specific details concerning questionable payments were disclosed to the board of directors or its legal affairs committee.

In March, 1976, ITT issued a "Special Report" purporting to disclose the results of its internal investigation; it stated that during the period from 1971 through 1975, payments "aggregating approximately $3.8 million were made to assist in developing or improving business opportunities and relationships in those countries." According to the SEC, this report, which was included as part of ITT's annual report to shareholders for the year 1975, was false because, "in fact, questionable payments in a substantially greater amount had been made by ITT." Subsequently, in July, 1977, ITT reported that the questionable payments involved $8.7 million, not $3.8 million, as previously reported.

In the course of its findings the Securities and Exchange Commission made passing reference to the apparent failure on the part of ITT's general counsel as well as independent counsel in the conduct of their special investigation. Here I put the same challenge to the lawyers on the SEC staff that I have put to my colleagues in the accounting profession, "Have you or will you be forwarding the file in this matter to the appropriate disciplinary committees of the bar associations for their inquiry into the competence and diligence of the lawyers who pursued this special investigation?"

By now you must know what the consequences were for all this naughtiness. Of course, it was a consent decree whereby ITT neither admitted nor denied the allegations, tra la, tra la, tra la.

Oh yes, ITT will create another investigative committee and presumably, ITT will be enjoined from violating the laws of our nation—otherwise the Geneen machine rolls along unobstructed and uninhibited.

But I have another complaint—one which the SEC did not raise. ITT's independent auditor, which failed to blow the whistle, was and is Arthur Andersen and Co. Arthur Andersen and Co. turned up as the white-knight accounting consultant to Lockheed's Special Review Committee probing the grease in that entity. You might remember that in my discourse on that sad saga I inquired as to why Arthur Andersen did not probe more diligently the rationalizations by Lockheed's auditor (Arthur Young & Co.) regarding that auditor's failure to decry misdeeds. Is it not likely that Arthur Andersen was mindful of Scripture which enjoins, "Let him who is without sin blow the first whistle"?

Neither Arthur had a vision of Excalibur! I maintain that the SEC should refuse to allow special reviews pursuant to an accord with the Commission or a court (pursuant to an SEC action) to be undertaken by an accounting firm identified with any similar action (concluded or pending) before the Commission.

The FCPA Enactment

To put an end to these "grease" practices, the Congress enacted the Foreign Corrupt Practices Act of 1977 (FCPA). This legislation was designed to prohibit what President Carter called "ethically repugnant and competitively unnecessary" conduct. Along with prohibiting companies from engaging in certain corrupt practices with respect to foreign officials, the act amends Section 13(b) of the Securities Exchange Act of 1934 to require reporting companies to make and keep accurate books and records and to establish and maintain a system of internal accounting controls which meet certain objectives.

Corrupting the FCPA

Surely, this legislation should have given rise to a hosanna from my colleagues in practice; the Congress had given legislative approval to our auditing standards pertaining to internal control. Our corporate clients were told that henceforth their endeavors to mislead us might lead to criminal indictments and even convictions. This was something which many of my colleagues were urging in the wake of Corporate Watergate. How did the accounting profession respond to this new congressional mandate?

Sadly, this new cloak of authority and legitimacy for our profession was too heavy for our shoulders. In any event, my colleagues determined to join with corporate managements in resisting the endeavors by the Securities and Exchange Commission to implement the legislation.

An obituary for the brave new world created by the FCPA appeared in the January 19, 1980, *Economist:* "SEC-Softer Yet: A staged retreat by the Securities and Exchange Commission threatens to become a rout as it thinks again about how to interpret the accounting provisions of anti-bribery laws."

The reason for this lament was the negative response from the business community (and their stalwart professional representatives) to the April, 1979, SEC proposals to give effect to the accountancy provisions of the 1977 enactment. Even these proposed regulations were watered down. All that was to be required was: First, that the books, records, and accounts accurately and fairly reflect, in reasonable detail, the transactions and disposition of assets, and, second, that companies must devise and maintain a system of internal controls.

The SEC then, in line with what it saw as Congress's intent, also proposed that, after December 14, 1979, annual reports should contain a statement from management saying the internal controls provided "reasonable assurance" of achieving their objectives, and a year later should contain an auditor's certified opinion on this management statement.

Those familiar with the history of the legislation might recall that when, in 1976, the FCPA was going through the congressional mill, the then SEC Chairman Roderick Hills stated flatly: "upon passage of this legislation we would, of course, impose a requirement upon outside auditors that they certify the adequacy of such (internal) controls."

This promise notwithstanding, in November 1979, the SEC, now under President Carter's Chairman Williams, withdrew the proposed implementation rules for further deliberations. This abdication of responsibility by the SEC (permitting a corresponding abdication by my colleagues in the accounting profession) has not induced distress among my colleagues.

The FCPA: "RIP"

If the foregoing was the obituary for the SEC's endeavors to implement the congressional mandate insofar as the internal control provisions of the FCPA were concerned, its requiem was "sung" in a June 6, 1980, "Statement of Management and Internal Accounting Control: Withdrawal of Proposed Rules."

According to this promulgation, the SEC's decision to abort the proposed certification requirements was motivated, in part, by its "determination that the private sector initiatives . . . have been significant and should be allowed to continue."

The Commission will be studying the progress of these "private initiatives" over a three-year period, and then will give further consideration to any required rule making.

Spring, 1980, most certainly afforded the Commission a solid basis for hoping that the private sector will, in fact, proceed to develop the initiatives for effective disciplining of the internal control system, at all levels of the corporate structure, and that the independent attesting auditors would proceed diligently to point up and act with intrepidity to weed out any misuses and abuses of corporate resources—even if such misuse and abuse should occur at the highest levels of their clients' organization.

After all, did not the spring of that year produce the miracles wrought by Genuine Risk and Temperence Hill?

11

Disorder in the Courts

The matter of *U.S. v. IBM,* regardless of its ultimate outcome, is destined to make history in the annals of jurisprudence; this antitrust action has been in progress longer than any other case of any kind in any forum. As of spring, 1980, for example, there were more than 100,000 pages of actual courtroom testimony—not including the huge volume of exhibits and papers generated during depositions and pretrial proceedings. In total the pagination must run into the millions.

Destiny has thrust me into the vortex of these proceedings as an expert witness in behalf of the defendant, International Business Machines Corporation. Casting my characteristic modesty aside, it is likely that I was the only person in the universe capable of serving as such witness in a very special context. That this is not a mere conceit can be readily demonstrated.

The Department of Justice (DJ), in its complaint against IBM, asserted that the company's marketing, pricing, and manufacturing practices had impacted adversely on two groups of competitors—computer leasing firms and peripheral equipment manufacturers. IBM countered by asserting that these two groups of entities suffered not because of IBM's practices but because Briloff wrote critically about their accounting practices—computer lessors in 1968, and peripheral equipment manufacturers in 1970.

Throughout days of deposition followed by weeks of testimony in the courthouse, I was called upon to explain in detail how I came to write about Leasco, Levin Townsend, *et al.,* in the first group (in "All a Fandangle") and Telex Corporation in the latter group ("Tomorrow's Profits").

Lease Accounting Shenanigans

My principal jibe at the computer lessors' accountings was that it was childs' play for them to show enormous profits—rental revenues were concentrated in the early years of the equipment rentals, while the principal cost, i.e., the depreciation, was being spread equally over a decade or longer. This patent mismatching, I said, was destined to produce a sorry end for the company's accountings—sooner, rather than later, they would be subjected to what is euphemistically referred to as "big bath accounting," that is, washing dirty accounting off the books. This would come to pass when the undepreciated costs shown by the books would appear absurdly high in relation to the then potential stream of rental revenues which might still be anticipated.

As to the peripheral equipment manufacturers (PEMs), the point I made in my condemnation of Telex was that the corporation was abusing the standards of accounting for "manufacturer-lessors," those who manufacture a product and then put it out on lease rather than selling it. Under the prevailing logical field rules, assume that a manufacturer produced a widget which cost $100 to produce and carried a $175 list price. Instead of selling it, the PEM leased it to, say, General Motors Corporation for a guaranteed period of five years at a rental of $35 annually (after which time GM could buy the widget for $1 or less), and assume that there were no gimmicks in the lease, the accounting field rules have permitted the PEM to book this transaction as the equivalent of a sale, even though it is a lease.

If this were the case, the PEM would book sales revenues of $175, offset it by the $100 cost, and $75 would drift down to the bottom line. Clearly, given these circumstances, economic reality (ignoring for this purpose the fact that there might be a "time value" applied to the deferral of the payment over a five-year period) would dictate that the $75 was as good as earned when the lease agreement with GM was entered into.

Now, then, what happened? At first the PEM had a five-year, full-payout lease contract. But then, the lease period shrank precipitiously. Meanwhile, there were all kinds of strings associated with the lease.

Another wrinkle in the manufacturer-lessor accounting ploy allowed the PEM to sell the equipment that was subject to the short-term lease to a financial institution. Presumably the sales transaction should permit the manufacturer to book the transaction as a sale—even if such booking on the lease per se might be challenged.

But here you must be made aware of the fact that the putative sales agreement typically carried so many strings, including requirements that the PEM remain involved in the marketing, servicing, and re-leasing of the equipment, and that the economic risks remained with the manufacturer.

Consequently, the sales contract notwithstanding, the accountant's commitment to substance over form (where the two diverge) should have dictated that the transaction with the financial institution "purchaser" be booked for what it really was—a financing arrangement.

Had they not perpetrated the charade, the reported profit would have been far less felicitous—the company would have been constrained to limit its reported revenues to the $35 rental, offset by depreciation of $20 (the $100 cost spread equally over five years for this purpose)— hence, a net of but $15 instead of $75.

To make matters worse, since these companies were assigned price/ earnings multiples as high as 100 by Wall Street, any earnings drop would have been devastating—even if Wall Street kept the stratospheric ratios. But as we should know, when the emperor's true state becomes discernible, not only do his clothes disappear but even worse, the public's perception changes drastically.

That is how my "Tomorrow's Profits" piece served to unclothe Telex (and as a consequence the raiment of other PEMs came under closer scrutiny).

It was IBM's assertion that the ripple effect produced by my writings induced a deterioration in the share prices of the companies—and that in turn triggered reductions in the financial resources made available to them by investors, banks, underwriters, and others in the financial community. Further, since the potential for booming stock prices was an important bait in executive recruitment (e.g., through stock option and stock bonus plans), the ability to lure such talent was also adversely affected.

It was to testify to all this—how and why I wrote, how I believed and believe in what I wrote, how my "prophecies" came to pass, or at least came home to roost—that I was called upon to be the witness for the defense.

To counter the position advanced by IBM, the government sought to discredit my testimony on two fronts. First, they alleged, there was no absolute proof of the causal connection between my writings and the dire consequences which ensued. If one were to assume an "efficient market," one which is omniscient and ubiquitous, there was nothing about my condemnations which might not have already been known by the wise men who set prices and values for company shares. This argument must be left for response or refutation by empirical evidence and by testimony of those who did, in fact, factor in my writings in their evaluations—if for no other reason than because they realized the shell game to which they may have been privy would soon end.

What was shocking to me was the intensive and expensive endeavors on the part of the lawyers for the Department of Justice to discredit my testimony on the basis that:

1. Whatever merit my writings might have, I endeavor to write with a commitment to "fairness"—hence, a standard which may vary at times from the prevailing norms.
2. In any event, the practices of the companies subjected to my attack were entirely correct, proper, true, and just at the time—so that my condemnation was unwarranted.

The Department of Justice's Distaste for Fairness in Accounting

To prove its "fairness" point, the Department of Justice lawyers confronted me with the *Business Week* book review and the Cohen Commission criticisms of me alluded to in the initial chapter of this book.

I might understand this obloquy if it emanated from the pragmatic practitioners of accountancy, or even from my colleagues in academe who act as apologists for the practitioners. But the same Department of Justice pressed the same fairness precept in obtaining criminal convictions of accountants in the Continental Vending and National Student Marketing fiascoes. Their attack on my commitment to fairness is obscene—and even worse.

But it is the government's endeavor (in the case against IBM) to justify the accounting practices of the computer lessors and peripheral equipment manufacturers which I found woefully incongruous. Not only have events of the intervening years demonstrated beyond question that the PEM accounting practices were fakes, but it is these very practices which the government, acting through its Securities and Exchange Commission, moved to exorcise immediately following my 1970 writing (not necessarily because of that writing).

The Department of Justice lawyers took up the cudgels in behalf of the Memorex Corporation, a high-flying PEM of the late 1960s and early 1970. Why the government determined to do so is not clear, except that it was possibly getting encouragement and important assistance in the development of its case from Lawrence Spitters, head of Memorex during the years when it was moving up.

What did Memorex do that the SEC found so abhorrent as to cause it to file a complaint against the company (as well as Spitters and Gordon E. Pilcher, another Memorex executive) in 1971? A judicial proceeding terminated by a consent decree followed. Prior to 1970, Memorex was primarily engaged in the manufacture and sale of magnetic tapes, disc packs, and television recording tapes. It also manufactured certain computer peripheral equipment, mainly disc drive products, which it had been selling to computer manufacturers who, in turn, marketed this equipment along with their own computers under their own name.

Memorex's Sales to Independent (Sic!) Leasing Corporation

In early 1970 Memorex began leasing computer peripheral equipment directly to end-users. For this purpose Memorex required a substantial amount of new financing. In late June, 1970, Memorex incorporated Independent Leasing Corporation (ILC) to serve as a vehicle through which Memorex would borrow the substantial funds needed for its leasing business. This borrowing was to be achieved by having major financial institutions lend money to or purchase the securities of ILC. ILC would turn the funds over to Memorex in return for the ostensible transfer of title to ILC of computer peripheral equipment that Memorex had leased to end-users. Memorex accounted for that transfer as a sale and recognized current income from the sale to ILC. This income could not properly be recognized as an incident to the lease of the equipment to end-users.

In soliciting such funds, Memorex represented to prospective lenders to ILC and purchasers of ILC securities that although the arrangement was to take the form of providing capital to ILC, in reality the participating institutions would be extending credit to Memorex. This arrangement was for the financial reporting purposes of Memorex. The terms of the agreements would make the loans to and investments in ILC the obligations of Memorex. The agreements that were effected among Memorex, ILC, and the lenders and other investors were designed to achieve these objectives.

Prior to December 29, 1970, ILC had no funds other than those provided directly and indirectly by Memorex. Memorex's efforts to obtain financing culminated on December 29, 1970, with the execution of a network of agreements setting forth the terms under which funds were furnished to Memorex through ILC. These agreements provided, among other things:

1. Most of the funds which were to be furnished by the financial institutions would be in the form of loans to ILC. A substantially lesser

amount of funds was to be in the form of purchases of stock of ILC.

2. The bulk of the equity investment in ILC was to be made by Memorex and Memorex was also required to furnish additional funds in the form of subordinated loans.

3. Memorex, under the terms of the agreements, was required to transfer to ILC computer peripheral equipment subject to leases obtained by Memorex and meeting certain specified terms, and in return Memorex was to receive funds from ILC representing the purported purchase price of such equipment.

4. Memorex had a contingent obligation to furnish additional subordinated capital pursuant to a formula designed to assure the financial institutions of repayment of their loans to and investments in ILC.

5. Memorex had an option to acquire all the ILC stock in return for a specified amount of cash and warrants to purchase Memorex stock, and the financial institutions owning ILC stock had options to exchange their ILC stock for Memorex stock at a specified rate of exchange.

6. Memorex was required to maintain and service the equipment transferred to ILC, and in the event that such equipment went off-lease, Memorex was required to use its best efforts to re-lease the equipment, giving the re-leasing of such equipment preference over the leasing of any of its other equipment.

Consequently, in the final days of 1970, various financial institutions loaned money to or purchased stock in ILC. Prior to that date Memorex had effected transfers of leased equipment to ILC and had reported those transfers as sales and recognized and reported current income from those transactions in various accounting periods.

According to the SEC, "Because of the relationship between ILC and Memorex, it was false and misleading for Memorex to report, in its consolidated financial statements, the transfers of equipment to ILC as sales and to recognize profit from the transactions."

Memorex's Accounting Called to Account

The first overt manifestation of the scheme appears to have been in a November, 1970, letter to shareholders which informed them of a restatement of the earnings previously reported for the nine months ended September 30, 1970. This interim report had disclosed sales of $79 million and net income of $6,126,000.

The interim report included a letter to shareholders which read as follows:

> Shipments of computer peripheral equipment products in the third quarter increased sharply. . . . The nine months' sales include $14,111,000 of computer peripheral equipment products sold to Independent Leasing Corporation, a new corporation organized to purchase peripheral equipment which Memorex manufactures and markets under leases to computer users. Efforts are currently underway to complete the permanent financing of ILC by long-term loan arrangements with commercial banks and other financial institutions and by private sale of a majority interest of its equity to these institutional investors and a minority interest to Memorex. Payment to Memorex for ILC's purchases is dependent upon the success of such efforts and will be made when ILC's financing is completed.

The SEC thought the report was something of a canard because it was based on the improper inclusion of purported sales and profits; in fact, sales and earnings were actually less than they were for the same period in 1969.

It appears that Memorex tried, during 1970, to adopt the accounting gimmickry which Telex had, for a while, gotten away with. But Memorex was found out, and had to recast its nine-month 1970 interim statements.

But even then, as the SEC emphasized, Memorex and Spitters sought to develop a cover story—that by year-end all would be well, so that the ploy would work *nunc pro tunc.* That Mr. Spitters did not know when the "jig was up" is evidenced by yet another allegation in the SEC complaint:

> On March 9, 1971, Spitters, acting on behalf of and as president of Memorex, made a speech before the New York Society of Security Analysts. In his speech, he first referred to a speech made three years earlier before the same body in which he had projected sales of $100 million dollars by 1970 and then stated,
>
> "In 1968, our growth carried from $34 million to $57 million. In 1969 to approximately $75 million in net sales and revenues and in the year just ended, 1970, to approximately $120 million of net sales and revenues. Slightly more than one third of the 1970 $120 million net sales and revenues were sales to the leasing company which Memorex has recently capitalized to finance leases of our computer equipment customers, finance the leases of the computer equipment which we manufacture and market to our users. Thus in 1970, we exceeded by a substantial margin the growth target which

we fixed three years ago. And this accomplishment has given to us not only an immense pride but it's given us encouragement to again set for ourselves ambitious and new growth objectives. I should tell you that I regret very much that we have yet under consideration with our auditors and with the Securities and Exchange Commission the method of accounting for Memorex's profit on these sales during 1970 to the leasing company. . . .''

This 1971 speech, the SEC asserted, was false and misleading in that, among other things:

1. Memorex's net sales and revenues for 1970 were not $120 million, but were no more than approximately $79 million;
2. Memorex had not enjoyed the substantial growth in sales and had not met the sales projections as claimed by Spitters; and
3. He omitted to state:
   (a) that it was improper to recognize any income or profits from the purported sales to ILC;
   (b) Memorex's net income for 1970 had declined substantially as compared to prior years;
   (c) that the staff of the Securities and Exchange Commission had indicated to Memorex that it was the view of the staff that Memorex was required to issue financial statements on a combined basis with ILC so as to exclude the purported sales to ILC and profits therefrom.

This kind of stonewalling was probably deemed essential by Mr. Spitters to maintain Memorex's fading image as a glamour, concept corporation. Remember, even after the emperor's true condition was discerned by the mob, according to Andersen (Hans Christian), "The Emperor writhed, for he knew it was true, but he thought the procession must go on now. So he held himself stiffer than ever and the chamberlains held up the invisible train."

Further, the company's and Spitters' concurrence in a consent decree should lead to the inference that they pleaded *mea culpa*. Once again, Mr. Spitters did not know when to stop—instead, he joined forces with the Department of Justice lawyers in an endeavor to restore his credibility, again, *nunc pro tunc*. Collectively they sought to prove that the Memorex-Spitters 1970 accounting ploy was entirely proper back then and only the fantasizing by Briloff (joined in by the SEC) put the company's efforts in a bad light. This historical reconstruction asserted that Memorex was right in its views based on the state of the accounting art back in 1970, even though it might have been changed since.

DJ's Expert Witness

The government and Spitters found themselves an ally in this expedition. Alan K. McAdams, an associate professor of economics at Cornell University, became the government's accounting guru in the *U.S. v. IBM* litigation. His testimony included the following:

Q. [counsel for the government] On a slightly different subject now, do you recall testimony concerning a change in accounting practices accomplished by Memorex Corporation?

A. [McAdams] Yes, I do.

Q. Briefly, in a brief summary, what do you recall about that?

A. I recall that Memorex had attempted to establish an independent leasing company, whose management control was not in the hands of Memorex, and that the objective of doing so was to create a vehicle which could provide outright purchases of Memorex-produced products in order that Memorex could show accounting profits from transfers of its products into the marketplace, in that instance into the market for disk drives and their associated controllers for attachment to IBM systems and, in addition to those products, other products; that Memorex had negotiated such an arrangement and had created a corporate entity which would permit, under the accounting rules which were then extant as of 1970, Memorex to recognize transfers to the ILC as outright sales, and thus reflect profit from the rapid build-up of Memorex products in the marketplace, which took place when Memorex entered the plug-compatible market in June of 1970.

I recall Mr. Sprouse's letters, and Mr. Sprouse is a gentleman who taught at Stanford when I was visiting at Stanford, and he was the Director of the Executive Program at Stanford when I participated in the Stanford Executive Program—a man I know well. Mr. Sprouse's assessment of the Memorex accounting was that it was proper under then-existing accounting procedures.

There was a controversy that seemed to have its origin in one problem, and that was that Memorex made an (interim) report of its profitability in the third quarter of 1970, prior to the final funding of the ILC, but after the incorporation of the ILC, and with full disclosure that the final funding had not taken place.

Memorex restated that accounting report, indicating what its profitability would be if it accounted for—if the ILC did not exist, and that was a problem that was anticipated if the ILC were not funded.

The ILC was funded before the end of the year, 1970, and it is my understanding of accounting principles that one is required under accounting principles to report (interim) statements, financial statements, on the basis that one anticipates to be using for the year as a whole. The Memorex [interim] report fell within that category.

The funding of the ILC did not clear the controversy. Rather, the controversy seemed to shift then to a different question, and that was a question as to whether it was proper for Memorex to account for its transfers to the ILC as outright sales or whether those should be reported as essentially risk leases.

There was then a requirement for Memorex to report on the latter basis, although accounting principles to that date had confirmed the approach of Memorex. And the fundamental principles did not change for approximately a year; nonetheless, Memorex was required to account in a way different from the then extant principles.

That is my understanding, in rough outline, of the controversies. There were some relationships with stockholders leading to stockholder suits as a result of the SEC problems and so forth.

Q. Thank you.

I find this rewriting of history absurd. Let us remember that in early 1971 Memorex (with Spitters' concurrence) prepared the 1970 accounts so as to exclude the sales to its captive ILC from the income account to the extent such sales were not realized by transactions with lessees or purchasers outside the Memorex-ILC circle.

Arthur Andersen's Refusal to Accommodate Memorex

This is not a case where Memorex's auditors had concurred with the Memorex-Spitters views back in 1970–71 but were bludgeoned into the income-exclusion determination by a misguided SEC. One of my most agreeable moments on the witness stand was to sing praises for Arthur Andersen and Co., Memorex's independent auditors.

It would appear from documents introduced in the *U.S. v. IBM* litigation that Arthur Andersen might have concurred in Memorex's accounting game plan in 1970, prior to the Telex disclosures. But by year end the firm was unalterably opposed to the inclusion of not-really-earned income from the ILC transactions. In a January, 1971, letter to the corporation, its accountants made clear the reasons why:

The agreements between Memorex and ILC and its lenders and investors are complex and involved. In many respects, the independence of ILC as a separate, decision-making operation is evident. At the same time, Memorex is required to invest approximately 70% of the equity in ILC initially, remains obligated under many provisions of the arrangement throughout the initial term of ILC's existence (as covered in the next paragraphs), and finally can be required subsequently to acquire ILC and assume its liabilities as co-obligor. The provisions of the arrangement which obligate Memorex and which we consider significant in arriving at an accounting conclusion are as follows:

1. Commitment to manufacture and market equipment with a total selling price to ILC of $196.9 million by December 31, 1972.
2. The existence of certain obligations should the Master Sales and Maintenance Agreement be terminated.
3. Investment of 70% of the equity for a 10% voting interest. Further investment of $18.5 million in subordinated notes increases Memorex investment to almost 90% of total subordinated debt and capital stock.
4. Possible conversion of subordinated notes into equity of ILC under certain circumstances. . . .
5. Agreement by Memorex to maintain ratio of current assets to current liabilities of at least two to one, and ratio of unsubordinated debt to tangible net worth of not more than 1.25 to one.

*   *   *

10. The option of Memorex to purchase all the Class A and C shares for 300% of the original amounts paid in therefor during the first calendar quarter of 1974. In the event this option is not exercised, the interest rate on the promissory notes is increased from 12% to 17%.
11. The option of the Class A and C shareholders to exchange their shares for Memorex shares, one share for 22.222 shares of Memorex (maximum 80,800 shares), from January, 1973, to December, 1977.

These conditions, requirements, and contingent obligations, in our view, result in a financial interdependence between Memorex and ILC which precludes the immediate recognition of profits on intercompany sales. Sales between unrelated entities normally transfer the economic risks of ownership to the purchaser. It seems clear that the combined economic risks of ownership by Memorex and ILC run to the recovery of all costs, over a period of years, through rentals or sales to third parties. Since the various provisions of the agreements between Memorex and ILC effectively insulate the "Lenders" and the "Investors" from risk (other than the ultimate risk of insolvency of Memorex), we are unable to see that there has really been a transfer of risk from Memorex to ILC. Accordingly, we believe the profits attributable to the sales to ILC should be deferred and taken into income by Memorex over the period during which ILC's costs and expenses (including interest) are recovered from lessees (estimated by Memorex to be approximately 48 months).

Memorex's Search for a Second Opinion

In apparent despair Memorex turned to Ernst & Ernst in the hope of getting a different opinion. That firm, in a January 22, 1971, letter demolished Memorex's hopes; that letter concluded: "In conclusion, I am certainly sympathetic with your problem. However, my answer to your question must necessarily be based upon the anticipated Memorex-ILC relationship which you expect to be as parent and subsidiary in the near future."

The only person that Spitters was able to induce to go along with him was Robert T. Sprouse, then a professor at Stanford University. A couple of years later Professor Sprouse found himself elevated to the august Financial Accounting Standards Board, where he still sits. The only way I can rationalize his concurrence is that he lost sight of our substance over form precept. In any event, Mr. Spitters in early 1971 rejected the Sprouse view and submitted the 1970 Memorex financial statements excluding the unearned portions of the transactions with ILC.

And now some years later Mr. Spitters has persuaded the Department of Justice to restore his credibility and virtue, to make it appear that his 1970 accounting game plan was right and proper and that the SEC had sought to compel his company to adopt an accounting practice which was not then the accepted standard. He induced the United States government to foster internecine battle between the Department of Justice and the Securities and Exchange Commission.

The "Entrepreneurial Subsidiary" Gimmickry

My involvement in the IBM antitrust litigation also made me acutely aware of some other accounting games played by Memorex during its years of boom—games played with the concurrence of its independent auditors. Memorex attracted certain high-level personnel by structuring for them what Mr. Spitters called "entrepreneurial subsidiaries." Briefly stated, these subsidiaries would be formed by Memorex making a nominal contribution of, say, $50,000 to purchase shares representing a 50 percent ownership; the person being hired would make a corresponding investment for an equal number of shares. A collateral agreement would allow Memorex to swap 50,000 shares of its stock for the employee's shares in the entrepreneurial subsidiary. As it turned out, these new subsidiaries operated at close to break-even—that is, their operations were integrated into the Memorex mainstream—so that at the times when Memorex exercised its swap options, these subsidiaries had book values essentially equal to their original capitalization.

Now let us see how this phenomenon had a salutary effect on the Memorex bottom line—thanks to the then-permissible (however questionable) pooling-of-interests practices.

From the various documents in evidence I developed the following tabulation of the spreads between the book values of the entrepreneurial subsidiary shares acquired in the swap and the Memorex shares given in exchange:

Subsidiary Company	Year of Exchange	Number of Memorex Shares	Total Market Value at Time of Issue	Amount Booked by Memorex	Differential (Cost Suppression)
Peripheral Systems	1968	75,000[a]	$5,625,000[a]	$ 50,000[b]	$ 5,575,000
Image Products	1970[a]	73,356[a]	5,960,165[a]		
		30,000[ad]	1,616,250[ad]	174,079[c]	11,015,461
Storage Products	1970[a]	40,000[a]	2,805,000[a]		
		15,000[ad]	808,125[ad]		
					$16,590,461

[a] Source of data: Form S-16, June 11, 1971, pages 1–2
[b] Source of data: 1968 Annual Report, p. 32 (Acquisition of Remaining Interest in Peripheral Systems Corporation)
[c] Source of data: 1970 Annual Report, p. 33 (Acquisition of Minority Interests in Subsidiary Companies)
[d] Represents shares issued subsequent to 1970 on the basis of an "earning-out" arrangement.

What does this table imply? In the 1968 Peripheral Systems swap, $5,625,000 of Memorex stock was given to the employees who invested $50,000 to form that subsidiary. Given the circumstances of the formation and collateral arrangements, I interpret the $5,575,000 spread as representing additional compensation for the employees involved—to pay them for their contribution during the period from the formation of the entrepreneurial subsidiary to the time when the swap for Memorex shares was consummated.

This inference notwithstanding, the books of Memorex would show a zero cost for these services insofar as this transaction is concerned. How come? "Dirty pooling" permitted Memorex to make believe that the acquisition of the employees' half interest in Peripheral Systems cost it only $50,000 rather than the $5,625,000 in stock given up on the exercise of the option. Again, this is because the accountants told

Memorex it could pick up the acquired shares at the book value according to Peripheral Systems books ($50,000) and to disregard Memorex's actual economic cost.

The same invidious comparisions can be made between the actual cost incurred by Memorex to acquire Image Products and Storage Products and those amounts required to be booked by Memorex after applying dirty-pooling practices—leading to the suppression of over $11 million in costs incurred by it. If we were to factor in these suppressed compensation costs into Memorex's 1968 and 1970 income statements, we come up with some devastating consequences:

	1968	1970
Income as reported before deducting the suppressed costs	$4,939,000	$ 3,183,000
Deduct the suppressed cost for employee compensation	5,575,000	11,015,000
Net loss as revised	$ 636,000	$ 7,832,000

Note that the additional employee compensation cost was subtracted from the net after-tax income as reported for the respective years; thus I did not reflect any reduction for any possible tax saving flowing from this added cost layer. This was because the Memorex exchanges for the employees' interests in the entrepreneurial subsidiaries were structured as taxfree exchanges. As a consequence, the acquiring corporation (Memorex) does not get a stepped-up tax basis by reference to the value of its shares given up on the swap. (This was, undoubtedly, part of the deal with the employees—only by reason of this taxfree structure could they harvest the enormous amounts of compensatory income as a capital gain. The euphemism "entrepreneurial subsidiaries" was truly inspired. The question remains as to exactly who were the entrepreneurs in this context.)

And so Memorex succeeded, by using dirty pooling, to get away with a $16 million cost suppression. I would have been disposed to let bygones be bygones, except that the Department of Justice, majestically representing the government, determined to justify Memorex's accountings as the model of chastity.

The DJ Found a Dirty Pool in IBM

To discredit my condemnation of the Memorex practices in this regard, the Department of Justice lawyers, presumably using all the investigative and intelligence facilities at their command, dug up the fact that

IBM itself had used dirty pooling in 1964 when it issued about $69 million of its shares for the stock of Science Research Associates, Inc. (SRA). The pooling-of-interests mystique allowed them to book the cost at but $6 million—suppressing $63 million of that cost. Without in any way justifying this pooling ploy, I explained that had IBM rejected pooling and followed the purchase-accounting alternative, the $63 million would have been charged to an asset account entitled "excess of cost of acquired subsidiaries over the book value thereof at the time of acquisition" (a long-winded synonym for goodwill). That $63 million could then have been kept on IBM's books in perpetuity—or written off in some year or years when the company determined the goodwill was no longer that good.

But then, proceeding on the assumption that IBM did book the $63 million and determined to spread it over a decade (an extraordinarily brief period even by present standards), the impact on its reported year-to-year earnings over the decade 1964–73 would have been one percent or less. While IBM's accounting for SRA was dirty pooling, I said, the accounting followed by Memorex was the "dirtiest" pooling.

Memorex's creative accounting game plan called for the use not only of dirty pooling and front-end loading of income (aborted during gestation, thanks to the intrepidity of its auditor); it also involved the rear-end loading of enormous bundles of research and development costs, as well as of marketing and lease-acquisition costs. These deferrals, all contributing to Memorex's euphoric earnings during the years when it was racing for its apogee, were washed out in the year of its big bath in 1973. I do not quarrel with the appropriate deferral of costs to permit their matching with the revenues reasonably expected, but the magnitude of Memorex's deferrals (especially when related to its revenues, income, and shareholders' equity) raised serious questions. The questions were not effectively answered by the circumstances of the ultimate write-offs. I would not resurrect these questions a decade later were it not for the fact that the Department of Justice sought to interpose its (and Spitters' and McAdams's) views of proper accounting practices against the Securities and Exchange Commission.

The moral of this Memorex accounting controversy is clear. It stands for a reaffirmation, if one were needed, of what the Accounting Principles Board had postulated as a basic feature of financial statements. In its Statement No. 4, Feature 12, it stated:

> *Substance over form.* Financial accounting emphasizes the economic substance of events even though the legal form may differ from the economic substance and suggest different treatment.

*   *   *

Usually the economic substance of events to be accounted for agrees with the legal form. Sometimes, however, substance and form differ. Accountants emphasize the substance of events rather than their form so that the information provided better reflects the economic activities represented.

Given this traditional wisdom, it is incredible that Memorex's management indulged itself in the notion that the ILC ploy qualified as a completed transaction—in substance as contrasted with form.

While the foregoing is incredible, I find the following absolutely shocking.

An Incredible SOP from the AICPA

Eight years after the Memorex unfrocking, the prestigious Accounting Standards Executive Committee (AcSEC) of the American Institute of Certified Public Accountants issued an awesome-sounding Statement of Position (SOP) designated as 78–8, entitled "Accounting for Product Financing Arrangements."

This SOP (dated December 26, 1978) was prefaced by a letter to the Chairman of the Financial Accounting Standards Board advising him that the AcSEC had labored long and hard over a difficult accounting dilemma and had determined that a new (sic!) standard needed to be released.

What was this awkward dilemma which had confronted the philosophers in the Institute's hierarchy? According to the initial paragraphs of the SOP:

> A number of methods have been developed whereby an entity finances inventory of product or materials without reporting in its balance sheet the liability or the related inventory. For example, a company transfers ("sells") a product to another party and in a related transaction agrees to repurchase the product or processed goods of which the product is a component at a specified price over a specified period. The other party ("transferee" or "purchaser"), using the product and at times the financing arrangement as collateral, may borrow against the value of the product from a lending institution or other credit grantor and remit the proceeds to the company as payment for the product. As the terms of the financing arrangement are fulfilled by the company making the original transfer ("sale"), the transferee ("purchaser") reduces its borrowing from the financial institution.

It seems the hanky-panky which had been exorcised at Memorex eight years previously was being perpetrated in other instances—and under the noses of the independent auditors.

If any SOP called for "trash canning" (see pages 69–70), this was it. Most certainly the condition described by the prestigious AcSEC called for accountants with standards, rather than a new "standard of accounting."

But the FASB determined to respond by granting a general amnesty. It promulgated FASB Statement No. 32 (September, 1979) captioned "Specialized Accounting and Reporting Principles and Practices in AICPA Statements of Position . . ." The amnesty and absolution took the following form:

> 10. The specialized accounting and reporting principles and practices contained in the AICPA SOPs . . . listed in Appendix A [which includes 78–8] are preferable accounting principles for purposes of applying Opinion 20.

The FASB has thereby, at least insofar as the SOP 78–8 condition is concerned, decreed that the exorcising of the prevailing perversity is merely to shift to another accounting principle, albeit a preferable one. This is the kind of innocuous treatment sought unsuccessfully by Touche Ross when its Gelco mischief was exposed (see pp. 123–125).

I maintain that the exorcising of the SOP 78–8 mischief demanded that the entities and auditors who may have been involved should have been constrained to proceed with the correction of errors rule and, as a consequence, called upon to say *mea culpa* and to restate the accounts for the prior periods.

But the FASB, like AcSEC, was desirous of permitting the companies and their auditors who distorted and misapplied GAAP to "get their feet out of the bear trap" gracefully. Whether such an attitude of compassion without justice will serve as a deterrent to subsequent abuses in other contexts is seriously open to question.

Suffice it to say that when companies and their auditors develop a vested interest in fakes, they (the fakes) die hard.

12

"Deep Throat" in the Executive Suite

September, 1976, was an especially busy period for Saul Steinberg, the boy genius who transformed his father's rubber goods business into a glamorous concept company (Leasco), and in 1968 used that inflated stock to acquire Reliance Insurance Company, an old-line Philadelphia-based insurance company. At the same time Steinberg was undoubtedly brooding over the fact that a New York appellate court told him that he had to make good on a pledge to a Long Island school—a pledge on which he sought to renege, pleading hard times. And in Chapter 3 we learned how in that fateful month he was giving hot tips to his secretary and others close to him to buy shares in Pulte Homes—while he was selling off a bundle of shares in that company, of which he had been a director.

Even with these major burdens he found time to direct his legal counsel to institute suit against *Barron's* and me because he was unhappy about my July 19, 1976, article in that magazine. I was critical of what I sensed were the motives for a then-contemplated issue of a new preferred stock by his insurance company.

A Synopsis of the "Whose Deep Pocket?" Article

What was there in the article to cause Steinberg to make it into a federal case? That article, "Whose Deep Pocket?," was inspired by a Reliance Insurance preliminary prospectus released in June, 1976, in contemplation of a $50 million issue of preferred stock by the insurance company. The points made by the article included the following:

210

1. Because of the dependence by the Reliance Group (the parent company) on Reliance Insurance's resources, a hefty share of the funds expected to be raised on the offering will find their way to Group.
2. The insurance company's affairs had been the subject of serious concern to various regulatory agencies; accordingly, various procedures (which I had characterized as artificial respiration) had been undertaken to shore up the company's "policyholders' surplus."
3. Because an insurance company is a regulated entity, a so-called full consolidation of Reliance Insurance's resources into Reliance Group's financial statements was an improper accounting procedure, I asserted.
4. As a consequence of unraveling the full consolidation, Group's stockholders' equity (excluding Insurance) was shown to be in a very substantial negative or deficit position.
5. Cited the point disclosed by the prospectus that because of the parent company's heavy reliance on the Insurance resources, after the new preferred will have been sold, the insurance company's board of directors (coincidentally consistent with that of Group) would be asked to vote an increased upstream dividend of $4 to $10 million annually.
6. Took issue with the way in which several special-feature preferred stock issues within the Group ambit were being reflected in the financial statements. Indicated that in my view these securities were merely thinly disguised debt and should be accounted for as such.
7. I made brief reference to what I considered to be an excessive carrying value for the computer equipment which was being leased by Leasco.
8. Criticized the underlying economics and especially the accounting treatment surrounding a complex transaction whereby Leasco sold its existing computer-lease receivables to a consortium of banks headed by Continental Illinois. The proceeds from these sales were used to repay existing bank loans to Continental Illinois and others.
9. I concluded by asserting that ultimately the policyholders would wind up footing the bill for this contemplated financing, with the benefits slated not for them but for the Reliance Group.

Reliance Takes Umbrage

What is there in the foregoing which could cause Steinberg to take umbrage? Let Judge Charles L. Brieant (of the Federal District Court,

Southern District of New York) summarize the plaintiff's analysis of my writing:

> . . . Plaintiff alleges various false or misleading statements which result in defamation by implying in the broadest terms that Insurance, in its official filings, has falsified the purposes of its public offering.
>
> These various statements can be divided into several categories. Plaintiff alleges that . . . the article (a) falsely implied that the amount of the prospective common stock dividends was misstated in the prospectus; (b) falsely stated that the preferred offering was detrimental to Insurance and beneficial only to Group; (c) falsely stated that Insurance's "earnings power" had "sharply diminished," thereby impugning Insurance's ability to service the preferred offering while paying common stock dividends; (d) falsely or at least incorrectly described Provident's interest in Commonwealth, thereby accusing Insurance of accepting a worthless pledge; (e) erroneously implied by the use of the term "artificial respiration" that Insurance was financially "near death"; (f) was written with omissions and innuendo which falsely substantiated the claim that Insurance was financially unstable and that Group's "accounting gimmickry" might force Insurance into an uneconomic stock offering; and (g) contains false and misleading statements as to Group's financial stability which falsely substantiate the theme that the preferred offering was improperly induced by Group to Insurance's detriment.

There was one word which took on a special role in the litigation. The second sentence of the fourth paragraph of my article, quoting from the preliminary prospectus, read:

> Initially, according to the plan, "the $47 million of net proceeds will serve to increase Reliance Insurance's Statutory Policyholders' Surplus, thereby momentarily increasing its underwriting capacity."

In fact the word "momentarily" did not appear in the preliminary prospectus, but had been inadvertently inserted by me during the course of revising successive drafts of the article. On learning of this aberration, *Barron's* published a correction in the issue immediately following the publication of the article. It seems that Steinberg and his counsel could not comprehend nor accept the fact that mortals can err. This will become apparent as the saga unfolds.

In his opinion, Judge Brieant observed that: "Viewed most favorably to plaintiff, the complaint alleges that the article was published at a time when plaintiff had filed a preliminary registration statement for sale to the public of two million shares of a proposed new Series A cumulative preferred stock issue."

A Preliminary Bout with "Confidentiality"

Before we observe the main event, it should be noted that there was a preliminary bout. When the issues were joined, *Barron's* counsel and mine demanded that the outraged plaintiffs produce various documents which we deemed necessary for the proper pursuit of our defense. Reliance and its counsel demurred, insisting that the documents we demanded were confidential. While Reliance and counsel might have been willing to disclose those documents to my counsel (possibly even to me if I were to take a "vow of chastity" insofar as these sensitive papers were concerned), they refused to produce them openly and above board. When my counsel refused to enter into any agreement compromising my right to review and use the information as I deemed appropriate, Reliance's counsel ran to the court for a protective order to ensure the confidentiality of the documents.

Judge Brieant, after hearing the opposing arguments, came forth with a spirited opinion upholding the concept of freedom of information insofar as the conduct of publicly owned corporations is concerned.

In the course of his opinion rejecting Reliance's plea for protective custody, Judge Brieant determined:

> . . . Since the parties were unable, although requested by the Court, to stipulate to an order of confidentiality, plaintiff sought a protective order . . . which would limit the use by defendants' attorneys of "(a)ll non-public information and documents ascertained and produced by plaintiff pursuant to discovery, including deposition testimony, answers to interrogatories, and documents produced. . . ." The order sought would forbid defendants' attorneys from disclosing "to any person other than such attorneys" the information and documents so described, but would allow disclosure of "financial information to parties, representatives of the parties and experts as necessary for purposes of this action. . . ." Finally, the requested order would prohibit "defendants and their employees and agents" from using any such information and documents "in any publication, address, lecture or other medium of public dissemination, except as such information is a matter of public record or is otherwise known to the defendants and their employees and agents." Thus, plaintiff is not objecting, at this time, to the scope of defendants' discovery; it is merely asking that the fruits of that discovery remain confidential.

What reasons did the plaintiff advance for an order of confidentiality warranting a couple of affidavits?

> . . . Public dissemination of the confidential non-public information "might be harmful to plaintiff and to the investment community." For exam-

ple, it is argued that incomplete or misleading information, such as internal memoranda, might result in an artificial impact on the market in plaintiff's securities.

To this argument Judge Brieant responded sardonically, "How the disclosure of truth can ever harm the 'investment community' is not clear, but we will assume that such disclosure might harm the plaintiff." Which documents did the plaintiff wish to suppress?

These include: (a) correspondence with government regulatory agencies; (b) "cash flow forecasts" of plaintiff for the period 1969–1978; and (c) "cash budgets" of plaintiff for the years 1975–1977, with projections through 1979. These last two categories consist of internal management projections of the plaintiff's financials for the present and future.

Why are they afraid of subjecting these documents to Briloff's benign scrutiny?

Plaintiff suggests that if defendants did not have the claimed animus against plaintiff in July, when the offending article was published, they probably have it now, having been hauled into court to justify their previous article. Much of the information sought in pre-trial discovery, while necessary to prepare for trial, may also furnish grist for the journalistic mill. Plaintiff contends that receipt of this information will likely inspire Briloff to write another article derogatory of plaintiff's management, or perhaps even defamatory, holding Reliance up to opprobrium, and damaging its relations with customers, investors, and creditors.

To all this the court responded forthrightly:

Defendants contend correctly that if this Court grants the protective order sought by plaintiff, it would, in effect, be ordering a "prior restraint" of the freedom of the press, thereby violating their First Amendment rights.
    . . . Such a prior restraint may be constitutional, but one seeking such relief bears a "heavy burden of showing justification for the imposition of such a restraint."

We Proceed to the Main Event

In the wake of this pre-trial proceeding, Reliance did begin to disgorge some, but only some, of the documents demanded of it. We then proceeded to the main event—depositions (including five full days of my testimony, wherein I conducted a tutorial, under the penalties of perjury, for Reliance's lawyers on the complexities and vagaries of double-entry accounting), briefs, and reply briefs. My counsel and that for

Barron's proceeded to file a motion for summary judgment, petitioning Judge Brieant to throw the case out of court. This he did in a September 14, 1977, *Memorandum and Order.* Its opening gambit, "After exhaustive pre-trial discovery, upon a mound of papers submitted by both sides exceeding in volume those usually resulting from a plenary trial, defendants have moved for summary judgment. . . ."

The court recapitulated the background facts and the substance of the article which offended Saul Steinberg. The opinion then went on to say:

> Strong public policies exist in favor of the right to publish such critiques as those contained in Dr. Briloff's article. Our federal securities laws are based on the theory that full disclosure will protect the integrity of the market place. The disclosure has tended to become so "full" in some situations, as to bury in legalese, in the interests of total accuracy, facts and possibilities flowing therefrom which should be simply stated in plain English and their possible consequences made known to potential investors. . . . Exposing to the public in plain language that which was either implicit in the circumstances surrounding the offering, or buried in the prospectus and other public filings of the Reliance companies . . . is an important function of a free financial press, which should not be inhibited by judgments for damages of the sort sought here.

The misquoted "momentarily," on which Reliance rested so much of its allegation that I was motivated by actual malice when writing the article, was also dealt with by Judge Brieant:

> The word "momentarily" did not appear in the preliminary prospectus. When this error was brought to *Barron's* attention, a correction was made in the following week's edition.
>
> The word "momentarily" adds little to the thrust of the sentence. . . . "Momentarily" in this context means "at any moment: momentarily liable to occur." Implicit in the preliminary prospectus is the suggestion that the dividend-paying ability of Insurance would be improved, and that availability of funds for dividends would in fact occur momentarily, after completion of the offering. But the word did not belong in quotes.

A Corporation as a "Public Figure"

With "momentarily" out of the way, we are led to the critical issue of libel implicit in the litigation. In this regard it became necessary for us to demonstrate that Reliance Insurance and its affiliated entities comprised a "public figure." While a president of the United States, justices

of the Supreme Court, congressmen, kings, and emperors are such figures in the context of the laws governing alleged libel by publications
protected by the First Amendment, the question was raised as to whether
corporate entities are subsumed in that category. On this score Judge
Brieant's opinion determined:

> It is now well accepted that the plaintiff's status determines the standard
> of proof that such plaintiff will be required to present in making a defamation
> claim. If the plaintiff is a public official or public figure, then the plaintiff
> will have to show that the defendant published false statements against him
> with "actual malice," a word of art discussed below. If, on the other hand,
> the plaintiff is not a public figure, then he need only establish a minimum
> degree of fault in order to establish liability. . . .

Brieant then said:

> A public figure is one who has voluntarily invited close public scrutiny
> by thrusting himself into the public arena. Finally, *Gertz* sets forth two categor-
> ies of public figures: public figures for all purposes and those whose lives
> are only public in limited circumstances.

The Supreme Court of the United States has opined on the public
figure question as follows:

> Those who, by reason of the notoriety of their achievements or the
> vigor and success with which they seek the public's attention, are properly
> classed as public figures . . . [*Id.* at 342].

Following a detailed analysis of the standards set forth in various
cases for determining the public figure issue, Judge Brieant concluded:

> We find that plaintiff is indeed a public figure. It is a large corporation
> with more than a billion dollars in assets. Nearly all of its common stock is
> owned (through Financial) by Group, a publicly held company whose shares
> are traded on the New York Stock Exchange. There has been great public
> interest in Insurance and its affiliated companies over the past several years,
> particularly with respect to the circumstances surrounding its acquisition.
>
> Indeed, plaintiff's role in society is such that it is a figure generally in
> the public eye. I find that plaintiff is a public figure in the general sense,
> and also in the specific context of its decision to make a $50 million public
> stock offering.

Reliance raised a tangential issue, as intriguing as it was specious.
From the opinion:

> Reliance argues that it should not be treated as a public figure because
> it was, at the time of the libel, "in registration" and therefore lacked the

media access to counteract the libel which is normally available to a public figure, and one of the theoretical underpinnings for the "actual malice" rule. We find nothing . . . which would remove "public figure" status from an offeror during the brief time it is in registration. . . .

The Court doubts that the SEC Release cited, upon which it [Reliance's argument] is ostensibly based, intended to prevent an issuer in registration from denying or disputing a defamatory article. It should be possible so to word a denial as not to constitute an offer to sell. To the extent the SEC purports to deny an issuer this fundamental right, that would appear to be a usurpation of power, and violation of the issuer's First Amendment rights. . . .

Finally, Insurance argues that it is not a public figure since it did not "thrust" itself into the media. This is simply untrue. By its very nature as a large publicly held, government-regulated corporation, and additionally because of its voluntary decision to make a public stock offering, Insurance has, in fact, thrust itself into the public eye.

Judge Brieant reiterated his strong support for the *Barron's*-Briloff endeavors, in categoric terms:

We must acknowledge that the public interest is well served by encouraging the free press to investigate and comment on business and corporate affairs in the same manner as it would report on other public issues. As we observed in *Reliance Insurance Co. v. Barron's*, 428 F. Supp. 200, 205 (S.D.N.Y. 1977):[1]

"Investigative reporting is not limited to the impeachment of presidents or the exposure of licentious congressmen. The public interest is served equally when reporters find a 'Deep Throat' in the executive suite, and when an accounting professor spotlights for the financial press, in common language, business dealings he regards as improper, improvident or unfair to investors. Whether his conclusions are right is to be resolved generally in the free marketplace of ideas."

When such reporting concerns the financial transactions of a large public corporation, the public interest in maintaining the free marketplace of ideas must outweigh plaintiff's claim to the sanctity of private status.

Was There Evidence of "Actual Malice"?

Since Reliance was deemed to be a public figure, it became necessary for the court to determine whether my writing of the article evidenced "actual malice." In asserting that it did, Reliance pointed to the "momen-

[1] This refers to Judge Brieant's March, 1977, opinion on the "confidentiality" issue.

tarily" misquote to demonstrate irresponsibility and worse. In this regard it cited the case of *Goldwater v. Ginzburg* to prove that even public figures can prevail in libel actions where the defendant had manifested irresponsibility and reckless disregard of the facts and here, once again, I was plagued by "momentarily"; and once again the court came to my defense, thus:

> Since plaintiff has been unable to point out any other example of misquotation or falsification of a hard fact (as distinguished from an opinion), evidence of error(s) alone is insufficient to raise a factual question on the issue of actual malice in the context of this case. We must affirm the longstanding principle that inaccuracy itself will not demonstrate "actual malice" in a libel case. Even if there were a dozen errors in this article, mistakes or bad judgment will not substitute for knowing falsehood or reckless disregard as to falsity, when the uncontradicted testimony reveals that the author and publisher held the good faith belief that the article was correct and truthful.

Judge Brieant rejected Reliance's reliance on the *Ginzburg* precedent:

> It is at this point that we consider the status and reputation of the author. Dr. Briloff is an acknowledged expert in the field of accounting as evidenced by his full-time profession as a Professor of Accounting and by his many publications and lectures in the field. The source of this article was therefore of known quality.
>
> Dr. Briloff is an expert in accounting, the relevant discipline, who gathered much material concerning Insurance, reviewed that material, and then published his own opinion of Insurance's stock offering. This is not the case of an unreliable informant . . . or of a conceded nonprofessional giving a psychiatric opinion *(Ginzburg)* who publish their opinions as fact without any basis in fact. Although Dr. Briloff's opinions may have been erroneous, they cannot be said to have been uttered with actual malice as above defined.

After considering some collateral aspects of the "actual malice" issue, Judge Brieant concluded:

> Since the Court has found that plaintiff is and will be unable on a trial to demonstrate the required "actual malice," defendants' motion for summary judgment on the libel claims is granted. The claims for intentional tort and negligence pleaded under state law add nothing to the libel or defamation claim and summary judgment is also granted as to them.

Reliance's 10(b) Canard

Now Judge Brieant had to address himself to another issue raised by Reliance in its complaint. Saul Steinberg and his colleagues (especially his lawyer, Robert Hodes), representing the epitome of truth, fairness, and absolute candor in matters involving the securities of publicly held corporations, asserted that the article had an adverse affect on the then-proposed preferred stock offering by Insurance. To this allegation the court responded:

> Because of our conclusions above we probably need not reach a tantalizing question sought to be posed by this complaint, namely: Could there ever be a case where a newspaper which has no financial interest in a securities transaction could be found liable for a violation of Rule 10b–5 because of a false report published bearing on securities offered for sale? . . . Here, the Rule 10b–5 claim must fail if only because plaintiff has been unable to establish that there is a genuine issue of material fact as to the required element of scienter. . . . We have already found that neither Dr. Briloff nor *Barron's* acted with such reckless disregard for the truth. Therefore, for that reason alone, plaintiff is unable to sustain a cause of action based on Rule 10b–5.

The court labeled this allegation in the complaint as a ploy, thus:

> In addition, the Court concludes that the allegation of a violation of Rule 10b–5 is being pleaded here as a method of circumventing the higher evidentiary threshold developed by the Supreme Court to limit state actions for libel. This is a misuse of the securities laws. Plaintiff's case, if it has one, is a libel action pure and simple. The securities laws, and particularly Rule 10b–5, were not developed with the intention of overlapping or reinforcing the law of libel, nor to inhibit the exercise of freedom of the press.

Whereupon Judge Brieant decreed that our petition for summary judgment would be granted. Reliance's counsel then filed a petition to the court for rehearing on the grounds that the court had not given adequate weight to the "momentarily" misquote.

In October that petition was rejected, and for the first time in this *cause célèbre* Reliance and its counsel evidenced good judgment—they failed to pursue the right to appeal the decision to the Circuit Court of Appeals.

So Reliance's endeavors to discredit my writing efforts were thwarted. This suit occasioned substantial material and psychic burdens for *Barron's* and me. One cannot be certain whether Saul Steinberg's ego was bruised. But one thing is certain: The lawyers came out ahead!

According to the 1978 proxy statement of Reliance Insurance Company, its attorneys, Willkie Farr & Gallagher (of which Mr. Hodes is a principal partner), received fees aggregating $212,713 during the year ended December 31, 1977 (i.e., the year when the litigation was in progress). I do not know how much of this was for the suit against me.

Nor do I know how much of the $237,681 in fees garnered by the law firm from other entities in the Reliance Group may have been attributed to this action. Suffice it to say, a hefty price was paid by the insurance company and presumably the policyholders in an endeavor to chill free and open expression.

Insights from the Litigation

A few footnotes to these proceedings may be of interest, and I will address myself briefly to them. A number of intriguing insights were obtained as a result of the litigation. Also subsequent developments cast additional light on the operations of the Steinberg empire.

To begin with, this litigation illuminates the earlier litigation of *Feit v. Leasco Data Processing Equipment Corp.*, where Federal District Judge J. Weinstein commented acerbically on the nature and content of the prospectus, thus:

> In at least some instances, what has developed in lieu of the open disclosure envisioned by the Congress is a literary art form calculated to communicate as little of the essential information as possible while exuding an air of total candor. The masters of this medium utilize turgid prose to enshroud the occasional critical revelation in a morass of dull, and—to all but the sophisticates—useless financial and historical data. Their earnest effort is to satisfy the SEC's requirements in the most uncommunicative possible way. In the face of such obfuscatory tactics the common or even the moderately well informed investor is almost as much at the mercy of the issuer as was his pre-SEC parent. He cannot by reading the prospectus discern the merit of the offering. . . .

In the course of his opinion, Judge Weinstein overtly criticized Messrs. Steinberg and Hodes for their lack of candor in the 1968 prospectus pursuant to which Leasco acquired Reliance. There are some manifestations of corresponding sins of omission in the 1976 Reliance Insurance prospectus.

When $4 to $10 Million Means $10 Million—Period

For example, the prospectus referred to the fact that after the successful offering of the insurance company's new preferred stock, the directors of that company (who were then consistent with those of the parent companies) would be asked to increase the subsidiary's dividend payment by some $4 to $10 million. It turned out that at the moment when the prospectus writers alluded to $4 to $10 million, Reliance Group's management knew it was going to be $10 million—and nothing less than that. Among the documents reluctantly disgorged by the plaintiffs in the action against *Barron's* and me was "6/11/76—Reliance Group Incorporated Cash Flow Forecast, January 1, 1976, through December 31, 1978." You will notice that this forecast was compiled prior to the actual offering of the new preferred stock. According to that document, the upstream payout by the insurance subsidiary is increased by about $2.5 million quarterly—$10 million annually. This is made explicit in Note II B to the forecast:

> The Reliance Insurance dividend is assumed to be increased in the third quarter of 1976 from its present level of $16,000,000 on an annual basis by $10,000,000 to $26,000,000 on an annual basis. The projection also assumed $10,000,000 increase in the annual dividend rate in the third quarter of 1977. Although it is anticipated that in the future Reliance Insurance will pay common stock dividends in the range of about 40% to 60% of consolidated net investment income, . . . for *projection purposes only* assumed no dividend increases after 1977.

I suppose $10 million might, by some stretch of the imagination, be rationalized as coming within a $4 to $10 million range; yet I cannot refrain from alluding to Judge Weinstein's opinion for the Steinberg-Hodes sins of omission and commission incident to the critical filings with the Securities and Exchange Commission.

The proceeds from the August, 1976, preferred stock offering were still warm in the insurance company's hands when its representatives hot-footed it down to the offices of the Insurance Department of the State of New York to obtain permission to hike the dividend by the amount projected in the cash flow forecast, i.e., the $10 million figure. An immediate and angry response from the Insurance Department indicated that the proposed sharp increase was "not yet justified by underwriting and investment results." The New York Insurance Department went on to state: "While this [increased dividend] might be helpful to the parent company [Group] and its debt obligations, it is certainly not in the best interests of the insurers in the Group. . . ."

The Insurance Department of Pennsylvania also learned of the proposed dividend increase, and on September 1, 1976, the Commissioner of Insurance of Pennsylvania wrote to the Chairman of the Board of Reliance Insurance indicating his view of the proposed dividend increase: "I am therefore shocked to learn that within weeks of receiving approval from my department on the stock issue, you have decided to consider an increase of approximately $10 million in dividends to your stockholders." In addition the letter detailed reasons why the proposal was "imprudent."

Because of these two letters the Board of Directors of Reliance Insurance did not increase the dividend at its September 7, 1976, meeting. Nevertheless, at its meeting on October 21, 1976, the Board of Directors of Reliance Insurance declared an increase in dividends on its common stock in an amount of approximately $10 million on an annualized basis for a total annual dividend of approximately $26,000,000.

This action by the board prompted further discussions with the New York and Pennsylvania insurance departments. On behalf of the New York Insurance Department, the state Attorney General threatened to file suit against Insurance seeking an injunction to prevent the payment of such dividends. Under threat of this litigation, an interim agreement was reached between Reliance Insurance and the New York Insurance Department and the Pennsylvania Insurance Department to the effect that Insurance would withhold payment of such dividend to Reliance Financial pending resolution of the differences between Reliance Insurance and the regulatory agencies.

Apparently these differences were resolved and payment of the dividend was permitted in early 1977, but in withdrawing its objections to the payment of such dividend, the Insurance Commissioner of Pennsylvania reiterated his concern about the dividend policy of Insurance:

> Thus, we and the New York Insurance Department expressed grave concern over the precipitous increase in dividends declared on common stock of Reliance almost immediately after receipt of proceeds from the preferred stock. The concern was, and continues to be, that such proceeds would inure to the benefit of the company's parents, Reliance Finance [sic] Services Corporation and Reliance Group, Inc., rather than the public and policyholders of Reliance and its subsidiary insurance companies.

As the article emphasized, Reliance Insurance's ultimate parent was in urgent need of liquidity; sadly, the article (like the prospectus) neglected to point up the special pressure on Group resulting from the fact that it had "suspended" the payment of dividends on its outstanding preferred stock from the first quarter of 1975. Consequently, in September, 1976, it was confronting default for the sixth consecutive quarter on its preferred stock dividends. So what? Well, according to the provisions of those stock issues, the holders of each preferred issue are entitled to elect two directors to Reliance's Board of Directors when the dividends on their shares are in default for six quarterly periods. And if this were to happen, Saul Steinberg would have to sit with four directors on his board not of his choosing. They might even act independently, possibly even aggressively.

This compelling urgency to get the increased dividend was not disclosed in the 1976 prospectus and, *mea culpa,* though I was aware of it at the time, it somehow escaped my pen as I was writing the "Whose Deep Pocket?" essay.

As it developed, the regulators' temporary reluctance to permit the $10 million hike caused some problems because, according to press reports, Group had negotiated some bank loans ostensibly predicated on the increase. But all's well that ends well. The corporation broke the string of six during the fourth quarter of 1976, and then, in May, 1977, cleared up the entire accumulated arrearages—paving the way for a resumption of dividends on the common stock in the fourth quarter of 1977.

The "Whose Deep Pocket?" article and its legal aftermath made accounting history in yet another way. Under Item 5, registrants must include in their annual filings with the Securities and Exchange Commission a statement of legal proceedings in which they may be involved. This section typically carries a summary of proceedings in which the corporation is the defendant—thereby permitting stockholders and others to take note of any contingencies facing the corporation.

The 1976 forms 10-K for Reliance Group, Reliance Financial, and Reliance Insurance included this pronouncement:

> On September 14, 1976, Reliance Insurance commenced an action in the United States District Court for the Southern District of New York against *Barron's* (sued in the name of Dow Jones & Company, Inc.), Dow Jones & Company, Inc., and Abraham J. Briloff. This action is based upon the publication of an article by Mr. Briloff in the July 19, 1976, issue of *Barron's.* It is alleged that the article, which appeared shortly before Reliance Insurance's recent preferred stock offering, contained false, misleading, and libelous statements which caused Reliance Insurance to increase the dividend yield on the preferred stock issue. Reliance Insurance seeks to recover $7,500,000 in compensatory damages and also seeks appropriate punitive damages for commercial libel and violations of the anti-fraud provisions of the securities laws. On October 21, 1976, Dow Jones & Company, Inc. served its answer generally denying the allegations and asserting several affirmative defenses. On December 8, 1976, Abraham J. Briloff served his answer generally denying the allegations and asserting several affirmative defenses and partial defenses. Discovery proceedings have been commenced by the parties to the litigation. Messrs. Willkie Farr and Gallagher, general counsel to Reliance Insurance, have not expressed an opinion as to the outcome of this action.

The corresponding Item 5 in the following year drops that paragraph. Regrettably, Steinberg, *et al.*, lacked the grace and sense of fair play to state in that section that the litigation they began with such fanfare was tossed out of court by summary judgment. (It would also have been of interest to Reliance's policyholders and shareholders to know how many thousands of dollars Hodes's firm had collected for bringing the matter to court.)

Saul Steinberg on Top of the *Financial World*

Divine justice does reward virtue and punish wickedness—demonstrated by events in the life of Saul Steinberg during 1978 (aside, of course, from the Pulte matter discussed in Chapter 3). He was on the cover of the December 1 issue of *Financial World*, which carried as the feature article "The Regreening of Saul Steinberg." How did this embarrassment of riches come about? It would appear that the insurance commissioners of the various states set out to fill the coffers of the insurance companies that they regulate. They accomplished this by granting enormous rate increases and permitting a much narrower selection of risks by the companies. As a consequence, Reliance Insurance's earnings increased dramatically, with a corresponding impact on the price of the shares of the parent company.

As it happened, in the spring of 1978 Reliance Group had outstanding some 6.5 million warrants entitling the holders to purchase the company's shares at $32 a share. When, in mid-1978, Group shares moved to a price above $32, 5.8 million of these warrants were exercised, throwing to Reliance $187 million in cash.

Thereafter the company reacquired 1.1 million of its shares for about $38 million and another 3.6 million for $124 million; Group appears to have used another $19 million to reacquire some preferred stock. As a consequence Reliance was left with but $6 million of fresh cash— and one million of additional common shares outstanding.

The Leasco Spin-Off

The epithet "boy genius" has regularly been thrown at Reliance-Leasco's mentor, Saul P. Steinberg, though at times with tongue in cheek. I've applied the epithet to him myself on frequent occasions. However, in the following incident there is no question that Steinberg deserves the title.

In the spring, 1979, he engineered an extraordinary *tour de force*. Reliance Group consolidated into a single package, Leasco Corporation, the computer-leasing operations theretofore conducted by Leasco Computer, Inc., and Leasco Europa, Ltd. (the domestic and foreign operating entities respectively). In May, Reliance Group shareholders received, ostensibly as a taxfree distribution, one Leasco Corporation share for each six Reliance shares then owned by them.

At its inception the new Leasco was essentially comprised of a single tangible asset, namely, the IBM systems 360/370 computer hardware which had been accumulated over the years and which had gone through the leasing, re-leasing, and re-re-leasing process. Because of the cash stringencies which had prevailed for the Reliance operations and other factors impacting on the computer-leasing industry, there was relatively little recent replenishment of the hardware.

The structuring of Leasco Corporation, predicated on the December 31, 1978, balance sheets of the component enterprises, reflected this computer equipment at $30.4 million. The new corporation was burdened with long-term notes of $16.3 million offsetting this asset plus an additional obligation to Reliance Group in the form of $25 million in mandatory-redemption preferred stock—an aggregate long-term obligation of $41.3 million.

To provide an initial capitalization of $10 million for the common stock to be distributed to the Reliance shareholders, Leasco was endowed with cash and receivables (net of other liabilities) of $20.9 million. Do take my word for it, the debits did precisely balance the credits.

We move along to September 30, 1979, by which time Leasco Corporation was spun off, made independent, liberated, free, and autonomous. It was now owned separately by the public and traded over the counter. Of course, those Reliance shareholders who sold neither Reliance nor Leasco during the intervening months continued to own one share of Leasco for each six shares of Reliance—but that initial relationship need not have continued. Some may have sold one or the other; others may have bought one or the other. And then there are those who owned neither to begin with but bought shares of either or both of these corporations. Be that as it may, the new Leasco opened for trading on April 17, 1979, at $14 and closed on September 30, 1979, at $26. During the intervening months the stock had traded as high as $28 a share and as low as $11.

Since there are about 1.5 million of these shares outstanding, it meant that the inspired professional investors of Wall Street put a price tag on Leasco's common shares of more than $40 million at one point and almost that sum at the end of this period of reckoning.

Where is the pot of gold which appears to have bedazzled the market makers? Well, let's first look at Leasco's income statement for the period ended September 30, 1979. (Here are the data reflected by the nine-month statement included in Leasco's form 10-Q, even though it includes a couple of months prior to the actual restructuring of the new subsidiary.) The operations of these nine months were stated as follows (in millions):

Revenues:	
Equipment rentals	$20.0
Earned income on direct financing leases	2.7
Interest and other income	3.8
Total revenues	$26.5
Costs:	
Depreciation on computer rental equipment	18.6
Interest	2.0
Selling, general, and administrative	5.2
Foreign currency translation	.2
Total costs	$26.0
Income	
Before income tax	.5
Income tax benefit	.2
Net income	$ .7
Dividend requirements re preferred stock	1.9
Net deficit for common stockholders	$ 1.2

So far one is hard-pressed to see the bonanza for the common stockholders which might warrant the high-falutin' prices assigned by the inspired professional investors. Is there something lurking in the balance sheet which enthralled Wall Street? That statement according to the 10-Q read as follows as of September 30, 1979 (in millions):

Assets		Liabilities and Shareholders' Equity	
Cash (assets including time deposits)	$37.8	Notes payable	$ 9.8
Accounts and direct finance receivables	15.7	Accounts payable and accruals	3.9
Computer rental equipment	16.3	Deferred income	2.5
		Mandatorily redeemable preferred stock	25.0
Other assets	4.1	Income taxes (principally deferred)	5.7
			$21.9
Total Assets	$73.9	Secured notes payable	17.6
		Common stock equity	9.4
		Total liabilities and shareholders' equity	$73.9

But, ah!, the sophisticated investor would tell us that it is not the negative bottom line that should determine the value in this kind of a situation; instead, he says, look at the cash flow, i.e., add back the non-cash cost for the depreciation, and ergo!—instead of a negative $1.2 million we have a positive $17.4 million.

That kind of euphoria, however, ignores entirely the cost outflows which are inextricably related to the computer equipment which is the generator of the cash inflows. There is the obligation to pay off the notes, long-term and short-term, as well as the $25 million of preferred stock which Reliance impacted into Leasco.

But yet, it might appear that it is precisely the utilization of the "cash flow," during the interval that it is still in Leasco's possession, that the Reliance management may have had in mind for the spin-off.

It could, of course, use its resources in the interim to buy new equipment to put out for rental and thereby rejuvenate its portfolio. But, as it turns out, Saul P. Steinberg's group has other ideas for the utilization of Leasco's cash resources before it is assigned to pay off its $25 million indebtedness to Reliance Group. According to the September 30 form 10-Q, Leasco bought no fewer than 250,000 shares of Reliance Group for $12 million (i.e., at $48 a share).

Steinberg Finds a Catch 22 in APB Opinion 18

The Steinberg genius doesn't end there, because he has even found a catch 22 in Opinion 18 of the Accounting Principles Board, which according to the 10-Q would permit Leasco's earnings to be injected from quarter to quarter and year to year with a very high-potency stimulant. Thus, from the 10-Q:

> SUBSEQUENT EVENT. On October 19, 1979, the Company purchased 250,000 shares of common stock of Reliance Group, Incorporated, . . . This represents approximately 3.2% of the outstanding common stock of Reliance Group. Several of the Company's directors and officers are also directors and/or officers of Reliance Group. Since Reliance Group and Leasco are, in effect, being controlled by the same officers and directors, under generally accepted accounting principles the equity method of accounting is appropriate and will be used for the investment in the common stock of Reliance Group.

I have learned a lot about accounting from Saul P. Steinberg over the past decade. He taught me how to make $200 million in debt disappear from his company's balance sheet, how to front-end load income, how an ordinary loss can come forth as an extraordinary minus, and how a consolidation can be used to give his enterprise the appearance of affluence beyond what I had considered appropriate under the circumstances. And if he gets away with the APB Opinion 18 ploy, I will have learned something more.

The APB Opinion, released in March, 1971, entitled "The Equity Method of Accounting for Investments in Common Stock," is, for all its faults, an essentially logical precept. It informs us that where a corporation has a 20 percent or greater investment in another corporation (dubbed the "investee"), then the former should, generally speaking, reflect year-by-year its proportionate share of the investee's income or loss.

That opinion also provided that even where the investment falls short of the 20 percent standard, but where through a common management the investor nevertheless controls the investee, something like a monkey on a string, the equity method (i.e., picking up investor's equity in the investee's results) should also prevail. Until this particular Leasco ploy, I knew of no instance where the monkey on the string was able to turn around to absorb the proportion of the income of the string-puller. In short, as in other instances, Steinberg is somehow capable of making essentially good accounting precepts stand on their heads. And he has, in the past at least, apparently managed to get his prestigious auditors and audit committees to go along.

This Opinion 18 maneuver was the subject of an *Inside Wall Street* column of the December 31, 1979, issue of *Business Week*. Included in that story were the following:

> Steinberg personally received 86,481 shares of Leasco from the spinoff, and during the spring and summer he increased his holdings to 655,257 shares of the 1.46 million outstanding. In fact, he now has effective control of 50.7% of Leasco shares.

*   *   *

> *Stock price surge.* To be sure, this accounting measure will fatten Leasco's reported profits. Reliance, for example, had a net profit of $73 million in the first three quarters of 1979. In the fourth quarter it could earn $100 million in extraordinary income alone from its proposed sale of CTI International Inc. to Gelco Corp. . . . Leasco's 3.2% of that extraordinary profit would be more than $2 a share. Of course, these are bookkeeping earnings, not cash. . . .
>
> (A) source points out that Leasco's decision on the equity method was purely optional and may have been designed to promote the stock. "Perhaps Steinberg wants to take Reliance private through Leasco," says still another

source. Leasco stock jumped to 35½ from 28 (it sold at 11¾ earlier this year). It now trades around 34, which means that the total market value is close to $50 million.

* * *

The prospectus from last spring is equivocal about Leasco's plans and certainly says nothing about buying Reliance stock or using the equity accounting method. Briloff points out that Leasco did not obtain a tax ruling in advance on the spinoff, as is customary. "The IRS would have wanted a more specific business plan," he says.

The foregoing critical commentary on Leasco's most recent accounting ploy was predicated on the company's report for the quarter ended September 30, 1979; I was hoping, possibly even expecting, that when the more objective, knowledgeable, independent certified public accountants concluded their rounds at year end this latest manifestation of creative accounting would be tossed out.

Alas, the year-end report did come forth, showing as a plus to the income account "Equity in net income of Reliance Group (Note 5) $651,000." The note 5 essentially duplicated the "Subsequent Events" note included in the 10-Q.

Nor did the independent, attesting, certifying auditors have any qualms regarding this $651,000 income injection—at least not if you judge by their certificate. Instead, that document is "as clean as a hound's tooth."

In despair I telephoned a high-level staff person at the Securities and Exchange Commission; surely, I thought, that regulatory agency would put God back into His Heaven, making the world right again. Alack and alas, I was informed that the awesome SEC had in fact had the accountants in to discuss the issue here in question. The accountants pointed out the catch 22 in APB 18; as a consequence the sovereign, majestic United States government was constrained to pay homage to that provision—no matter how strained the application and incongruous the consequence.

Troubles in Paradise?

As of mid-1980, it might have appeared that Saul P. Steinberg should be "sitting on top of the world," making of it "his oyster." After all, his wealth (at least on paper) would undoubtedly have to be written, as the saying goes, "in nine figures"; more importantly, he sits at the apex of a power structure based on well over $2 billion of resources—

comprised principally of his insurance empire of other people's money. This power base permits Steinberg to threaten the managements of holding companies, financial institutions, and other insurance companies. He is able to go forth to do battle with other acquisitive emperors (e.g., Victor Posner of Sharon Steel fame) for rich lodes of liquidity sequestered in other entities.

But then, at the very moment of his greatest triumphs Saul P. Steinberg might be likened to the hero of a Greek tragedy.

Putting aside for the present the most serious allegations contained in a Reliance Group shareholders' derivative action brought on by his estranged wife, Steinberg's conduct is put into serious question in various proceedings growing out of his hot pursuit of a franchise in behalf of a company controlled by him to construct and maintain bus shelters in the city of New York.

It appears that some years ago a company called Bus Top Shelters, Inc. obtained such a franchise, and thereby its entitlement to substantial advertising revenues, on an interim basis. Then, Steinberg's company, Convenience and Safety Corporation, was formed and thereupon proceeded to wrest the franchise from Bus Top.

So far, so good, all this might be seen to be in the spirit of American captalistic free enterprise. But not so, as soon becomes clear from a May, 1980, indictment handed down by a federal grand jury in Manhattan. That proceeding was instituted against Jack E. Bronston, an erstwhile New York State senator who thus stands accused of mail fraud as an incident to a breach of fiduciary duty by his law firm to shareholders of Bus Top.

According to the indictment, that fraud and breach (and involvement by our "tragic hero") was as follows:

4. . . . During the period of time relevant to this indictment, the minority investors, represented by the Rosenman Colin firm, invested approximately one million dollars ($1,000,000.) in Bus Top. The profitability of that investment was dependent upon Bus Top's obtaining a long term franchise from the City of New York.

5. Convenience and Safety Corporation ("C&S") was incorporated in the State of Delaware on approximately June 6, 1977, at the direction of the defendant JACK E. BRONSTON. During the time relevant to this indictment, C&S became a major competitor for the New York City bus stop shelter franchise.

6. Saul P. Steinberg ("Steinberg"), at all times relevant to this indictment, was Chairman of the Board of C&S and a close associate of the defendant JACK E. BRONSTON.

There then followed the allegations to support the Justice Department's two-count indictment against Senator Bronston, to wit:

7. From early 1977 . . . the defendant JACK E. BRONSTON, and others to the Grand Jury known and unknown, unlawfully, wilfully and knowingly, would and did devise and intended to devise a scheme and artifice to defraud and for obtaining money and property by means of false and fraudulent pretenses, representations and promises from the persons to be defrauded, to wit: the minority investors in Bus Top and Bus Top.

8. It was a principal object of the scheme and artifice that the defendant JACK E. BRONSTON, in complete disregard of the fiduciary duty he as a member of Rosenman Colin [a law firm] owed to the Bus Top minority investors, would and did advise, promote and advance the interests of Steinberg and C&S, a major competitor of Bus Top, in seeking to obtain for Steinberg and C&S a long term bus stop shelter franchise from the City of New York, to the detriment of the Bus Top minority investors.

9. It was a part of the scheme and artifice that the defendant, JACK E. BRONSTON, as a partner in the Rosenman Colin firm, would and did confer, discuss and attend meetings in connection with Rosenman Colin's representation of Bus Top's minority investors.

10. . . . that the defendant, JACK E. BRONSTON, at the same time would and did advise and promote the interests of Steinberg and C&S in their efforts to obtain a long term bus stop franchise and noted in his diary for 1977 and 1978 to bill C&S for numerous meetings, telephone conferences, letters and other services he rendered on their behalf.

11. . . . on approximately October 28, 1977, the defendant JACK E. BRONSTON wrote a letter to Richard Wells, the Executive Assistant to Harrison J. Goldin, the Comptroller of the City of New York, on his New York State Senate letterhead, in which BRONSTON stated that it was not in the public interest to renew Bus Top's then existing franchise. BRONSTON noted in his diary to bill C&S for the time spent drafting this letter.

12. . . . on approximately June 27, 1978 the defendant JACK E. BRONSTON would and did receive a personal check from Saul Steinberg, made payable to BRONSTON, in the amount of $12,500.

13. . . . the defendant JACK E. BRONSTON would and did conceal from, and fail to disclose to, the Bus Top minority investors and Bus Top the fact that he was advising and promoting the interests of Steinberg

and C&S in their efforts to obtain a long term bus stop shelter franchise from the City of New York.

Adding to Steinberg's legal difficulties is a report from the Commissioner of Investigations of the City of New York probing the circumstances of the bus shelter franchise; thus:

> On the particular question of the role of the Convenience and Safety Corporation in this matter, the Board of Estimate should be advised that on January 28 and 29, 1980, after a lengthy process of repeated requests and finally pursuant to subpoenas issued by the Department of Investigation, the active principals of that firm—Mr. Saul Steinberg and Mr. Henry Silverman—were brought to the Department to give testimony on a large number of extremely relevant facets of this department's investigation.
>
> Each man refused to answer any question on any aspect of the bus shelter franchise matter on the basis that the answers might compel them to be witnesses against themselves. Both men cited this constitutional privilege on the stated advice of counsel.
>
> The New York Court of Appeals has recently unanimously ruled in *Marine Midland Bank v. Russo,* _____ NY 2nd _____; _____ NYS 2nd _____ (New York Law Journal, p. 1 and 7, April 7, 1980) that it is proper to draw the inference that one who asserts this Fifth Amendment privilege does so because the information he possesses is harmful to his cause.
>
> The Board of Estimate, we believe, should ask the advice of Corporation Counsel as to whether this refusal to testify by these two men should be considered to be grounds for disqualifying them and their firm from bidding on a new contract, particularly since the contract involved is not for routine supplies or goods or services but instead is for the granting of a discretionary franchise for the highly lucrative use of the public way for the provision of a public service.

For the reasons implicit in the foregoing assertion by Investigation Commissioner Stanley Lupkin, it is my view that the Commissioners of Insurance of the States of Pennsylvania and New York (who are importantly involved in overseeing the insurance aspects of Steinberg's Reliance empire) should study the record being developed in the Federal Court (with the active participation of the Federal Bureau of Investigation and the New York City Department of Investigation) to determine Steinberg's fitness to fulfill his awesome responsibilities for the deployment of billions of dollars of other people's moneys.

This kind of maneuvering entitles Steinberg to the encomium of "genius"—benign or diabolic, I leave the judgment to history.

13

A House Divided

The year 1977 may be remembered as the accounting profession's year of agonizing reappraisal. It began auspiciously enough with the release of *The Accounting Establishment,* the staff study of the Subcommittee on Reports, Accounting and Management of the U.S. Senate's Committee on Governmental Affairs (the Metcalf Committee). The study begins as follows:

> The accounting establishment in the United States is primarily comprised of the nation's eight largest accounting firms, certain influential CPA professional organizations and business lobbying groups, and a few Federal agencies—most notably the Securities and Exchange Commission.

The significance of the subcommittee's undertaking in this connection is indicated by the staff:

> Historically, Congress and the public have regarded accounting as an arcane subject, better left to accountants themselves. Continual revelations of wrongdoing by publicly owned corporations have caused a new awareness of the importance of accounting practices in permitting such abuses to occur. Unexpected failures of major corporations have led to requests for substantial assistance to such companies from taxpayers. Accounting practices ultimately involve social issues that affect the Nation's economic welfare.

To dramatize its findings the staff study included the following chart outlining the various relationships among the sectors comprising the accounting establishment:

**CONTROL OF THE "BIG EIGHT" ACCOUNTING FIRMS AND THE AICPA
OVER ACCOUNTING STANDARDS APPROVED BY THE SEC**

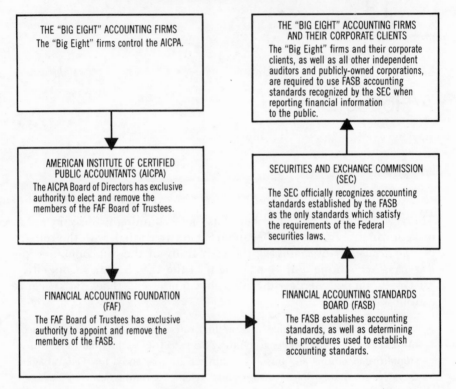

Findings of the Metcalf Staff Study

Among the findings in the Metcalf Committee's Staff Study bound to trigger the AICPA's knee-jerk response were:

1. The Big Eight accounting firms dominate the accounting profession. These firms "effectively control the power structure [of the AICPA], and use the AICPA to advance their collective interests." That conclusion is all the more disturbing because of its accompanying finding:

AICPA is the largest professional association of CPA's and the most important private group affecting the practice of accounting. It dominates all significant aspects of accounting because the profession is largely self-regulated and government authorities have recognized policies and procedures established by the AICPA as representing decisions by the accounting profession.

2. The staff found that fully 85 percent of the 2,641 corporations listed on the New York and American Stock Exchanges are clients of the Big Eight firms. (The staff study preceded the recent merger of Touche Ross & Co., one of the Big Eight, with J. K. Lasser & Co., one of the next seven largest accounting firms, which further increased the percentage of control. Also Ernst & Ernst, another Big Eight firm, has merged with S. D. Leidesdorf & Co.) Those clients accounted for about half of the $2.55 trillion in sales for U.S. manufacturing, trade, and retail sectors and about 84 percent of the $75.4 billion of corporate profits after taxes.

3. The staff study noted that certain activities of Big Eight firms impaired their independence and that performance of executive recruitment and other ancillary, nonaccounting services further bound the auditor to the client.

4. As a result of its study, the staff made a series of sixteen sweeping recommendations, including increased governmental supervision of auditing standards and performance. These recommendations were predicated on the premise that

> The Federal Government has an important responsibility to ensure that publicly owned corporations are properly accountable to the public. Existing accounting practices promulgated or approved by the Federal Government have failed to fulfill that responsibility adequately. . . .

Just two months previously (October, 1976) the Subcommittee on Oversight and Investigations of the House of Representatives' Committee on Interstate and Foreign Commerce had promulgated its *Report on Federal Regulation and Regulatory Reform.* This report included (in Chapter 2, on the Securities and Exchange Commission) a critical commentary on the accounting profession and its standards. (This subcommittee, chaired by Congressman John E. Moss, is accordingly referred to as the Moss Committee.)

Throughout the spring of 1977 the Metcalf Committee held hearings on *The Accounting Establishment;* these proceedings (and collateral documents) are assembled in a 2,176-page volume entitled *Accounting and Auditing Practice and Procedures.*

What caused all of this congressional brouhaha revolving about the accounting profession—a profession which had been accorded benign neglect by the legislators? It is undoubtedly because the year reflected a culmination of forces which had been festering during the preceding half-dozen years. These forces would include the unanticipated collapse of Penn Central, Equity Funding, National Student Marketing, and a bevy of major Wall Street brokerage firms.

Then, too, there was the disclosure that many of the most prestigious of American corporations had sequestered off-balance-sheet funds undetected by their independent auditors—funds used for illegal or at least highly questionable purposes by the highest echelons of the corporate hierarchies. And Congressman Moss's experiences during the hearings on the Energy Policy and Conservation Act of 1975 made it clear that creative accountants are capable of producing almost any number which their clients may have in mind. (It was this revelation which caused the Congressman to introduce Title V into that Act, requiring that standards of accounting by oil and gas producing companies be developed within two years after the passage of that Act. This aspect is considered in Chapter 4.)

In his 1977 testimony before the Metcalf Committee, SEC Chairman Harold M. Williams observed that the accounting profession should be afforded a period of time to respond to the challenges raised by the staff study, subject to the SEC's disciplinary and standard-setting powers under existing law. He promised to report back to the Congress periodically on the profession's efforts to achieve reform in the areas focused upon in the staff study, and on the SEC's oversight role.

Chairman Metcalf closed the hearings by stating that "the ball is in the court of the accounting profession." The clear implication was that action had to be taken by the profession to reduce the domination by the largest accounting firms, to increase competition for auditing business, and to provide more effective means of assuring that the highest standards of auditing practice are implemented and maintained.

The AICPA's Knee-Jerk Response

Confronted with these congressional challenges (as well as some from within the profession, e.g., from a committee of the American Institute of Certified Public Accountants, its Commission on Auditors' Responsibilities), the Institute responded in late summer of 1977 with a resolution of Council—to establish within the AICPA a Division of Firms which, in turn, would be subdivided into an SEC-Practice Section and a Private Company Practice Section. (These sectors might be euphemistically referred to as the Big League and the Bush League, respectively.)

The AICPA's move was so impetuous that it did not even take pains to obtain the approval of its members to a by-law change to effect the apartheid process—instead, it proceeded entirely on a September 17, 1977, resolution of Council—a group which the Metcalf staff study, as noted, criticized as being the alter ego for the accounting establishment.

This impetuosity angered a number of members of the Institute, who were not prepared to accept cavalier treatment from the hierarchy, and they instituted legal proceedings in the Supreme Court of the State of New York. All that the lawsuit demanded was that the democratic process be pursued so that the membership might determine whether this division of the ranks should be implemented.

It was the view of the aggrieved members of the AICPA that the move would legalize the prevailing power structure.

The litigation instituted by the small and regional firms to compel a membership referendum failed; the division of the house has been implemented and is, at least for now, a fact of life for the accounting profession.

The structure of the Big League sector might be seen to have two keystones: a Public Oversight Board and a system of peer review.

The Public Oversight Board (POB), according to its charter, is to be composed of five venerable gentlemen, "including, but not limited to, former public officials, lawyers, bankers, securities industry executives, educators, economists, and business executives."

The POB created under the aegis of the AICPA during 1978 was comprised of:

> John J. Mc Cloy, Esq., Chairman
> Ray J. Garrett, Jr., Esq.[1]
> Professor William L. Cary
> John D. Harper
> Arthur M. Wood, Esq.

Each of these distinguished gentlemen has earned high marks within the American establishment (albeit not necessarily the accounting establishment).

The Role of the POB

The role of the POB in the implementation of the objectives of the SEC-Practice Section include:

1. Monitor and evaluate the regulatory and sanction activities of the peer review and executive committees.
2. Determine that the peer review committee is ascertaining that firms are taking appropriate action as a result of peer reviews.

[1] Mr. Garrett died in February, 1980.

3. Make recommendations to the executive committee for improvements in the operations of the section.
4. Engage staff to assist in carrying out its functions.

What has this impressive POB wrought during the first year of its operation (the period from its inception until spring, 1979)? That year was devoted principally to:

1. Organizing, defining its role, and recruiting its staff.
2. The advising on policy matters during the development of a peer review program to be considered presently.
3. Monitoring initial peer reviews.
4. Studying the question of the scope of services provided by CPA firms and preparing and publishing a report containing recommendations on the subject.
5. Considering the question of what action should be taken by the section in the event of an alleged or possible audit failure involving one of its member firms.

A New PR System

The other keystone is the system of peer review (PR) provided for the SEC-Practice Section. At this juncture it should be noted that PR is not a new phenomenon for the accounting profession; such a system of review is undoubtedly a precondition for any calling aspiring to professional stature.

In Chapter 2 extensive consideration was given to the puerile efforts of the profession in its implementation of the Code of Professional Ethics governing the accounting profession.

Thus, the accounting establishment set up the Public Oversight Board and a system of peer review to answer the challenges which confronted the profession in mid-1977. What have been the reactions to this establishment response?

The report of the Metcalf Committee after extensive hearings on the accounting establishment concluded:

> During the accounting hearings, subcommittee members were pleased to hear pledges from the accounting profession and the SEC that public concerns can be met without the need for new legislation. The SEC also pledged to inform Congress of progress on accounting matters through comprehensive periodic reports. All parties agreed that oversight by Congress is a valuable catalyst for achieving needed reforms. . . .
>
> The subcommittee believes there are many talented and dedicated people in the accounting profession who are eager to make the profession's perfor-

mance meet this ideal. Subcommittee members prefer that the profession itself achieve reforms in cooperation with the SEC. It must be remembered, however, that the public has reasonable needs and expectations which must be satisfied, and the amount of time for achieving reforms is not unlimited. Therefore, the subcommittee expects the accounting profession and the SEC to act in a timely manner to implement the policy goals in this report.

Senator Lee Metcalf died shortly after that report was rendered to the Senate. The focus for attention regarding developments in the accounting profession shifted to the House of Representatives, where the Moss Committee determined to hold hearings on Regulatory Reform— Securities and Exchange Commission. There were extensive presentations before this Committee, including those by the AICPA and others who were to be identified with the SEC-Practice Section created by the September 17, 1977, resolution.

"You Scratch My Back . . ."

During the course of these hearings Dr. John C. Burton, a former Chief Accountant of the Securities and Exchange Commission, observed that, in his view, the AICPA's revised organizational structure would not be adequate to provide the institutional stability required by the profession. He then set forth a number of reasons why the new program would not meet the required objectives, including:

1. The AICPA does not have legal authority to maintain effective surveillance and discipline of members of the profession.
2. Even if the Institute's system were to survive legal attacks, any sanctions would lack the force of law. And if the SEC were to endeavor to formalize such sanctions, it would necessarily have to proceed with its own investigation under Rule 2(e) of the Commission's rules. (As we should know from the Ernst & Ernst–Westec saga, retold in Chapter 3, this is, at best, an attenuated proceeding, capable of extending beyond a decade.)
3. There are serious problems of public perception of the new program. "The AICPA program under which major accounting firms will review each other is likely to be seen as a process of mutual back-scratching."
4. Although the Public Oversight Board is a prestigious body, "it is highly unlikely that a part-time group can, either in fact or perception, provide an effective substitute for statutory regulation."
5. The governing body of the SEC-Practice Section is the Executive Committee, hence, a group comprised of representatives of the firms engaged in such practice. Consequently, standards would be set by

those who have a vested self-interest—the standards would not be subject to review by any governmental agency.

The Moss Committee was not especially impressed by the AICPA's endeavors. In June, 1978, the Committee introduced H.R. 13175:

> To establish a National Organization of Securities and Exchange Commission Accountancy, to require that independent public accounting firms be registered with such Organization in order to furnish audit reports with respect to financial statements filed with the Securities and Exchange Commission, to authorize disciplinary action against such accounting firms and principals in such firms . . .

Pursuant to its commitment to the Metcalf Committee, the Securities and Exchange Commission issued annual reports to the Congress in 1978 and 1979 on "The Accounting Profession and the Commission's Oversight Role." These reports expressed guarded optimism for the profession's ability to fulfill its responsibilities for self-regulation. They did, nonetheless, point up some of the SEC's serious misgivings with the structure of the SEC-Practice Section. The mood of the Commission was effectively summarized by Commissioner John R. Evans in an October, 1979, address:

> . . . For the last two years in its July Report to Congress, the Commission has identified certain attributes which we believe the peer-review process must possess, yet the profession's response has not been satisfactory. One of these attributes relates to Commission access to the working papers of the peer-review process. In my opinion, just as an auditor cannot certify to the accuracy and completeness of financial statements without access to underlying documents, the Commission cannot fulfill its oversight role responsibly without access to work papers. Access is not merely desirable, it is essential if the process is to have the integrity necessary to be effective. Secondly, the Commission continues to maintain that the peer-review process cannot arbitrarily exclude "problem" engagements. I believe the Commission may seriously consider withdrawing its support for the peer-review process rather than risk the erosion of credibility that could result from reporting to the Congress again after three years that these significant issues still have not been resolved. It would be a mistake to assume that the Commission's patience to date with the slow progress being made is in any way due to a lack of resolve that our concerns must be satisfied.

A POB–SEC Colloquy

By way of conclusion to this "House Divided" essay I will juxtapose the "last words" on this issue (at least as of this writing) from the POB and the SEC.

First, from the conclusion to the POB's 1980 report:

The Board believes that in the past year the Section has shown continued strong commitment to the success of its self-regulatory program. This is evidenced by (1) further progress in developing and administering its peer review program, (2) adoption of an initial program for surveillance and disciplinary action in cases of alleged or possible audit failure, (3) the review of the auditor's work environment, (4) efforts to enlarge membership of the Section, and (5) continued attention to the scope of services issue. The SEC continues to be supportive with its constructive criticism and comments.

The Section will face many challenges in 1980–1981 to make its programs more effective. The Special Investigations Committee will have the opportunity to develop surveillance and investigatory procedures. The increased activity in peer reviews will require a major expenditure of time by the profession and the Board. The Board believes, however, that the experience thus far gained will enable the profession to make continued progress in 1980 and the years ahead.

For the SEC's views I had expected to rely on the Commission's 1980 Report to the Congress—a document scheduled to be released by June 30. Regrettably, the last days of June found the Commission still deliberating, possibly even still negotiating a detente with the POB on certain controversial aspects. As a consequence, I am constrained to rely on a "preview," as disclosed by the weekly newsletter of one of the Big Eight accounting firms, to wit:

Public Oversight Board

The Commission continues to be concerned that the POB has not yet assumed the type of leadership role with respect to the self-regulatory effort that it must [assume] for the structure and process as a whole to function effectively. The Commission and its staff continue to provide significant impetus to the Practice Section's development of its self-regulatory program.

In our view, the profession—and, in particular, the POB—must be willing to fully assume this initiative (i.e., internalizing the capacity for self-assessment, criticism and correction) in order for meaningful self-regulation to exist.

Peer Reviews

Commitment to meaningful, in-depth peer reviews by independent and objective reviewers is a prerequisite to the success of the profession's self-regulatory program. Accordingly, any delay in the effective implementation of the peer review program is a serious threat to the whole structure of self-regulation.

At the time of its July 1979 Report, the Commission expected a significant number of peer reviews would be conducted during 1979. In fact, however, only 40 peer reviews were conducted. The pace must be accelerated and the first cycle completed by the end of 1981. . . . The profession's willingness to react appropriately and timely is particularly important, since over 400 peer reviews are expected to be conducted during the next two years.

Access to Working Papers

The issue of Commission access to peer review working papers is a difficult one, and we appreciate the profession's concerns for client confidentiality . . . the SEC staff's review of the peer review process has been limited to a review of the oversight files of the POB.

As indicated in our 1979 Report to Congress, this indirect access to the peer review program, based on a concept of total reliance on the POB and its staff, is not consistent with the Commission's view of its oversight responsibilities. It is vital that an arrangement for Commission staff access to peer review working papers be agreed upon.

Finally, a personal note. I wish the Institute and the profession as a whole good fortune in this noble experiment—at least it represents a recognition of the existence of cracks in the profession's foundation. Further, these cracks are not merely discernible by academicians from their ivory towers—they are now seen to exist by the hierarchy of our profession who sit in glass skyscrapers.

14

Who Will Guard the Guardians?

This question was raised by the Roman satirist, Juvenal, two millennia ago; it is appropriate to ask it again, in this context of corporate accountability.

We will take as our point of departure for this discourse a "Management Report" included with the 1979 Financial Statements of the United States Steel Corporation:

> The Corporation believes that the accompanying consolidated financial statements of United States Steel Corporation and Subsidiary Companies have been prepared in conformity with generally accepted accounting principles. They necessarily include some amounts that are based on best judgments and estimates. The financial information displayed in other sections of this Annual Report is consistent with that in the consolidated financial statements.
>
> The Corporation seeks to assure the objectivity and integrity of its financial records by careful selection of its managers, by organizational arrangements that provide an appropriate division of responsibility and by communications programs aimed at assuring that its policies and methods are understood throughout the organization.
>
> The Corporation has a comprehensive formalized system of internal accounting controls designed to provide reasonable assurance that assets are safeguarded and that its financial records are reliable. Appropriate management monitors the system for compliance, and the internal auditors independently measure its effectiveness and recommend possible improvements thereto. In addition, as part of their examination of the consolidated financial statements, the Corporation's independent public accountants, who are elected by the stockholders, review and test the internal accounting controls

on a selective basis to establish a basis of reliance thereon in determining the nature, extent and timing of audit tests to be applied.

The Board of Directors pursues its oversight role in the area of financial reporting and internal accounting control through its Audit Committee. This committee, composed solely of non-management directors, regularly meets (jointly and separately) with the independent public accountants, management and internal auditors to monitor the proper discharge by each of its responsibilities relative to internal accounting controls and consolidated financial statements.

Protective Insulation at U.S. Steel

In the view of management, the following steps are presumed to assure the effectiveness of corporate governance at United States Steel:

1. Careful selection of its managers.
2. Organizational arrangements that provide an appropriate division of responsibility.
3. Communications programs aimed at assuring that its policies and methods are understood throughout the organization.
4. Establishment of a comprehensive formalized system of internal accounting controls designed to provide reasonable assurance that assets are safeguarded and as to the reliability of its financial records. Appropriate monitoring by management of compliance with the system.
5. Internal auditors independently measure the effectiveness of the system and recommend possible improvements thereto.
6. The Corporation's independent public accountants, who are elected by the stockholders, review and test the internal accounting controls on a selective basis.
7. The Board of Directors pursues its oversight role through its Audit Committee.
8. The audit committee regularly meets (jointly and separately) with the independent public accountants, management, and internal auditors to monitor the proper discharge by each of its responsibilities relative to internal accounting controls and consolidated financial statements.

Given all of this protective insulation and immunization, it might be expected that the end product would be as pure as new-fallen snow. Why the Securities and Exchange Commission and several other regulatory agencies should have found fault with the consequences of this elaborate and undoubtedly costly process for 1978, for example, defies comprehension. Be that as it may, this new departure in reporting to shareholders is consistent with the recommendation contained in the Final Report of the AICPA Commission on Auditors' Responsibilities.

Approbation for This New Development

In its 1979 Report to the Congress, the SEC expressed its approbation for this new development. In addition, the Commission proposed rules that would require public reporting on the effectiveness of systems of internal accounting controls. The Financial Executives Institute has similarly endorsed this report, and has issued a set of guidelines for its preparation.

If this new rulebook for reporting corporate activity makes clear that management, not independent auditors, is responsible for the choice of accounting principles on which to operate and for supervision of accounting activity, the innovation might prove salutary. If the changes are brought to public attention, financial statements might then be stripped of the aura of certitude, and, more important, auditors will be relieved of the burden of discerning fairness. Ostensibly the independent auditor might then be seen as doing little more than countersigning the managerial options from the Book of GAAP.

Fairness Anathematized

Complementing the managements' report developments, the Auditing Standard Board, in mid-1980, proceeded to a radical change in the auditor's standards report or certificate. The new format would read as follows (based on the July, 1980, draft version):

> The accompanying balance sheet of X Company as of [at] December 31, 19XX, and the related statements of income, retained earnings and changes in financial position for the year then ended are management's representations. An audit of financial statements is intended to provide reasonable, but not absolute, assurance as to whether financial statements taken as a whole are free of material misstatements. We have audited the financial statements referred to above in accordance with generally accepted auditing standards. Application of those standards requires judgment in determining the nature, timing and extent of testing and other procedures and in evaluating the results of those procedures.
>
> In our opinion, the financial statements referred to above present the financial position of X Company as of [at] December 31, 19XX, and the

results of its operations and the changes in its financial position for the year then ended in conformity with generally accepted accounting principles.

Notice the absence of the references to the statements' fairness and consistency with those of the preceding years.

But Then, Who Needs the External Auditors?

To the extent this message becomes clear, the investing public (possibly also corporate managements) might then be inclined to inquire whether the independent, external auditor is cost efficient. This was the question discussed in *Accountancy* (the publication of the United Kingdom chartered accountants) for November, 1977. In the article "The External Auditor: His Role and Cost to Society," Professors Richard Briston and Robert Perks noted that criticism of the auditing profession was not a new phenomenon. Briston and Perks set out "to consider the functions of the external auditor, the cost to society of having these functions performed, and the alternative methods available for achieving the benefits which are claimed for the external audit."

After considering the costs incurred in the audit process, the authors concluded that the advantages are probably not as great as is often claimed, because the importance of the original role of protecting the shareholder has considerably diminished, given the vast improvements in financial accounting and internal control in this century.

> Furthermore, [according to Briston and Perks] the threat of fraud has lessened with the improvement in both commercial standards and internal control. The main areas of misconduct have been the manipulation of profit rather than the traditional misappropriation of assets; and even where this has been detected, it has tended to result from the collapse of the company rather than from the investigations of the auditor.
>
> . . . As far as auditing is concerned, it should be recognized that the current structure is repetitious and outmoded, and that it represents from a national viewpoint a massive misdirection of scarce resources to have highly trained professional accountants checking the work of other highly trained accountants when that work has normally been checked internally by yet other highly trained accountants.
>
> The whole emphasis of the audit should be shifted towards the audit of the management of the company. This, after all, is what investors and all other user groups are primarily concerned with. It seems absurd to check twice over that the accounting records are technically correct when there is no check whatsoever on the efficiency with which a company is operated.

For Audit Committees of Boards of Directors

The process of corporate accountability for publicly owned corporations is moving at an accelerating rate to include among their boards of directors duly constituted audit committees.

In its 1977 Report, *Improving the Accountability of Publicly Owned Corporations and Their Auditors,* the Metcalf Committee urged the adoption of this proposal by all publicly owned corporations. In the view of the Committee, "Audit committee members should be free of any significant involvement with the management of a corporation, such as commercial or investment banking relationships, outside legal counsel, management consulting, or major commercial relationship."

The major purpose of such a committee should be "to handle relations with the independent auditor, improve internal auditing controls, and establish appropriate policies to prohibit unethical, questionable, or illegal activities by corporate employees."

The New York Stock Exchange, which had been considering such a policy, moved to require that all domestic corporations listed on the exchange create audit committees by July 1, 1978. The SEC, in its July, 1979, report to the Congress, commended the NYSE for its action and indicated that the National Association of Security Dealers and the American Stock Exchange were considering corresponding actions. The report made reference to the Commission's revised proxy rule which would require "disclosures as to the composition of audit committees and the functions they perform."

The AICPA had established a special committee to study the feasibility of introducing an auditing or ethical standard which would require that publicly owned corporations create independent audit committees. That special committee of the AICPA concluded, in December, 1978, that the organization was powerless to mandate such audit committees. In its report, the special committee indicated that it had been advised by counsel that the imposition of an audit-committee requirement in the absence of a reasonable foundation would expose the AICPA and its members to a risk that established antitrust principles would be violated. The AICPA pointed out, however, that it "continues to support the establishment of audit committees and is prepared to support efforts by others having authority to require audit committees where such requirements give due recognition to a reasonable cost-benefit relationship."

I believe the AICPA was overly concerned about the antitrust and other implications of a firm position on audit committees. I see no reason why the independent auditor's detailed audit of the audit committee's structure and operation should not be an essential extension of the auditor's study of his client's internal-control organization and functioning.

I would, in fact, expect the independent auditor to comment critically where he finds the presumptive independent, conscientious, and effective audit committee to exist merely as a paper committee. In short, if the independent auditor finds the members of the independent audit committee to be other than really independent as the auditor judges independence, I expect him to make that fact known, and to tell why. And if he finds the committee functioning in a manner inconsistent with the standards presumed for such a committee, I would expect him to blow the whistle, just as he undoubtedly would if he found the bookkeeper dipping into the petty cash box.

True, such a cussed independence on the part of the independent auditor might make him *persona non grata* with a less-than-independent audit committee. Such a committee might even go looking for another auditor; but virtue is not necessarily free from cost.

What is the role of the audit committee? What are its functions? A frame of reference for such a committee may be found in the decree settling the litigation brought by the Securities and Exchange Commission against Killearn Properties, Inc. That determination directed that an audit committee be formed comprised of "at least three persons who shall be members of the Board and outside directors . . ." and have the following responsibilities:

i. It should review the engagement of the independent accountants, including the scope and general extent of their review, the audit procedures which will be utilized, and the compensation to be paid.

ii. It should review with the independent accountants and with the company's chief financial officer (as well as with other appropriate company personnel) the general policies and procedures utilized by the company with respect to internal auditing, accounting, and financial controls. The members of the committee should have at least general familiarity with the accounting and reporting principles and practices applied by the company in preparing its financial statements.

iii. It should review with the independent accountants, upon completion of their audit, (a) any report or opinion proposed to be rendered in connection therewith; (b) the independent accountants' perceptions of the company's financial and accounting personnel; (c) the cooperation which the independent accountants received during the course of their review; (d) the extent to which the resources of the company were and should be utilized to minimize time spent by the outside auditors; *(e)* any significant transactions which are not a normal part of the company's business; *(f)* any change in accounting principles; *(g)* all significant adjustments proposed by the auditor; *(h)* any recommendations which the independent accountants may have with respect to improving internal financial controls, choice of accounting principles, or management reporting systems.

iv. It should inquire of the appropriate company personnel and the independent auditors as to any instances of deviations from established codes of conduct of the company and periodically review such policies.

v. It should meet with the company's financial staff at least twice a year to review and discuss with them the scope of internal accounting and auditing procedures then in effect; and the extent to which recommendations made by the internal staff or by the independent accountants have been implemented.

vi. It should prepare and present to the company's board of directors a report summarizing its recommendation with respect to the retention (or discharge) of the independent accountants for the ensuing year.

vii. It should have the power to direct and supervise an investigation into any matter brought to its attention within the scope of its duties (including the power to retain outside counsel in connection with any such investigation).

In addition, the Audit Committee shall have the following special duties, functions and responsibilities:

viii. Review, either by the Committee as a whole or by a designated member, all releases and other information to be disseminated . . . [by the company] to press media, the public, or shareholders . . . which concern disclosure of financial conditions of and projections of financial conditions. . . .

ix. Review of the activities of the officers and directors of Killearn as to their future dealing with the company and take any action the Committee may deem appropriate with regard to such activities. . . .

Mr. Justice Goldberg's Proposals

When, in late 1972, Arthur J. Goldberg resigned from membership on TWA's board of directors, he described the difficult plight of a conscientious director, saying, "The outside director is simply unable to gather enough independent information to act as a watchdog or sometimes even to ask good questions. When presented with the agenda of the board meeting, the director is not basically equipped to provide any serious input into the decision. Realistically, it has already been made by management. . . ."

To help remedy this condition he proposed the establishment of a "committee of overseers of outside directors." Such a committee would be "generally responsible for supervising company operations on a broad scale and make periodic reports to the board." To permit the effective fulfillment of the committee's responsibilities, the former justice proposed:

> To perform these duties adequately this committee would need authorization to hire a small staff of experts who would be responsible only to the board and would be totally independent of management control. In addition, the committee should also be empowered to engage the services of consultants of the highest competence.
>
> As the eyes and ears of the directors, these independent experts and their staff assistants and consultants would look into major policy questions and report to the committee and through them to the board as a whole before decisions are taken on management recommendations.
>
> The fundamental responsibility of these experts, staff, and consultants would be to provide an independent source of expertise for the board. . . . In addition, it would reassert the position of the board as a focal point for creative policy input for corporate decisions.

*   *   *

> The membership of this group of expert advisers should include representatives from widely divergent areas of expertise.
>
> For technical aspects of product-line development, scientific advisers should be recruited. For a look at future markets and the desires of the public, a demographic expert and consumer adviser should be consulted. To ensure compliance with truth-in-advertising standards, an outside advertising consultant might be utilized.
>
> Other possible experts might include an independent auditor to assure the soundness of the accounting techniques used by the corporation and a disinterested independent financier (for example, a retired executive of an investment banking house) to ascertain whether the operations are being frugally financed.
>
> Finally, some employee representatives might be consulted for their independent view of the performance of the corporation from their perspective. Permanent staff assistants to the overseer committee could perform most of the investigative work necessary for the use of the experts.

In short, such a committee of the board should be capable of probing and judging the decision making of the corporate enterprise to assure its optimal functioning in behalf of shareholders, creditors, employees, governments, and the public in general.

Senator Metzenbaum's Proposals

Also of interest in this connection are the provisions of a bill introduced by Senator Howard Metzenbaum in April, 1980. That bill (S. 2567), *The Protection of Shareholders' Act of 1980,* was intended "to establish Federal minimum standards relating to composition of corporate boards, duties of corporate directors, audit and nomination committees, shareholders' rights and for other purposes."

This bill would apply to publicly owned American corporations with 500 or more shareholders and with substantial properties or sales volume (as defined by the bill, Section 3).

To begin with, such corporations would be constrained to elect to their boards of directors a majority of independent directors, i.e., those who have no conflicting entangling alliances with the corporation or its chief executive (as defined by Section 5).

And then, the affected entities were to be required to have audit committees comprised entirely of such independent directors; S. 2567 then sets down certain of the duties of that committee, to wit:

Audit Committee

Sec. 6. (a) The board of directors of an affected corporation shall establish and maintain an audit committee composed solely of persons who are not described in subsection (b) of section 5 of this Act.

(b) It shall be the function of the audit committee, in addition to any other functions agreed to by the board of directors, to—

(1) review the arrangements and scope of the independent audit examination;

(2) review, upon completion of the audit, the following items with the principal firm of independent auditors engaged by the affected corporation:

(A) any report or opinion proposed to be rendered in connection with the audit;

(B) the extent to which the resources of the affected corporation were and should be utilized to minimize the time spent by the independent auditors;

(C) any significant transactions detected during the audit which were unrecorded, unauthorized, or not adequately supported;

(D) any material change in the affected corporation's accounting principles;

(E) all significant adjustments proposed by the auditor;

(F) the scope of the auditor's examination; and

(G) any recommendations which the independent auditors may have with respect to improving internal accounting controls and choice of accounting principles;

(3) investigate and make recommendations concerning the cooperation which the independent auditors received from officers and employees of the affected corporation during the conduct of the audit;

(4) subject to the approval of a majority of the outstanding shares of the affected corporation, hire and dismiss the independent auditors and determine the compensation which they shall be paid;

(5) inquire of appropriate company personnel and the independent auditors as to any instances of deviations from the affected corporation's established codes of conduct and periodically review such policies;

(6) meet with the affected corporation's chief financial officer and other appropriate personnel at least twice a year to review and discuss with them the general policies and procedures utilized or proposed to be utilized by the affected corporation with respect to internal accounting controls, including the internal audit function;

(7) direct and supervise an investigation into any matter brought to its attention with the scope of its duties;

(8) review executive perquisites;

(9) report on the committee's activities in the annual report to shareholders; and

(10) review, either as a committee of the whole or by a designated member, all releases and other information to be disseminated by the affected corporation to the press media, the public, or its shareholders which concern disclosures of financial condition and results of operation, or forecasts of such information, of the affected corporation and its subsidiaries.

(c) Pursuant to performing the function specified in paragraph (6), the audit committee shall have the power to retain outside counsel in connection with any investigation.

A January, 1979, New York Stock Exchange publication reported on a questionnaire directed to the 1,700 members of the American Society of Corporate Secretaries (hence, identified with publicly owned corporations required to report to the SEC). According to that study, "audit committees are entirely comprised of non-management directors for 92 percent of respondent companies, 96 percent of New York Stock

Exchange respondent companies." Further, the Exchange report cited the fact that it was subsequently determined that "only one New York Stock Exchange respondent company's audit committee was not entirely comprised of non-management directors."

How did the survey define "non-management director?" This critical phrase, for purposes of the questionnaire, meant "any person who is independent of management and free from any relationship that, in the opinion of the board of directors of the company, would interfere with the exercise of independent judgment as a board member." This definition involves tautology. It would be of at least academic interest if the proxy material and annual reports which list the ostensibly non-management directors provided in reasonable detail a statement of the relations such members and/or their firms may have had with the corporate entity over the past five years, say.

I consider the survey especially significant since the New York Stock Exchange requirement for an audit committee was specifically rephrased to exclude the requirement for independent directors; the phraseology used in the Metcalf Committee report cited early in this chapter should have been adopted as the standard for determining independence. Regrettably, the Exchange bowed to expedience in the face of stiff opposition—and accepted the definition of "non-management director" in the corporate secretaries' questionnaire.

I will close this segment on a positive note: There is little question that an independent audit committee as suggested by the Metcalf Committee report, functioning along the lines implicit in Arthur Goldberg's proposals, devoting adequate time to the fulfillment of its responsibilities, would contribute to the corporate entity's optimal performance. Such performance could go far to restore the public's confidence in the private sector—and in the public sector too (since so many of the failings in the latter in recent years are rooted in aberrations by the former).

Myths vs. Realities

Ironically these new proposals to advance corporate governance and accountability do little more than return full circle to what was presumed in this regard in a more bucolic period in history. For example, when Francis W. Pixley, at the turn of the century, described the role of the auditor (in Great Britain), he noted that "The Shareholders [he wrote it with a capital S] of a Company may, therefore, be said to have two representatives of their interests . . . the Directors, [and] *their* Auditor" [emphasis mine].

Some forty years ago the late Justice William O. Douglas discerned the disparity between the myth and reality regarding corporate boards of directors. He observed that when the ordinary citizen or the ordinary stockholder thinks of the board of directors, he thinks of them "as distinct from and superior to the management." Such a view presumes that the directors are of such caliber that management will seek their advice and that they "will exercise independent judgment on corporate problems." Douglas then concluded that "this kind of director is too often nothing more than a myth."

This problem is exacerbated by the accelerating concentration of share ownership in disembodied funds of various kinds (mutual, trust, pension, insurance, and the like), and also by the acquisitive takeover pursuits of conglomerates and other entities bent upon empire building.

The remarks by Senator Metzenbaum when submitting his S. 2567 to the Senate on April 16, 1980, included the following:

In theory, a major responsibility of a corporation's board of directors is to carefully monitor corporate policy in order to prevent abuses of this kind. But in fact, a very large number of corporate boards do not exercise meaningful oversight and control over management. "Directors," complained William O. Douglas as early as 1933, "do not direct."

In a 1975 survey of 394 of the country's largest corporations. Korn/ Ferry International—a New York executive recruiting firm—found that boards averaged only seven meetings per year. "In most large corporations," Korn/ Ferry reported, "the board meetings have withered, through neglect, into a ritualized 1- to 3-hour ceremony with much of the time being consumed by a pro forma review of operations by the president or vice presidents and equally routine approvals of the capital appropriations that management wants."

Perhaps the best illustration of the failure of many corporate boards to exercise meaningful oversight and control over management is the Penn Central failure. At the time of the collapse in June 1970, Penn Central was the largest railroad in the country and the sixth largest industrial corporation overall. Within a 2-year period, shareholders watched their shares plummet from 86½ to 2¾. A director who joined Penn Central in December 1969 gave the following, devastating description of board attitudes:

They sat up there on the eighteenth floor in those big chairs with the (brass name) plates on them and they were a bunch of, well, I'd better not say it. The board was definitely responsible for the trouble. They took their fees and they didn't do anything. They didn't know the factual picture and they didn't try to find out.

In testimony before the Senate Commerce Committee a few years ago, former SEC Chairman Roderick Hills summed up the situation as follows:

> Too many boards are dominated by inside directors. Even where there are significant numbers of outsiders on a board, they are all too often old friends of the chief executive office who would rather resign from the board than severely criticize or vote to oust their old friend.

When it is recognized that corporate accountability extends to all of society, these endeavors by the NYSE, the SEC, the Congress, and it is hoped, even by the AICPA, should have a salutary effect. But, in truth, the answer to Juvenal's question must be, "The ultimate guardian of the guardian must be the guardian himself." If there is not something of a "born-again morality," all this tinkering will be an expensive voyage to Erewhon.

15

Quo Vadis?—IV

The numeral designation in the title denotes that this is the fourth occasion when, at the conclusion of a comprehensive presentation of accomplishments and disappointments in the realm of corporate accountability and accounting, I proceeded to set down my considered views as to how society's expectations might be best fulfilled.

From the vantage point of the early 1980s, I see evidence of some progress, however slight and inadequate, in the areas considered here. When I reflect on the greater public awareness of the role and responsibility of the accounting profession, on the profession's self-regulatory endeavors and corresponding commitment to change, on the renascence of the board of directors as an active representative of the shareholders' interests (as distinguished from management's), especially on the interpositioning of the audit committee between management and the independent auditor—there might well be reason for rejoicing.

Then why not close with a hymn of praise? First, of course, because the optimal condition does not yet prevail. And, I suppose, even if it did, I am inspired by the Browning philosophy, "Ah, but a man's reach should exceed his grasp, or what's a heaven for?"

With this challenge in mind, *quo vadis?* I will restate some of the exhortations, pleas, and proposals made in the preceding chapters, including:

1. A major reconsideration of the accounting for business combinations (Chapter 6).
2. A sharp delineation between the independent audit function and the assortment of consultative services which might conflict with such function (Chapter 9).

3. An end to ambivalent consent decrees which have become the hall-mark of the SEC's enforcement process (Chapter 3). Should the practi-calities of the judicial or administrative process nevertheless demand the continuance of such inconclusive determinations, then, at the least, the traditional phrase "without admitting or denying" should be proscribed. Instead, the defendant or respondent should be con-strained to state affirmatively which of the alleged facts are admitted and which denied. Such a statement is no more than what is required of litigants whenever they enter a plea or respond to interrogatories. Why should the consent decree, coming after a long and expensive investigation by the Commission's staff, be terminated by something less than that which may result from litigation generally?

4. A reversal (by legislative enactment, if need be) of the *Hochfelder, Redington, Aron* line of judicial decisions (Chapter 3).

5. Greater independence, integrity, and intrepidity on the part of the independent auditors and all others responsible for corporate gover-nance and accountability.

Beyond these recommendations, I advance the following transcen-dent proposals:

To Make the Independent Auditor Responsible

First: I look for a radical reversal in the determination of underlying accounting precepts and their implementation in practice. Should pre-cepts be determined in the public or the private sector? The popular response favors the latter. To my mind, arguments for this course are sterile. As I see it, accounting principles are a synthesis; they represent the conglomeration of sociology, history, economics, communications, philosophy, law, mathematics, taxation, and then, too, accounting con-verging on itself. Accounting principles draw from every conceivable discipline—certainly every one among the behavioral sciences.

When we reflect on the performance record of the FASB, we find it to be essentially oblivious of the implications of the term "standards." For example, the rules (not the standards) promulgated for research and development costs, foreign currency translation, accounting for equity securities, leases, restructured debt, oil and gas producers—all are consistent with this quest for certitude—a quest for a chimera.

I would unshackle accountants from the bonds of uniformity and leave it to the marketplace of ideas to judge the appropriateness of the generally accepted alternative precepts as they apply them in practice.

Insofar as the current noble experiment in standard-setting is con-

cerned, I would urge that the seven FASB members take a well-earned
sabbatical. During this period of rest, relaxation, and refreshment, let
them reflect on the "standard for standards" envisaged by Professors
Paton and Littleton in *An Introduction to Corporate Accounting Standards* (a
seminal work which undoubtedly inspired the Wheat Committee as it
was formulating the charter for the FASB). According to those professors:

> Standards should deal more with fundamental conceptions and general
> approaches to the presentation of accounting facts than with questions of
> precise captions, degrees of subdivision, and detailed methods of estimat-
> ing. . . .
>   . . . It should be possible to state accounting standards in such a way
> that they will be useful guides to procedures over a wide area of application.
> Whereas rules would be made to afford a basis for conformity, standards
> are conceived as gauges by which to measure departures, when and if depar-
> ture is necessary and clearly justifiable. Standards, therefore, should not pre-
> scribe procedures or rigidly confine practices; rather standards should serve
> as guideposts to the best in accounting reports. . . .

Should the FASB members nevertheless decide to be active, let them
come out of their temple and go down into the marketplace to see
where and how our reasonably good doctrine is being Greshamized.
Then let the FASB inform the Ethics Division of the AICPA of the
multiplicity of incidents where the auditors permitted GAAP plus GAAS
to be transmuted into Cleverly Rigged Accounting Ploys.

If we accept the concept of flexibility and alternatives in GAAP, we
confront the question: Who shall be responsible for choosing the alternatives from the Good Book of GAAP to be applied in a particular context?
Are the choices to be made by the independent auditor or shall the
responsibility remain with corporate management?

These questions were considered by the Moss and Metcalf committees; they have also been the subject of important deliberation by the
American Institute of Certified Public Accountants' Commission on Auditors' Responsibilities.

Here is where I would put an end to the painting of fakes—or at
least make certain that the fakes are not sold to the public. I would
want the independent auditor, on the basis of his credentials, professional responsibility, and integrity, to assert that from GAAP he has
determined the options and the particular alternatives that he deemed
to be *most appropriate* and *fairest* under the circumstances.

At present, the words used by the auditor when he "certifies" the
financial statements make it appear that this is precisely what he is doing;

but as we saw in the initial chapter, the words in the auditor's certificate about the statements presenting fairly the financial condition and results from operations may be specious. I urge that this appearance become reality. I would put the profession's performance where our fees are—in short, give the public that for which we are exacting billions of dollars each year.

Furthermore, the selection of the particular alternatives or options from the Book of GAAP should not be made in an environment of intimacy between the auditor and the client's management. I would have these determinations made consistent with the "sunshine standards" presumed to be applicable in governmental deliberations—"open covenants openly arrived at," a matter of public record. Management should not be permitted to manipulate a contrived transaction into a particular accounting alternative in order to achieve a preconceived accounting consequence. New wine in old bottles should be recognized by the auditor whenever it occurs, and he should thereupon apply a more appropriate, a fairer, alternative, to avoid misrepresentations and misapprehensions.

Reinforcing the Self-Disciplinary Process

Second: Radical change in the structure and operation of the disciplinary process for the accounting profession. As is evident from the discourse in Chapter 2, the accounting profession has been impotent when confronted with misfeasance and malfeasance and deleterious conduct by those who comprise its power structure. This impotence is the consequence of a number of factors and forces, among them:

1. It is the giant firms comprising the hierarchy who are capable of obtaining the most expert legal counsel (frequently as house counsel) to delay indefinitely, and ultimately to frustrate, the disciplinary process.
2. These firms are entirely capable of inundating the limited staff and other facilities of the profession's disciplinary apparatus with a record so enormous that the system gets helplessly bogged down.
3. Since the Director of the Ethics Division of the AICPA serves at the pleasure of the hierarchy within the organization, it could be politically disadvantageous to take a hard line where a firm within that power structure is involved.
4. Experience has demonstrated that just when an AICPA divisional director has learned his responsibilities and figured out how to gather the information needed to operate his division, he is transferred (pos-

sibly even promoted) out of that division. It may be true that a new broom sweeps clean; nonetheless, an old broom knows the corners.

The profession has determined to do something about self-regulation. The SEC-Practice Section in late 1979 created a Special Investigations Committee. According to its charter, the committee would be responsible for monitoring litigation against members of the SEC-Practice Section where there are allegations of audit failures pertaining to such practice. The committee would have the authority to investigate and to recommend corrective and disciplinary measures.

This is an important step; nonetheless, the problems identified with the disciplinary process within the AICPA generally are perpetuated.

In my view there is a need for a far more radical restructuring of the disciplinary process than that suggested by the foregoing. The hierarchy's oligopolistic hold on the AICPA must be broken in this realm at least. I urge the establishment of an independent disciplinary apparatus, adequately funded and fully staffed. Such an independent board would be expected to take notice, either on its own initiative or by referral from members of the profession or others, of deviations from established standards of conduct. I would expect such a board to proceed with an inquiry and judgment independent of (and probably also in advance of) any other proceedings before the courts or regulatory agencies. All the arguments advanced by the Wheat Committee report for the establishment of an independent board for the advancement of principles of accounting are appropriate, with even greater import for the advancement of the principles of the accountant than for those of accounting.

How such a professional integrity board would be constituted and financed I leave for future deliberation; I would not necessarily adopt the Financial Accounting Standards Board as my model.

Academic Responsibility and Irresponsibility

Third: For this proposal I take as a frame of reference the opening segment of an address (Spring, 1980) by SEC Chairman Harold Williams before an Accounting Research Center forum at Northwestern University. That speech, entitled "The First Thousand Days—and Beyond" began on the following note:

. . . I have always been concerned—and somewhat bewildered—by the fact that academia, although making many contributions, has not always provided the accounting profession with the significant ongoing expertise, criticism, innovation, creative ideas—and academic conscience—that it has provided, for example, to the professions of law and medicine. Many of the most crucial issues now before the profession—including independence, measurement, relevance, reliability, audit technology, display of information, economic consequences, summary indicators, and particularly the conceptual framework—are subjects which can greatly benefit from the unique contributions and perspectives associated with scholarly research and thought. . . .

My initial reaction to the remarks was to write them off as a mere rhetorical device intended to challenge his audience—presumably comprised of academic scholars. But this mood soon changed to one of indignation.

I know of my own direct knowledge of the ways in which the scholars in academia compelled the august Securities and Exchange Commission to take action regarding, for example, the pooling-of-interests excesses of the sixties, the conflict inherent in the performance of management consultation services by the independent auditor, debt masquerading as shareholders' equity (i.e., "Transient Preferreds"), accountings by computer leasing companies, franchisors, peripheral equipment manufacturers—and the list can be expanded by introducing the experiences of others.

Also, let the chairman call in his chief accountant and director of enforcement to find out how often they respond only after hearing or reading the cries of indignation from academics.

Further, the chairman has been crisscrossing the nation to spread the gospel of "economic reality" by reference to accounting for the effects of inflation. Putting my personal views aside, this is not a wheel discovered by the chairman nor by my colleagues in practice. The ideas come straight out of the writings of academics going back half a century or longer.

This prodding of the SEC might well be paralleled by a demonstration of the academicians' impact on the practitioners' sector of our profession. Had the chairman reflected but a moment on the early history of the Accounting Principles Board he would have recognized the ways in which the academics (e.g., Profs. Maurice Moonitz, Robert Sprouse, Perry Mason, John Myers, Arthur Wyatt, *et al.*) were desirous of leading the profession onward and upward. But then the heavy hand of pragmatism proceeded to a disavowal of these valiant endeavors. Some of the academics persisted in their endeavors; others determined to move to the greener, more fertile field—they joined the pragmatists.

And did not the chairman's own Commission confirm that the practitioners were to remain in the saddle by its adoption of Accounting Series

Release 150? And with whom does the chairman and his staff meet to expose their thinking informally and anticipatorily? As far as I can see, it is not academicians who are invited to come and chat with the chairman and his fellow commissioners; instead, I read of these briefings in the newsletters emanating from the major accounting firms comprising the accounting establishment.

And the chairman might also be faulted by the ways in which he personally and directly feels a compulsion to shape accounting theory in a particular fashion. If, in the realm of the law, for example, the Chief Justice of the Supreme Court were to go about the country indicating the way in which the judges were to do their judging on a particular issue and lawyers to prepare contracts, he would be branded as meddlesome or worse.

And if the Secretary of Health, etc., were to go about talking about how physicians and surgeons were to pursue their practice in a particular condition he (or she) would be anathematized by their profession.

Enough of this indignation and refutation of the chairman's remarks—whatever their intent might have been. He is absolutely right in his assertion that the academicians have been cowed into submission to the practitioners' sector of the accounting pursuit. We are so preoccupied in absorbing, teaching, and writing books about the "what is" in our discipline, that we hardly have the time or inclination to lift up our heads to probe the "what ought to be." Professor William T. Baxter of the London School of Economics has frequently lamented the fact that we are obsessed with drilling our students on the promulgations of the Accounting Establishment (Accounting Principles Board Opinions, Financial Accounting Standards Board Statements, Statements on Auditing Standards, and the like) that we have little, if any, time for reflecting on what we are all about, and why. The idea of exposing our students to the literature that helped shape our theory and practice appears to be beyond the experience of the classroom professor.

The Chairman is right, and this, in brief, is my third transcendent proposal: Insist that all students aspiring for entry to our profession be compelled to at least question, and possibly even to challenge, the doctrines emanating from the Establishment.

There are, of course, several serious caveats, to wit:

1. This kind of learning might be counterproductive for our students when they sit for their CPA examinations. After all, these are prepared and graded by the AICPA—they look for the answer (to be judged by a computer) in the official dogma.

2. Such an inquiring attitude, if developed by the student might be inimical

to his being recruited by a firm that wants productivity and client acceptance.

These caveats notwithstanding, the teaching and learning of accountancy by professors and their students can be a most rewarding, intellectually exciting experience. I urge that more of my colleagues in academia
and even those in practice sincerely dedicate themselves to the implementation of the thrust of Chairman Williams' opening gambit to his
spring, 1980, address before the Accounting Research Center.

A Call for a Joint Congressional Committee

Fourth: My most far-reaching proposal: I urge the creation of a joint
congressional committee on corporate accountability.

In my previous writings I recommended the creation of an overarch-
ing governmental agency (either as a trade court or a commission on
corporate accountability); developments during recent years dictate a
change in course. We see a new antiregulatory, antibureaucracy mood
on the part of our citizenry. Consequently the time is anything but ripe
for urging a new agency to be established.

But a significant change, which could not have been envisaged even
as recently as four years ago, is the extent and intensity of congressional
interest in the corporate accountability process in general, and accountancy in particular. When I was writing *More Debits Than Credits* in 1975,
it would have been beyond my expectations to contemplate the possibility
that committees of both houses of the Congress of the United States
would soon be launching major inquiries into the accountability-account-
ing process of American corporations. And yet this is precisely what
happened, beginning in spring, 1976, with the inquiry by the Subcommittee on Investigations and Oversight of the House of Representatives'
Committee on Interstate and Foreign Commerce and the Subcommittee
on Reports, Accounting and Management of the Senate's Committee
on Governmental Affairs. Also, there have been inquiries by the subcommittees on Antitrust and Monopoly and Shareholders' and Citizens'
Rights and Remedies (both of the Senate's Committee on the Judiciary).

These developments have demonstrated that the focus for oversight
over corporate accountability and accountancy might well lie in the Congress, with its broad powers of inquiry and investigation incidental to
its legislative role. Hence, the concept of a joint congressional committee
on corporate accountability.

Such a committee might be comprised of representatives from the
House of Representatives' Subcommittee on Oversight and Investiga-

tions and the Senate's Subcommittee on Governmental Efficiency (which inherited the accounting oversight responsibility from the subcommittee headed by the late Senator Metcalf), the committees of both houses of the Congress devoted to antitrust and monopoly (which in the upper house subsumes the responsibilities of Shareholders' and Citizens' Rights and Remedies), the committees on Finance, Ways and Means, banking, environmental protection, energy, transportation, etc.—in short, all committees which over the recent past have demonstrated an interest in the corporate accountability process.

To help launch the committee's activities, I would suggest a probe of what went awry with corporate governance and accountability at Chrysler, whose fiscal hemorrhaging appears to have caught everyone by surprise in early spring, 1979; in late February, 1979, Chrysler's auditors had no misgivings regarding their client's viability. Then in March, 1979, management disseminated to Chrysler's shareholders and to the world a euphoric message:

> During the year, cash and marketable securities increased from $409 million to $523 million. The total of short- and long-term debt at year-end was $1,265 million, compared to $1,594 million one year earlier. The company's working capital, its current ratio, and its debt-to-equity ratio were the best in five years. Shareholders' investment at year-end was $42.06 a common share compared to $48.51 a common share one year earlier.

This was followed by a statement of Management Actions to Strengthen the Company, including:

> As the result of steps taken during the past year, Chrysler Corporation enters 1979 in a considerably stronger position in many respects compared to one year ago. This strength is the result of three primary actions:
> (1) Through a series of innovative financial moves, the company concluded a number of significant arrangements to finance its record plant modernization and new product programs.
> (2) During 1978, the company essentially completed its program of restructuring its overseas investments.
> (3) The company strengthened its management team with the election of a new president, the reassignment of several senior executives to positions which make better use of managerial talent, and the acquisition of experienced consultants to assist in key areas having to do with quality and reliability.

Further, the corporation's independent audit committee was graced with persons prominently identified with high finance and sophisticated investment responsibilities. Assuredly one might have expected that they and their consultants should have had sufficient foresight to discern that which lay in the corporation's immediate future.

We must not forget that Chrysler had, for almost twenty years, been headed by persons who were distinguished alumni of Chrysler's independent audit firm.

In short, there are enough lines of inquiry to provide the joint committee envisaged by me with insight into the ways in which critical decisions and disclosures are determined in corporate America.

Such a joint congressional committee would be in the tradition of the Temporary National Economic Committee of the 1930s. As such it would provide an ongoing detailed analytical study of the nature and conduct of the evolving corporation.

The joint committee envisaged by me would not preempt the legislative and investigative functions of the many separate committees of the Congress which may be represented on this proposed consortium (any more than the Joint Committee on Federal Taxation preempts the committees on Finance and Ways and Means of the Senate and House respectively).

A joint committee on corporate accountability could avoid duplication of hearings and investigations into a particular area of national concern affected by the corporate sector of our society. From this shared experience the staffs of the various separate committees should be able to derive expanded, possibly new, insights into the nature and conduct of the corporate environment which could have a significant effect on the legislative proposals emanating from such committees.

The continuous process of study and inquiry anticipated by this proposal should have a salutary effect on the evolution of the corporate sector. This would be a consequence of the Brandeisian dictum that "Electric light is the best policeman, and sunshine the best disinfectant." The process of continuous and open inquiry should serve to elevate the standards for the governance and accountability by corporate managements, their boards of directors, and the various professions (law, accounting, actuarial, engineering, etc.) which are so vital to the functioning of corporate society.

The reports on the hearings, staff studies, and committee recommendations should inform and enlighten the legislature, scholars of the corporate environment, and the public—all to permit the checks and balances and eternal vigilance which are so vital to the preservation of our constitutional process and democratic society.

In short, I am searching for a *modus operandi* to institutionalize the activities and objectives of the Moss-Metcalf-Eagleton-Metzenbaum committee inquiries—and thereby make them permanent.

From Foreword to Coda

More than a dozen years ago the late Justice William O. Douglas graced my book, *The Effectiveness of Accounting Communication,* with a foreword. He captured there the essential spirit of my writing; but more important, his words and work have contributed significantly to my course of conduct and sense of commitment. Because it may contribute to identifying higher levels of consciousness toward which we might strive, and as a coda to this work, I quote relevant segments from that foreword:

[The book takes] me back to the days when corporation finance was my preoccupation and the teaching of accountancy a hobby. Of the questions posed the most fundamental is the accurate and true determination of the economic facts of corporate operations, and the interpretation, dissemination, and fair expression of such data to those who are entitled to know. The inability to determine the persons in interest to whom the attesting accountant holds himself to be responsible is alone destined to contribute to the deterioration of confidence in the accountant's product.

Looking back and beyond the present crises in accounting practice, this work searches for a definition of the true responsibilities of the auditor in terms of the economic society in which he practices. About a third of a century ago, Gardiner C. Means described the changes in the fundamental character of the "Modern Corporation" brought about through the growth of the corporate complex. This development has since been characterized by Adolf A. Berle as a "Power Without Property" dichotomy. It is in this context that the accounting profession must search for its ultimate identity. Unless it really comes to grips with these economic developments it will not be able to fulfill the role which is so vital to our society.

Nearly thirty years ago, while Chairman of the Securities and Exchange Commission, I advocated a system of paid directors to harmonize the various elements of public interest which converge in the modern corporation. I then observed that while "these elements may superficially appear to conflict, the fundamental interests of all social groups are identical over the long term." While the corporate officer should be expected to recognize these principles, he may be too close to his work to look beyond its immediate necessities. "But the paid director," I noted, "need not be afflicted with such nearsightedness. It would indeed be one of the defects which he would be paid not to have."

[*The Effectiveness of Accounting Communication*] seeks to vest the independent auditor with a pervasive obligation—one which extends beyond his parochial relationship to his client per se, and to all those entitled to have access to the full and fair disclosure of the facts of corporate activity. This, then, is the logical extension to the independent auditor of the role which I suggested for the "paid director." To that end, [the auditor is enjoined] to parallel the historian in the ways in which he develops his commitment and pursues his "call," and to develop a philosophy going beyond the all too prevalent "vulgar pragmatism."

The author demands an understandably high price of the attesting accountant, who is preparing himself to fulfill this essential role. He expects him to undergo a "ritualistic purging.". . .

The burdens which [the author] puts upon the profession are substantial; but, as he demonstrates, our economic society is in urgent need of this service. If the accounting profession does not respond effectively to the challenges presented, there may be little alternative but to have possibly a new profession fill the breach.

The functioning of our capitalistic society is rooted in confidence in those to whom power is delegated. That requires a functioning system of checks and balances; and that in turn demands the effectiveness of communication between and among the various elements in the society and system. In that communication the accountant should play a crucial role.

Notes

1. We Often Paint Fakes

P. 1   The Picasso-fakes anecdote: Arthur Koestler, *The Act of Creation,* Macmillan (New York), 1964, p. 82.

P. 2   The Montgomery quotation: Quoted by A. C. Littleton, *Structure of Accounting Theory,* American Accounting Association (Urbana, Ill.), 1953, p. 10.

P. 3   The criticism of my commitment to "fairness" in financial reporting: Carl L. Nelson, *Business Week,* March 8, 1976, p. 12. This criticism was cited with approbation by Report of the AICPA Commission on Auditors' Responsibilities, 1978, p. 13.

P. 4   *The Continental Vending* litigation: Refers to U.S.V. Simon, et al., 421 F 2d796 (CCA2, 1970).

P. 4   The A. A. Sommer, Jr. article: From his "Survey of Accounting Developments in the 60s; What's Ahead in the 70s?" *Business Lawyer,* November, 1970, p. 209.

P. 5   The Herzfeld litigation: *Herzfeld* v. *Laventhol,* 378 Fed. Supp. 112 (SDNY, 1974): affd., 540 Fed. 2d 27 (CCA2, 1976).

P. 6   Seidman Committee refers to: Special Committee on Opinions of the Accounting Principles Board. Its report was promulgated in 1965.

P. 7   Auditing Standards Board Hearings: "Summary of the Consensus of the Public and the Task Force on Issues Related to Revisions of the Standard Report, January 8, 1980," p. 2.

2. The Godfather

P. 12 The Code of Professional Ethics Reference: CCH *Professional Standards* # 55.03, re "Responsibilities to Colleagues."

P. 12   Re Code of Professional Ethics Rules 2.01 and 2.02: Included in CCH *Professional Standards* #s ET 201.01 and 202.02, respectively.

P. 13   The Russell Palmer speech: Included in the published proceedings of The Emanuel Saxe Distinguished Lecture Series, 1977–1978, pages 6–16.

P. 14   The Maurice Stans litigation: The case was docketed as Criminal Case No. 75-163, USDC District of Columbia.

P. 14   The review of the Stans book: By Harriet Van Horne, *New York Post,* December 28, 1978, final ed., p. 48.

P. 15   The quotations from Maurice Stans: His *The Terrors of Justice,* New York, Everest House, 1978, pp. 383–84.

P. 16   The *Washington Post* article: From page F3.

P. 17   The January, 1979 AICPA letters were signed by Daniel L. Sweeney, Director, Professional Ethics Division.

P. 18   The second AICPA letter: Dated April 21, 1980, signed by Donald J. Schneeman, Secretary.

3. The Enforcers

P. 19   The Metcalf Committee Staff Study: Subcomm. on Reports, Accounting and Management of the U.S. Senate Comm. on Government Operations (later Comm. on Governmental Affairs), Staff Study, "The Accounting Establishment," 1976.

P. 19   ASR 173: "Opinion and Order in a Proceeding Pursuant to Rule 2(e) of the Commission's Rules of Practice in the Matter of Peat, Marwick, Mitchell & Co.," July 2, 1975.

P. 24   Litigation re Steinberg's unfulfilled pledges: *Woodmere Academy* v. *Saul P. Steinberg,* 53 App. Div. 2d 156 (1976) Affd. 41 NY 2d 746 (1977).

P. 24   The Steinberg borrowings from Reliance Group: Reliance Insurance Company prospectus dated August 17, 1976, p. 43.

P. 24   The Steinberg bank loan: Reliance Insurance Company prospectus dated August 17, 1976, p. 40.

P. 24   Prior violations of Securities Acts: See *Feit* v. *Leasco,* et al., 332 Fed. Supp. 544 (EDNY, 1971).

P. 25   The ITT-Lazard Freres Administration Order: Published in the SEC Docket vol. 13, no. 6, October 25, 1977 (Release No. 14, 049, October 13, 1977), beginning at p. 316.

P. 27   The *Reeves* decision: Officially cited as 71 TC 727. The Circuit court references (per CCH Federal Tax Service) are as follows—Rev'd. CA-3, sub nom Herely, A. S.; (March 25, 1980), Vacd. and rem'd, CA-1, *sub nom* Chapman, E. S. (March 31, 1980).

P. 35   The SEC 1978 Report: "Securities and Exchange Commission Report to Congress on the Accounting Profession and the Commission's Oversight Role," July, 1978.

P. 35   The Touche Ross-SEC litigation: Refers to *Touche Ross* v. *SEC* 609 F. 2d 570 (CCA-2, 1979).

P. 37   ASR 153: "Findings, Opinion and Order Accepting Waiver and Consent and Imposing Remedial Sanctions in the Matter of Touche Ross & Co.," February 25, 1974.

P. 41   The *New York Times* article: (re Corp Crime), July 15, 1979, p. 1.

P. 43   The "reckless negligence" references: See e.g., Douglas S. Liebhafsky, "Accountants' Liability-Recent Developments," *New York Law Journal,* July 23, 1979, fns. 3 and 4.

P. 43   The Douglas-Bates article: William O. Douglas and George E. Bates, "The Federal Securities Act of 1933," *Yale Law Journal,* December, 1933, p. 171.

P. 43   The *Ultramares* case: *Ultramares* v. *Touche,* cited as 255 NY 170 (1931).

P. 45   The legislation proposed by Congressman Moss: HR 13175 entitled "A Bill to Establish a National Organization of Securities and Exchange Commission Accountancy and for Other Purposes."

P. 46   The Arthur Young Geotek litigation: Citations are: 426 Fed Supp. 715 (1977) affd. 590 F 2d 785 (CCA-9, 1979).

P. 47   Allegations re Geotek transactions: Securities and Exchange Commission brief on appeal.

P. 48   The *Aarons* decision: Cited as *Peter Aarons* v. *Securities and Exchange Commission*—U.S.—, Case No. 79–66, 100 S. Ct. 1945 (June 2, 1980).

P. 49   The Briston-Perks article: *Accountancy,* November, 1977, p. 48.

4. Fiddlers on the Roof

P. 57   In August, 1980, the FASB exposed for consideration by interested parties a revised "standard" for accounting for foreign currency translation. The principal provisions of this proposed phenomenon would include:

> Abandonment of the temporal method used in FASB Statement No. 8 in most situations, for the net investment or current rate method, whereby:
>
> All assets and liabilities (including inventories and fixed assets) are to be translated from the foreign entity's functional currency (the primary currency of the economic environment in which the entity conducts its operations) into the reporting entity's (parent or investor's) currency by using the current exchange rate in effect at the end of the fiscal period.
>
> All revenue and expenses are to be translated at a weighted average current exchange rate.
>
> Adjustments resulting from translating the foreign currency statements (called foreign translation "gains and losses" in FASB Statement No. 8) are to be accumulated and reported in a special section of stockholders' equity.
>
> This accumulated equity adjustment from translation of foreign currency statements is to be included in income in full or in part upon complete or partial liquidation of the investment in the foreign units,

and in the period that the liquidation occurs. Similarly, a loss would be charged to income upon impairment of the investment.

Foreign exchange gains and losses resulting from foreign exchange transactions are to be reported in current income with certain exceptions. (Foreign exchange transactions are those that result in an asset or liability that is to be settled in other than the entity's functional currency.)

Significantly, this proposal if adopted, would create yet another "whatchamacallit" in accounting—a number on the credit side of the equation which is neither a liability, nor shareholders equity. It would hold suspended in limbo the difference between two sets of numbers—a difference which the FASB cannot really comprehend.

P. 63 ASR 150: "Statement of Policy on the Establishment and Improvement of Accounting Principles and Standards," December 20, 1973.

5. Big Steel—Little Steals

P. 76 The Foremost-Sharon Steel litigation: Refers to *Foremost-McKesson Inc.* v. *Victor Posner*, et al., C 76–338, USDC, Northern District of California. Judge Poole's opinion has not been officially reported but was filed April 20, 1977.

P. 80 The SEC-Sharon Steel Litigation: *Securities and Exchange Commission* v. *Sharon Steel Corporation, NVF Company, Victor Posner*, et al., USDC, District of Columbia, 77-1631.

P. 82 The CCH Discourse on the "Dollar Value Method": 1980 CCH *Federal Tax Service* Par. 2964.0464.

P. 83 The SEC-LTV litigation: *Securities and Exchange Commission* v. *The LTV Corporation, Jones & Laughlin Steel Corporation, James J. Paulos*, USDC, Northern District of Texas, Dallas Division, Civil Action No. 3-78-1269.

P. 86 The "Link-Chain" Discourse: From 1980 CCH *Federal Tax Service* #2964.0462.

P. 88 ASR Interpretative Bulletin: Included in *Staff Accounting Bulletin, "Miscellaneous Disclosures—Topic 10."*

6. Jaws and Star Wars

P. 102 The Metzenbaum-Eastman dialogue included in Subcom. on Antitrust and Monopoly of the U.S. Senate Comm. on the Judiciary Hearings re "Mergers and Industrial Concentration," pp. 286 ff.

7. Fiddlers on the Roof

P. 111 The Gelco Stock Market Letter: This dissemination was from the Hayden Stone firm.

P. 128 Gelco management's refusal: In response to a final request prior to completion of this work that Gelco furnish the details of the Fleet Management Accounting Change, Vice President Schmidt wrote (July 9,

1980), stating ". . . our major competition in this business had made a similar change. . . ." Included with his letter was a page from the January 31, 1980, quarterly report to shareholders of the PHH Group Inc. Included thereon was the following reference to a "Change in Accounting Principle" which read, in part, as follows:

> . . . the company effected a change in its accounting for revenues from vehicle related services. . . . This change consists of the deferral of a portion of the revenues arising from the purchase of fleet vehicles for use by its corporate clients. . . .

If it was Mr. Schmidt's desire to confirm my hypothesis, I very much appreciate his endeavors. If, on the other hand, he sought to demonstrate that the front-end loading of income from the discount on purchased vehicles is endemic to Gelco's industry, then I leave it to the SEC and the independent auditing profession to determine how the matter is to be corrected. In sum, I do not accept the flow-through into income of the discount as an acceptable accounting precept.

I directed an inquiry to Mr. Frank J. Schmieder, Senior Vice President of the PHH Group. He replied by a letter (October 6, 1980) discoursing extensively on his company's accounting policies and practices.

I replied to Mr. Schmieder expressing appreciation for the time and effort which he devoted to my inquiry, however, I was constrained to observe that while he spoke "around and about" the accounting changes issue he never did provide me with the particular transactions whereby his company's fleet acquisitions permitted PHH to pick up income at the time of purchase, i.e., the accounting practice which appears to have prevailed prior to the charge.

8. Write-Offs or Rip-Offs

P. 132   The Arthur Andersen Compendium: *Disclosure of Replacement Cost Data—Illustrations and Analysis,* 1977.

P. 139   The Williams Speech: Entitled "Financial Reporting in a Changing Environment" FASB Conference (New York City, May 31, 1979).

P. 144   Congressman Vanik's 1980 Report: Published in *Congressional Record,* H. 5823—H 5828, June 27, 1980.

9. The Odd Couple

P. 149   The Metcalf Committee Report: Subcomm. on Reports, Accounting and Management of the U.S. Senate Comm. on Governmental Affairs. Report entitled *Improving the Accountability of Publicly Owned Corporations and Their Auditors,* 1977.

P. 152   The POB Scope of Services Report: Dated March 9, 1979.

P. 153 The Moss Committee 1978 Hearings: Subcomm. on Oversight and Investigations of the U.S. House of Representatives Comm. on Interstate and Foreign Commerce, "Hearings on Reform and Self-Regulation Efforts of the Accounting Profession."

P. 154 Accounting Series Release 264. "Scope of Services by Individual Accountants," June 14, 1979.

P. 158 The NBC-Associated Press survey entitled "April National Poll," #41, May 3, 1979.

P. 160 *The Effectiveness of Accounting Communication* reference: This is, generally, to pages 191–94 of that work (New York, Praeger, 1967).

P. 161 References to prior writings: See, e.g., *Unaccountable Accounting,* Chapter 11, "Riding Two Horses With One Backside," pp. 276–305 and *More Debits Than Credits,* in Chapter 10, "GAAP Potpourri," pp. 282–90.

P. 162 The Retail Credit Corporation litigation: The case is cited as Docket No. 8920, my testimony was given before the Administrative law judge in June, 1975.

P. 164 The Gustave Comprecht Report: Included in volume entitled *"Du Pont Laird Securities, Inc.,* et al., v. *Haskins & Sells, et al.,* Opinions on Reports of Haskins & Sells on Their Examination of the Answers to Financial Questionnaire and Statement of Condition of Francis I. Du Pont & Co. as of September 28, 1969, dated November 29, 1978.

P. 165 The Eagleton Hearings: Subcomm. on Governmental Efficiency and the District of Columbia of the U.S. Senate Comm. on Governmental Affairs; hearings entitled *Oversight of the Accounting Profession,* 1979.

P. 167 The AICPA Scope and Structure Report: "Report of the Committee on Scope and Structure," September 25, 1974.

10. Grease

P. 172 Gulf Oil Special Review Committee Report: This is officially described as "Report of the Special Review Committee of the Board of Directors of Gulf Oil Corporation" in *Securities and Exchange Commission* v. *Gulf Oil Corporation,* et al., Civ. No. 75–0324, USDC, District of Columbia.

P. 182 The Lockheed litigation: Refers to *U.S.A.* v. *Lockheed Aircraft Corp.,* USDC, District of Columbia, Cr. 79-00270.

P. 184 The Northrop Corporation Report: Included in Subcomm. on Multinational Corporations of the U.S. Senate Comm. on Foreign Relations, Hearings on Political Contributions to Foreign Governments, *Multinational Corporations* and *United States Foreign Policy,* 1975. (The section on the Northrop Corporation is included in the Appendix, pp. 393–932.)

P. 191 Chairman Williams speech: Entitled "The 1980s: The Future of the Accounting Profession," before the AICPA Seventh National Conference on Current SEC Developments, January 3, 1980.

P. 191 The SEC "Proposed Release": SEC Release No. 15772, April 30, 1979.

11. Disorder in the Courts

P. 193 The U.S. v. IBM litigation: Docket No. 69 Civ. 200 (USDC, Southern District, N.Y.).

P. 193 The *Barron's* articles cited by IBM: "All A Fandangle," December 2, 1968, p. 3; "Tomorrow's Profits," May 11, 1970, p. 3.

P. 196 SEC re Memorex *Securities and Exchange Commission* v. *Memorex*, et al.

P. 202 The Arthur Andersen letter: Dated January 26, 1971, addressed to Lawrence Spitters, and signed in the name of the firm.

P. 204 The Ernst & Ernst Opinion: Dated March 11, 1971, addressed to Gordon Pilcher, and signed by E. G. Zum Brunnam.

12. Deep Throat in the Executive Suite

P. 210 The Reliance Insurance litigation: *Reliance Insurance Company* v. *Barron's*, et al., 428 Fed. Supp. 200 (SDNY, 1977), the "March decision." 442 Fed. Supp. 1341 (SDNY, 1977), the "September decision."

P. 229 For an updating in the Leasco saga, see "Leveraged Leasco," *Barron's*, October 20, 1980, p. 4.

P. 230 The indictment against Senator Bronston was docketed as number 80 Cr. 224 (USDC, SDNY). On October 23, 1980, a Federal jury voted to convict Senator Bronston after a trial extending over eight days.

P. 232 The New York City Department of Investigation report from Commissioner Stanley Lupkin was contained in a press release dated April 16, 1980.

13. A House Divided

P. 235 The Moss Committee Report: Subcomm. on Oversight and Investigations of the U.S. House of Representatives Comm. on Interstate and Foreign Commerce," Report on Federal Regulation and Regulatory Reform," 1976. (The especially relevant segment in Chapter 2, pp. 15–54.)

P. 235 The Metcalf Committee Hearings: Subcomm. on Reports, Accounting and Management of the U.S. Senate Comm. on Governmental Affairs; Hearings on Accounting and Auditing Practices and Procedures, 1977.

P. 236 The litigation regarding the AICPA Division of Firms: Cited as In the matter of *Joseph Alam*, et al., against *American Institute of Certified Public Accountants*, Supreme Court of the State of New York, County of New York, Index No. 353/1978.

P. 238 Regarding the Moss Committee 1978 Hearings: See references to p. *Supra*.

P. 240 The Evans speech: Entitled "The Regulatory Framework for Public Accounting" before the Third Annual Intermountain Accounting Seminar, Logan, Utah.

P. 241   The POB 1980 Report: Public Oversight Board, Annual Report, 1979–
          1980, p. 28.
P. 241   The Big Eight Newsletter: Deloitte Haskins & Sells, *The Week in Review,*
          June 13, 1980.

14. Who Will Guard the Guardians?

P. 243   The SEC 1979 Report: "The Securities and Exchange Commission
          Report to the Congress on the Accounting Profession and the Commis-
          sion's Oversight Role," July, 1979.
P. 243   The Juvenal quotation: From his Satires, vi, *"Quis custudiet ipsos Custodes?"*
P. 245   Proposed Standard Auditor's Report: Based on submission to the mem-
          bers of the Board for final approval prior to possible submission to
          the AICPA membership.
P. 245   On September 10, 1980, the AICPA Auditing Standards Board promul-
          gated an "Exposure Draft" for comment by the Institute's membership
          on a revised form for the auditor's standard report. If adopted in the
          form proposed by that draft the auditor's "certificate" would thereafter
          read as follows:

> The accompanying balance sheet of X Company as of (at) December
> 31, 19XX, and the related statements of income, retained earnings,
> and changes in financial position for the year then ended are man-
> agement's representations. An audit is intended to provide reason-
> able, but not absolute, assurance as to whether financial statements
> taken as a whole are free of material misstatements. We have au-
> dited the financial statements referred to above in accordance with
> generally accepted auditing standards. Application of those standards
> requires judgement in determining the nature, timing, and extent of
> tests and other procedures and in evaluating the results of these pro-
> cedures.

(Opinion Paragraph)

> In our opinion, the financial statements referred to above present
> the financial position of X Company as of (at) December 31, 19XX,
> and the results of its operations and the changes in its financial posi-
> tion for the year then ended in conformity with generally accepted
> accounting principles.

P. 247   Report of AICPA Committee on Audit Committees: AICPA "Report
          of Special Committee on Audit Committees," 1978.
P. 248   The Killearn Properties, Inc. reference: CCH *Federal Securities Law Re-
          porter,* 1977–78 Transfer Binder, Par. 96,256.
P. 249   The Arthur Goldberg Statement: Originally published in *The New York
          Times* of October 29, 1972, Sec. 3, p. 1.
P. 251   Senator Metzenbaum's remarks: *Congressional Record,* April 16, 1980.
P. 253   The Pixley reference: Francis W. Pixley, *Auditors: Their Duties and Respon-
          sibilities,* London, Henry Good & Son, 1901.

P. 254 Justice Douglas' comment on directors: Included in James Allen, ed., William O. Douglas, *Democracy and Finance,* New Haven, Yale University Press, 1940, p. 49.

15. Quo Vadis?

P. 258 The Wheat Committee Report: Refers to report entitled "Establishing Financial Accounting Standards," Report of the Study of Establishment of Accounting Principles, AICPA, 1972.

P. 258 The Paton and Littleton work: W. A. Paton and A. C. Littleton, *An Introduction to Corporate Accounting Standards,* Chicago: American Accounting Association, 1940.

P. 262 Professor William L. Baxter's misgivings: His views were set forth most poignantly during the course of his Emanuel Saxe Distinguished Lecture at the Baruch College on February 13, 1979, entitled: "Accounting Standards—Boon or Curse?" As published in the 1978–79 compendium of those lectures, Professor Baxter's commentary on "Standards and Intellectual Training" included the following:

Standard and Intellectual Training

My paper has (I fear) done more to list problems than to solve them. But on one point I am clear. Let us agree for argument's sake that standards—particularly if issued with safeguards—may for a time do more good than harm in the world of practice. I still find it hard to feel anything but gloom about their effect on education.

The study of standards now plays a big part in any accounting curriculum. They must have a profound influence on students, just when these are at their most impressionable and uncritical. You have only to look at an up-to-date textbook to see how much weight is given to official pronouncements, how little to the economic reality that accounts are supposed to show. Standards are a godsend to the feebler type of writer and teacher who finds it easier to recite a creed than to analyse facts and to engage in argument. If an official answer is available to a problem, why should a teacher confuse examination candidates with rival views? Thus learning by rote replaces reason; the good student of today is he who can parrot most rules. On this spare diet, accounting students are not likely to develop the habits of reasoning and skepticism that education should instill.[7]

And the student will have little cause to abandon his passive attitude when he leaves the university and enters practice. Here too he must be the respectful servant of standards. We may indeed envisage a brave new world in which an accountant spends his whole life applying rules propounded by others—unless at last, full of years and honors, he himself ascends to the Accounting Principles Board, and then for the first time must face reality.

I am sorry to end so glumly. But the trend in accounting education must make one pessimistic. For many years, academic critics viewed accounting—wrongly, to my mind—as unworthy of a place in higher studies. It got in at last. Now that we are substituting rule-of-thumb for reason, one must sadly admit that our critics were right.

P. 263 The Trade Court concept: In my *Unaccountable Accounting*, pp. 310–13.

P. 263 The Corporate Accountability Commission concept: In my *More Debits than Credits*, pp. 422–27.

P. 266 The Foreword from Mr. Justice Douglas: In my *The Effectiveness of Accounting Communications*, pp. vii–viii.

Index

279